"Reflecting on a lifetime call for Christian unity, *Tear Down These Walls* is a must-read for anyone who has a ministry call of healing wounds in the body of Christ. This work invites us into the life-giving relationships made possible by a Christ who calls every part of his church to follow him more closely, and in that process to love their fellow Christians more deeply."

—**Alexei Laushkin**
Founder, Kingdom Mission Society

A fascinating and awesome book which—taking start from the narration of the biographical events that led the author to a lifelong commitment to the cause of ecumenism—provides an honest and insightful glance at the issues at stake in the journey to unity. Bridging past and future, personal conversion and ecclesial identity, biblical perspective and confessional sources from various Christian traditions, the book proposes the key concepts of a 'new ecumenism,' such as 'missional ecumenism,' 'cooperative love,' 'relational unity,' and calls for a concrete individual and communal involvement in the ecumenical enterprise that is costly, but possible.

—**Teresa Francesca Rossi**
Associate director, Centro Pro Unione, Rome

"Armstrong lays out his passion for ecumenism and rehearses much of his personal journey from a rigid, doctrinaire stance to an open appreciation of and readiness to work with (and learn from) Christians of all sorts of backgrounds. He invites readers to embrace what he has styled 'missional ecumenism,' an approach to seeking the unity of Christ's followers that is deeply relational and welcoming. This book offers renewed hope for the ecumenical future."

—**James R. Payton Jr.**
Professor, McMaster Divinity College

"Through his very rich faith experiences, Armstrong shares keen insights into the crucial work of the ecumenical movement for the twenty-first century. For anyone who wholeheartedly accepts Jesus' words, 'That they may be one,' *Tear Down These Walls* is an engaging and encouraging read. In a secularized world searching for answers, Christian unity is essential for the new evangelization. *Tear Down These Walls* provides a hope-filled framework for the task that lies before us: to give witness to the power of unity we have in Christ in overcoming the divisions that have plagued the Christian church for over one thousand years."

—**Mitchell T. Rozanski**
Archbishop of St. Louis, Missouri

"*Tear Down These Walls* is an ecumenical memoir in which John Armstrong (once again) invites us to participate in costly unity for the love of God and others. As a dear friend, John has helped lead me into a deeper historical, theological, and practical understanding of Jesus' high priestly prayer in John 17, and this great work has certainly contributed to that process. *Tear Down these Walls* will leave you challenged, convicted, and encouraged!"

—**Jeff Gokee**
Executive director, PhoenixONE

"Promoting Christian unity begins with spiritual ecumenism. Armstrong's theological story teaches that Christian unity is the result of grace, not works. The unity Christ wills for his church displays to the world a revelation about the nature of God. 'Missional ecumenism' is grounded in the nature of God expressed as 'relational love.' If Christians abide in God-love, the unity Christ prayed for will make it more possible for the world to believe."

—**Thomas A. Baima**
Provost, University of Saint Mary of the Lake

"This book helps one see how both the character of God (love) and the nature of the church are profoundly interrelated and expressed via relationships. Armstrong's stories and reflections help us make friendship—not buildings and programs—central in church life. These pages will motivate you to devote more time to personal relations with other Christians, for the ecumenical movement is a work of grace rooted in friendships."

—**Tom Ryan**
National director, Paulist Ecumenical Relations

Tear Down These Walls

Tear Down These Walls

Following Jesus into Deeper Unity

JOHN H. ARMSTRONG

Foreword by Richard W. McDaniel

CASCADE *Books* • Eugene, Oregon

TEAR DOWN THESE WALLS
Following Jesus into Deeper Unity

Copyright © 2021 John H. Armstrong. All rights reserved. Except for brief quotations in critical publications or reviews, no part of this book may be reproduced in any manner without prior written permission from the publisher. Write: Permissions, Wipf and Stock Publishers, 199 W. 8th Ave., Suite 3, Eugene, OR 97401.

Cascade Books
An Imprint of Wipf and Stock Publishers
199 W. 8th Ave., Suite 3
Eugene, OR 97401

www.wipfandstock.com

PAPERBACK ISBN: 978-1-7252-9807-1
HARDCOVER ISBN: 978-1-7252-9808-8
EBOOK ISBN: 978-1-7252-9809-5

Cataloguing-in-Publication data:

Name: Armstrong, John H.
Title: Tear down these walls : following Jesus into deeper unity / John H. Armstrong.
Description: Eugene, OR: Cascade Books, 2021 | Includes bibliographical references and index.
Identifiers: ISBN 978-1-7252-9807-1 (paperback) | ISBN 978-1-7252-9808-8 (hardcover) | ISBN 978-1-7252-9809-5 (ebook)
Subjects: LCSH: Christian union. | Ecumenical movement. | Church controversies.
Classification: BX8.3 .A65 2021 (paperback) | BX8.3 (ebook)

05/28/21

All Scripture quotations, unless otherwise indicated, are taken from *The New Revised Standard Version Bible*, copyright, 1989, Division of Christian Education of the National Council of Churches of Christ in the United Staes of America.

Contents

Foreword by Richard W. McDaniel | vii

Introduction | 1

Chapter One
The Road to the Future | 5

Chapter Two
My Long Slow Journey to Catholicity | 15

Chapter Three
My Search for an Elusive Truth | 23

Chapter Four
The Jesus Prayer for Our Unity | 31

Chapter Five
Our Greatest Apologetic | 40

Chapter Six
Christ the Center | 51

Chapter Seven
The Four Classical Marks of the Church | 59

Chapter Eight
Can Our Unity Be Restored? | 68

Chapter Nine
Sin Destroys Our Unity | 78

Chapter Ten
Sectarianism: Our Real Enemy | 87

Chapter Eleven
Why the Church Still Matters | 98

Chapter Twelve
For Christ and His Kingdom | 105

Chapter Thirteen
The Search for the Ideal Church | 116

Chapter Fourteen
Healing Schism through Costly Love | 127

Chapter Fifteen
Envisioning New Ways to Live as One: The "New Ecumenism" | 138

Chapter Sixteen
Missional-Ecumenism: A Paradigm for Unity | 149

Chapter Seventeen
Learning to Live Missional Lives | 159

Chapter Eighteen
Building Relational Bridges for Unity | 169

Chapter Nineteen
Models of Missional-Ecumenism | 180

Chapter Twenty
Costly Love, Costly Unity | 189

Glossary | 199
Appendix | 205
Bibliography | 207

Foreword

This book is as much autobiography as theology. It maps a faith journey from sectarian isolation to authentic community embracing the full family of God. Because John and I have shared it, I commend not only the discovery he chronicles, but the man who lived it. The backdrop is clear. In just three short decades, we have witnessed an unprecedented decline of the American church, raising an obvious question. Why? And its corollary: What must we do? In these pages John's answer points in an unexpected direction, "back to the future." It is the plan for reformation and renewal found in Scripture and widely practiced in the earliest days of the church. He uses the term "missional-ecumenism" to describe it. Here is how John uses this hyphenated word.

We are called to a unity that embraces *all* believers! Who can defend 45,000 denominations living largely in isolation and often unwarranted conflict, much less the preponderance of interpersonal discord found in church life today? Such incongruity cripples us within and explodes like a "blinding flash of the obvious" on all who witness us without. It was not so in the beginning and the unity of *all* believers is itself the high ground in Scripture.

True unity must be grounded in *God's mission*. Nothing less will do. The American church's historic focus on buildings and programs designed to exceed member expectations, grow membership, and sustain *ourselves* internally, has simply not worked. To focus there is to "major on minors." The mission that Christ passed to us is to live as "salt and light" in his kingdom, to love God so much that his love overflows us, into the lives of our "near ones," inseparably binding our faith to works and our teaching to practice as two sides of the same coin. This is a shared mission that we are called to advance together, as one. The unity John describes is no mere difference of degree. It is a difference of kind and its absence looms large, like an elephant in the church.

John has paid dearly for advocating "missional-ecumenism." Yet, the vision and strategy he presents are above reproach. Though not common practice, it is common sense. As we draw closer to God, we find ourselves closer to one another. This journey begins by simply sharing our lives with fellow believers in other faith traditions, coming to know them, respect them, and love them. It then grows into sharing together the very mission for which we were created. As with all relationships, life together is not easy or automatic. There are places of ambiguity and challenge. Yet, it is the way of love prescribed by a God of love. It is the only way that works! "By this everyone will know that you belong to me" (John 13:35).

Richard W. McDaniel
Principal, Collegiate Best Practices, LLC
Vice President Emeritus, Cornell University
CEO Emeritus/Cofounder, Collegiate Retail Alliance, Inc.

Introduction

A house divided against itself cannot stand.
—*President Abraham Lincoln, citing Mark 3:25*

Jesus espoused humility, servanthood of leaders,
and breaking down walls between people.
—*President Jimmy Carter*

Speeches are sometimes memorable. Some are even historic. Modern history is replete with examples of how spoken words have moved people to see the world more clearly. In elementary school I memorized what is perhaps our nation's most famous speech: "Four score and seven years ago . . ." We learned Lincoln's Gettysburg Address to better understand our divided past and embrace a vision rooted in sacrifice and courage.

Words do matter. Words still shape history and change lives. Just days after America was attacked at Pearl Harbor, President Roosevelt's words galvanized the nation. The president said the day Japan attacked Pearl Harbor, December 7, 1941, would become "a day that will live in infamy." As a twelve-year-old boy, I was challenged by the words of President John F. Kennedy's inaugural address: "Ask not what your country can do for you, but what you can do for your country." And who doesn't remember the moving words of Martin Luther King, Jr., spoken at the Lincoln Memorial on August 28, 1963: "I have a dream . . ." Some spoken words are just electric, especially if they contain images and metaphors that fill us with courage, hope, and promise.

In my lifetime, another presidential speech stands out in a remarkable way. The indelible image left on those of us who heard these words remains. For more than four decades the Cold War had threatened our planet with nuclear destruction. The symbol of our division was a concrete wall dividing East and West Germany. It was this wall that President Ronald Reagan spoke about in his memorable words of 1987.

> Behind me stands a wall that encircles the free sectors of this city, part of a vast system of barriers that divides the entire continent of Europe. . . . Standing before the Brandenburg Gate, every man is a German, separated from his fellow men. Every man is a Berliner, forced to look upon a scar. . . . As long as this gate is closed, as long as this scar of a wall is permitted to stand, it is not the German question alone that remains open, but the question of freedom for all mankind.
>
> General Secretary Gorbachev, if you seek peace, if you seek prosperity for the Soviet Union and Eastern Europe, if you seek liberalization, come here to this gate.
> Mr. Gorbachev, open this gate!
> *Mr. Gorbachev, tear down this wall!*

To this day the president's vivid metaphor—"tear down this wall"—inspires me. Whatever you think of President Reagan, his words were a strong, clear, and timely call for openness and peace.

When the Berlin Wall did come down in 1989, I remember where I was and the incredible joy I felt. I was watching how the power of Reagan's words changed the world. His metaphor of "the wall" perfectly described a moment that reshaped the world. Pieces of the wall are now a monument of remembrance in many parts of the world. A reunited and prosperous modern Germany demonstrates what happens when walls are torn down and people come back together.

My admiration for Reagan's words—"tear down this wall"—provides me a lively metaphor through which I express the theme of this book. Just as the Berlin Wall once divided a nation, and even a great deal of the wide world, so Christians have been divided from one another for centuries. This was profoundly true in my childhood world, where I grew up never really going to a friend's church, especially if that church was Catholic or Black. Christians had built their own walls through ideology, politics, ethnicity, race, gender, and denominationalism. Yet there is another story, one not so well known to most Christians. Over the last one hundred years many of these old walls of separation have been torn down. Others are falling before our eyes, but too few know or understand this important story. I will attempt to explain this modern history and encourage you to help others in tearing down these walls of division. I will then attempt to show you how to build friendship bridges in the very places where these walls once divided us.

My own story can be pictured by these walls. Mine is a story of being led by the Spirit to seek God's healing mercies with *all* Christians. From a narrowly parochial world and a separatist evangelical background, I was led on a life-transforming journey.

Looking back over my life, I realize I agree with the words of Frederick Buechner: "All theology is biography." Like history, theology gets a bad rap when it is taught merely as systematic ideas. But the theological story I will share is rooted in a long, slow journey into God's love.[1] I hope this story will prompt you to align your life with the central theme of this book—our relational unity in Christ's mission. So mine is a theological story and a personal memoir. All the stories I share are told to focus your imagination and prayer on Jesus' words in John 17:20–23:

> My prayer is not for them alone. I pray also for those who will believe in me through their message, that all of them may be one, Father, just as you are in me and I am in you. May they also be in us so that the world may believe that you have sent me. I have given them the glory that you gave me, that they may be one as we are one—I in them and you in me—so that they may be brought to complete unity. Then the world will know that you sent me and have loved them even as you have loved me.

To be sure, you have a story too. It includes deeply personal discoveries and choices. I share my story for two reasons. First, I want you to understand your own spiritual story in an entirely new way. Second, I want you to understand the mission of Christ in a life-giving way that grips your imagination. More specifically, I hope you will gain a whole new understanding of what it means to live the gospel of the kingdom faithfully in fellowship with the "one holy catholic and apostolic church."

Around the time of Ronald Reagan's words at the Berlin Wall I began to discover that my particular mission was to tear down walls that had kept churches and Christians from loving one another. It may sound simple, but it's not.

In 1981, as a thirty-two-year-old pastor, I began to experience a deep relational oneness with God *and* others. My new journey began in the context of an ever-growing post-denominationalism inside an emerging

---

1. Armstrong, *Costly Love*. I wrote this book to show what love is in Christian understanding and how this understanding continues to reshape my life and all that I attempt to do.

post-Christendom culture, even though few had yet been awakened to the serious decline and marginalization of the church in America. Because of this journey, I met a significant number of Christians who were discovering that we shared a common ancient faith, one that is greater than all of our historical and personal differences. C. S. Lewis appropriately called this shared faith "mere Christianity." The discovery I made did not pit the Bible against Christian **tradition**.* Rather, my discovery showed me how biblical faith was deeply rooted in the *living* Christian tradition, a tradition found in all the classical expressions of our one faith. It is this one faith that calls us to become a bold and prayerful people who envision a time when walls will be torn down. It calls us to a dream! Frankly, we live in a time when we can no longer afford to see other Christians as our enemies.

Many of us have drunk deeply from the wells of various Christian traditions other than our own. We have discovered far more good reasons to be together than to remain divided. The words of Martin Luther King, Jr. speak to the depth of our collective souls: "Life's most persistent and urgent question is, 'What are you doing for others?'" Indeed, what are you doing for others that will build them up in the love of Christ?

I sense a growing hunger for a profound renewal of Christian faith among many. I believe this will be a faith that is more about life lived well than about winning debates and building walls. I am convinced that what I have seen and lived for decades has not been ephemeral. It all points to someone and something far greater.

In 2010 I wrote a book with an intentionally provocative title: *Your Church Is Too Small: Why Unity in Christ's Mission Is Vital to the Future of the Church.*[2] This new book is a richer telling of the same story joined with the vision behind it. This vision has worked itself out in my life over the last eleven years, and this book includes that part of my theological story. In this new book I will undertake a serious recasting of my vision for the church. I hope you will agree at least with the overall arc of my story: Our church really is still too small if we embrace what Jesus taught us about his mission. I pray you will join me in becoming part of a growing movement of people who seek to live out this ancient story in our modern context. I have dared to pray, as a friend taught me years ago: *Dream a dream so big that it is destined to fail unless God is in it!*

---

* A glossary is provided in the back of this book with definitions of important terms. The first instance of each term found in the glossary is set in **bold** in the text.

2. Armstrong, *Your Church Is Too Small.*

Chapter One

The Road to the Future

*You can best think about the future of the faith
after you have gone back to the classical tradition.*
—*Robert E. Webber*

*No one dare do contemporary theology
until they have mastered classical Christian thought.*
—*Karl Barth*

The church today is undergoing a significant transition. In the early twenty-first century, the great shift in the growth and vitality of Christianity has moved from Europe and North America to the global East and South, e.g., Asia, Africa, and Latin America. Religious historian Philip Jenkins has given a compelling vision of what the wider Christian future might look like in his important book *The Next Christendom: The Coming of Global Christianity*.[1] He shows, through historical narrative and contemporary data, how rapidly these new expressions of the ancient Christian faith are growing.

The late Phyllis Tickle said the church was passing through a long multi-generational shift. She examined massive transitions in culture and in church life and practice, and how these changes came to be. Her passion

---

1. Jenkins, *Next Christendom*.

was to tackle the big questions about where we seem to be going. Anyone interested in the future of the church in America can find many things in her book *The Great Emergence* to stimulate better understanding of our present and near future.[2]

How life for the Christian church will be different in the years ahead may well depend on how the church responds to this story of unity. There is only one thing we can be sure of: The past is a prelude to the future and our Christian future will be very different than the post-Reformation world of modern Western church history.

The Past Can Lead Us to the Future

There is no doubt that new patterns of Christian faith and life are emerging in the church. I welcome these patterns, but I believe they desperately need to be rooted in the past—the Word of God understood as the story of God's love for us, the creeds *rightly used*, life as a **sacramental mystery**, and the deeply rooted practices of **spiritual formation**. I believe the famous Catholic theologian Karl Rahner got this right: "The devout Christian of the future will either be a '**mystic**,' one who has experienced 'something,' or he will cease to be anything at all."[3] We will see why this is so in the chapters that follow. God's purpose must be embraced and loved.

This thesis was captured by my friend and teacher Robert Webber in the words "ancient-future faith."[4] This is a way of saying the church must be deeply rooted in the past if it is to rightly embrace real hope for the future.

The incarnation of Jesus Christ in human history is *our* story. Christianity's view of the universe and human destiny rests upon *historical* events. Christians have always privileged these central facts and thus they have been *universally* recognized. These facts include the life, character, and teaching of Jesus. Yet above all other facts Christians have believed that the death, burial, resurrection, ascension, and coming again of Jesus are central to our faith. These are more than *mere* facts, but they are nevertheless essential facts (1 Corinthians 15:3–4). The true calling of the church, rooted in good theology and faithful ministry, must always start here.

From the very beginning Christians have confessed a faith that believes we are spiritually united with the glorified Christ through the gift of the Holy Spirit. This union results in our collective story, a story rooted in oneness. But our modern story often confuses us, and thus the church

---

2. Tickle, *Great Emergence*.
3. Rahner, *Theological Investigations VII*, 15.
4. See Webber, *Ancient–Future Faith*.

gives mixed signals. Our historical past sometimes embarrasses us, especially if we know our profound inconsistencies. To be faithful to our history and confession the church must understand that she is simultaneously just and sinful. Because we are sinful, the church has embraced and promoted practices that reveal our gross failure to follow Jesus: war, misogyny, injustice, anti-Semitism, colonialism, slavery, racism, et al. We have to be honest about our story. We have lived as if the central facts we confess are not really central. Nevertheless, as people of faith in Jesus, this story remains "our" story, with all our brokenness and failure.

In large portions of American Protestantism, Christian conversion is seen almost exclusively as an individual event. A sinner comes under the conviction of sin and is born again by asking Jesus into their heart. But in early Christianity, the central truth of spiritual birth was this: The new birth was a divine mystery of pure grace that introduced you to a family of forgiven siblings. Conversion was understood as a pilgrimage, not a one-time ticket to heaven. True faith is never discovered in your personal religious feelings but in these central historical facts that lead us to a life-changing experience of shared faith. Therefore, if we refuse to come to grips with our past, our present and future may *not* be distinctively Christian at all. The result will be new forms of man-made religion, with a host of bad ideas married to the spirit of our age. This will result in recycled heresies.

For almost two thousand years, Christians have lived this great mystery of apostolic faith, a mystery passed on through stories, sermons, creeds, and common practices such as baptism and the Lord's Supper. All of these were understood as expressions of their one faith. But in spite of these rock-solid facts, American Christians have a unique predilection to approach the Christian faith as if what we know today is vastly more relevant than what previous generations knew. This is naïve at best, dangerous at worst. It has led a generation of Christians to assume they know perfectly well who Jesus is, apart from any instruction in the ancient Christian tradition. As a result, America has become the primary breeding ground for new religions and a wide array of Christian **sects**. We have exported these spiritual novelties to Africa, Asia, and Latin America, resulting in thousands of new denominations and splinter groups and an almost unimaginable number of not-so-Christian churches and movements. Something about all this tribalism rightly disturbs younger Christians.

Building one's faith and life on various passages of the Bible, understood primarily through private experience, has resulted in nothing less than a confusing cacophony of Christian noise. This situation is precisely what I will challenge. The walls we have created around these projects must be torn down. But unless we understand what went wrong in the first place, we will be far more likely to leave these walls in their place. I will make a case for how the one church of Jesus Christ, ministering out of its spiritual unity in Christ and rooted in both history and core **orthodoxy**, can best live the faith and effectively serve Christ's mission.

The Scripture Is God's Supreme Witness to Christ

My foundational premise is that Scripture bears witness to the living Christ, who is the full and final revelation of God. Christ has promised to build *his* church (Matthew 16:18). Though Christians clearly do not agree about every aspect of how to confess this "once-for-all" faith, we all agree the church must be rooted in Scripture. All the great traditions of historical, incarnational, and confessional Christianity, East and West, flow from the church engaging actively with Scripture. But Scripture alone, without human life and community consensus, has been subjected to every human whim and fancy. History demonstrates the dangers of such an approach. The poet William Blake got our problem right when he wrote: "Both read the Bible, day and night,/ But thou read'st black and I read white."[5]

The better way forward beckons us to embrace our past in order to move into our future. We do this best by listening to the witness of the *whole* church through the *entire* story of the scriptural canon. (Marcionism, one of the earliest heresies in the church, was an appeal to throw off the Old Testament altogether as the story of a tribal god who was not consistent with the revelation we receive in Jesus Christ.) Yet we know that the church has been massively divided for well over a thousand years. We built huge walls that still keep us apart. These walls have hindered our listening and responding to each other in love.

The Scriptures are "the word of God [and thus] alive and active. Sharper than any double-edged sword, it penetrates . . ." (Hebrews 4:12). The Scriptures illumine the minds of God's people in every culture and context. This truth aligns with Karl Rahner's comment about becoming "mystics." Through Scripture we can freshly perceive truth as the Holy Spirit reveals Christ to our spirit. The whole church can come to know afresh God's wisdom and character through the Holy Scriptures. Christians believe that the Scripture is sufficient in all it affirms and authoritative for the Christian faith of all people everywhere.

But we must realize, as Rabbi Jonathan Sacks notes, that all religion is ultimately built on *hard texts* that "if taken literally and applied directly, would lead to results at odds with that religion's deepest moral convictions."

---

5. William Blake, "The Everlasting Gospel," ca. 1818.

This is certainly true for Christianity. We must then face this fact: There are passages in the Bible that, taken in isolation, are radically inconsistent with the larger and deeper commitments of Christianity. Such scriptural passages have been used throughout Christian history to demean the dignity of persons who bear God's image.[6]

But as I noted above, the Christian church is flawed, sometimes profoundly so. After all, the church is a worldwide fellowship of human persons with all their personal and collective flaws. But we remain Christ's church. He promised to build his church, and he has kept his promise—a promise he will continue to keep until he comes again.

A younger friend, who has also devoted his life to the vision I share, expresses what I too believe: "I love the body of Christ, not because I understand the entire body of Christ, but because Christ died for this body. I have a heart for Christian unity not because it is always practical, but because I know that our disunity is also a kind of crisis and that all is not as it should be."[7]

The Church: Unified and Diverse

During the first 1800 years of Christian history, almost no one understood the church as a myriad of independent and unrelated congregations and movements that interpreted the Bible as each saw fit. Even the sixteenth-century Protestant Reformers, especially the magisterial leaders like Martin Luther and John Calvin, understood there was an established historical foundation deeply rooted in the Scripture *and* the writings of the ancient church's earliest theological teachers. The so-called ecumenical **creeds** have been widely embraced as signs pointing to the central truths believed by a consensus of early church teachers. Thus the Apostles' Creed, Nicene Creed, and Athanasian Creed were continually appealed to by all the major Protestant Reformers. For them, a common faith was expressed in these earliest ecumenical creeds. The Reformers never encouraged people to pick through the Bible and concoct a better version of Christianity. *They understood that a text-based faith always had a history of interpretation associated with it.* This understanding is completely contrary to all forms of fundamentalism, which has produced a profoundly anti-traditional form of faith and practice of the Christian faith.

---

6. Sacks, *The Great Partnership*, 251–52.

7. Alexei Laushkin, written for a social media post. Alexei is the president of Kingdom Mission Society, a ministry committed to tearing down the walls of division (https://KingdomMissionSociety.org).

Growing evidence indicates that both an overly confident Enlightenment reading of Scripture, as well as the various reactions of modern fundamentalism, have separated us into our tribes and camps. But the church is coming together in new expressions of unity and diversity where peoples are reading the Scripture together. I believe these new expressions, small as they are in many places, will lead us to tear down many of the walls we constructed that kept us apart. This movement toward unity is the work of the Holy Spirit, reminding us that the church is God's creation. As we go along, I show how this new expression of unity in Scripture and **tradition** is being shaped by both mission and unity, which I call **missional-ecumenism**.

How the American Experience Went Bad

As I've indicated, I have no doubt the church in the West will undoubtedly experience a different future from our deeply divided past. The coronavirus pandemic, as well as the growing awareness of racial injustice and social divisions in America, have only added to our awareness that we cannot afford to go back to the way things were in the previous century. Add to these momentous changes the next generation's decline in church participation, and it becomes obvious things are changing quickly. The outcome may be mixed, leading to some amazing new stories of God's work in the world as well as widespread moral and spiritual confusion. A diluted understanding of the once-for-all nature of Christ the living Word could lead many to change virtually everything. There are scores of books that take this approach, arguing incessantly that the postmodern condition of our time requires a complete revolt against historic Christianity. I see a much better solution.

Much rethinking about the church is confused precisely because it seeks an *ideal* church, something Dietrich Bonhoeffer wrote about when he spoke of Christians seeking a "wish dream" Christianity.[8] Such "wish dreams" hinder humility and receptivity to others. They deny the actual reality of the historical church, with both its beautiful and ugly moments. (These "wish dreams" lead Christians back to one of the most virulent heresies in the early church: **Gnosticism**.)

I advocate a different approach, one rooted in **critical realism**. This approach involves a positive yet critical response to the past. It also allows the past to be properly linked with a biblically hopeful view about what God will do in the age to come. My critical realism is rooted in the study of Scripture, the story of the historical church, the foundation laid down by the

---

8. Bonhoeffer, *Life Together*.

earliest Christian leaders in the ecumenical creeds, and the various movements of the Holy Spirit that have renewed the church over two millennia. It is also centered in eschatology, or the future. The Christian church has never been a perfect community, but it is comprised of a redeemed people called by the gospel to continual repentance.

We can do better than arguing and demonizing one another. We can learn to *embody* the gospel, not just for ourselves but for the sake of the world. This is what Jesus taught his followers to pray for when he told them to seek God's kingdom first: "Our Father in heaven, hallowed be your name, your kingdom come, your will be done, on earth as it is in heaven" (Matthew 6:9-10). Jesus inaugurated his kingdom in order for us to bring good news to the whole world. Our mission is formed by this kingdom. Mark succinctly tells us what Jesus' coming meant: "Jesus came to Galilee, proclaiming the good news of God, and saying, 'The time is fulfilled, and the kingdom of God has come near; repent, and believe in the good news'" (Mark 1:14-15).

Clearly, we have done this mission imperfectly. But this must never become an excuse that hinders us from praying and working to do it better. Critical realism holds before us the priority of the kingdom of God and the commitment of Christ himself to complete the work he began with his disciples and carries on through us (see John 13-17).

The final book in the Bible makes plain what God will do before this present age ends. John was given a picture of Jesus and his throne in heaven (Revelation 5:9-10).

> You are worthy to take the scroll
>   and to open its seals,
> because you were slain,
>   and with your blood you purchased for God
> members of every tribe and language and people and nation.
> You have made them to be a kingdom and priests to serve our God,
>   and they will reign on the earth.

This theme of the Lamb redeeming men and women from every tribe, language, people, and nation has driven the modern mission movement, which is now reaching a profound crescendo in the third millennium. East and West, North and South, the **missional** theme of the Bible is transforming Christians of all persuasions. *This theme is one of a humble and serving victory of love.* It is not about getting a few troops to offer a one-time prayer and sign up for the right side in the afterlife. It is about a cross and a way of life, a way of life called into reality through the gospel of the kingdom that brings us together in a new family. Jesus told us the unity of the church must play a huge role in this transformation. This is why I argue that the future of the church is vitally connected to our unity in Christ's mission.

There is one reason I am not pessimistic about the long-range direction of the church: *It belongs to Christ.* Congregations flourish where the kingdom of God breaks into ordinary life. The church will accomplish God's purpose because Christ has won the victory. He will expand his kingdom to every nation and corner of the globe. This is our eschatology of hope! But why? Jesus said so. We live between two ages—"the already" and the "not yet"—the initial coming of Christ and his final appearing. When he comes again, he will bring the full and complete reality of his kingdom. So the church will yet play the decisive role in the great worldwide developments of history. What the church might look like, in terms of cultural forms, is anybody's guess. Futurists have a field day selling ideas about what this will be. We simply do not know. But Jesus is preparing his bride for a great wedding and celebration (Revelation 19:9).

What Is God Doing in Our Time?

Again, the Spirit seems to be taking us through a worldwide transition in which Jesus' prayer in John 17:20–24 is being answered in previously unheard of ways. While earlier movements for a unified church failed—at least in reaching large numbers of Christians within the churches—many elements of our recent past are gaining new expression, especially among evangelical and Pentecostal Christians who have generally not been involved with the wider church dialogue about unity. Meanwhile, mainline Protestants, as well as Roman Catholic and Orthodox churches, continue to work for unity in a number of fresh and creative ways. These developments particularly interest me. *How and where is the church actually discovering and seeking to live oneness, and how is this preparing the world to receive the gospel of the kingdom?* We must not grow weary. Remember, God can accomplish in one day what we think should take years, decades, even centuries. When it comes to this movement of the Spirit to restore our biblical unity, I ask: "Is anything too hard for the Lord?" (Genesis 18:14).

In trying to take the pulse of Christians and churches through a lifetime of reading, listening, traveling, and teaching, I have been afforded a wide view of God's diverse people. In America, we do not see *massive* change in our commitment to unity—at least not yet. But there is a serious searching, particularly among young people. Could the past be prelude to a very different future? I think so. I am convinced some Christians, and increasingly more congregations, are experiencing something previously unknown in

American church history: Catholics and Protestants are learning to interact with one another in gracious ways. They are forming friendships once dreamed impossible. Even within the Orthodox Church, similar relationships are forming. People in all three of the great Christian traditions are actually learning how to love one another. They are discovering that what unites them is greater than what divides them. As C. S. Lewis expressed it, "When all is said (and truly said) about the divisions of Christendom, there remains, by God's mercy, an enormous common ground."[9] I believe this movement toward unity is the work of God's Spirit. In embracing our common roots in **orthodox** confession, we are beginning to experience the reality that there is "one body and one Spirit . . . [and] one Lord, one faith, one baptism; one God and Father of all, who is over all and through all and in all" (Ephesians 4:4–6).

Less Optimism, More Hope

Christians in the West have lost a deep sense of their collective past. As a result, we suffer from a kind of spiritual amnesia that hinders our ability to faithfully move into the future with hope. This great loss overwhelms any normal sense of optimism. Such hope is *not* mere optimism. The loss of hope overwhelms any *normal* sense of optimism. Optimism describes a mental attitude characterized by confidence in our future success. (Christians easily confuse optimism with the gift of hope.) "But could it be," asks Michael Kinnamon, "that, in the absence of reasons to be optimistic, we discover greater humility and gentleness in our relations with sisters and brothers in other churches? Could it be that less optimism and more hope allows us to let go of favored projects and structures, while holding fast to those promises of God's reign that commonly compel us?"[10] Yes, our loss of optimism may well open a door to the Spirit in a way we could never have imagined. The Spirit can create a significant change in the coming generation, a generation that will need a new sense of identity all the more if it is to thrive in a post-Christendom culture.

---

9. Lewis, *Collected Letters,* "4 April Letter to Dom Griffiths."
10. Kinnamon, *Can a Renewal Movement?*, 159.

Questions for Discussion and Reflection

1. Why is understanding the past so important to the present and the future of the church? What happens when we ignore the past and plunge directly into a vision of the future?

2. Do you think the American church has become preoccupied with various methods for building the church rather than with worshiping the Christ who builds his own church? Why or why not?

3. What is meant by "walls" in the title of this book? Do you see any walls you have accepted, even passively, that need to come down? Name some of these.

4. How does hope differ from optimism, and how can this difference help us better embrace our future?

Chapter Two

My Long Slow Journey to Catholicity

Whoever tears asunder the Church of God, disunites himself from Christ, who is the head, and who would have all his members to be united together.

—*John Calvin*

Where Jesus Christ is, there also is the Catholic Church.

—*Ignatius of Antioch*

It was one of those moments when everything changes—both what had come before and what was to come. It was simple yet profound. It was too big to process at the time. The rest of my life has been an attempt to live what I knew in that unforgettable moment. The occasion was an ordinary Sunday morning worship service. We were saying the Apostles' Creed. I knew the words. I believed them. But I had never been particularly moved by them. They were just words we recited. But on this Sunday things unfolded very differently.

As I said the words of the creed, I was gripped by these words: "I believe in one holy catholic church." At that moment the Holy Spirit spoke to my heart in a quiet way: "John, do you *really* believe these words? If you believe them, then why don't you act like it?" The conviction of that moment was so powerful, I had to sit down. I wept. Questions flooded my mind. I knew God had spoken. But I had no idea how all of this was about to change my life.

Looking back, I now see that my long slow journey to **catholicity** became a life-changing reality that morning. Though I had experienced several dreams about what I thought was God's call to live and teach the truth of John 17 this moment was *the* turning point.

My First Journey: A Childhood Desire to Follow Jesus

I was born into a Christian home in which my parents deeply loved God, the Scriptures, and the local church we faithfully attended several times a week. I cannot recall a time when I did *not* care about God. Aside from several momentary periods of doubt, which I now see as healthy interludes, I have loved God for my entire life.

I have often pondered the words of Jesus and Peter in John 6:67–69 where we discover that many who "believed" in Jesus eventually abandoned him. Jesus asked his disciples: "You do not want to leave too, do you?" I identify with Simon Peter, who answered, "Lord, to whom shall we go? You have the words of eternal life. We have come to believe and to know that you are the Holy One of God." Perhaps you identify with this story too. Peter says he and the other disciples "have come to believe and to know." The Greek text literally reads: "We have entered a state of belief and knowledge that has continued until the present time." When we come to "know" Jesus, we enter into a state of knowledge more aligned with perceiving and experiencing than with intellectual facts. Such God-given knowledge is not the possession of information so much as the exercise of faith that flows from a transformed heart. Thus, to know God biblically is not to know *about* him in the abstract but to *enter into* his saving actions (Micah 6:5).

Reflecting on my life, I see that the question of *when* or *how* I "entered" into living faith is not important. Not everyone has a good answer to this question; many cannot pinpoint an exact moment. The *important* question is simpler: "Do you really *know* Jesus?" Another way to ask this is seen in how Jesus addresses Peter after the resurrection. Three times Jesus asked him: "Do you love me?" To know God, in Jesus Christ, is to love him. After seventy-two years, I have found that no one can satisfy or explain me like Jesus. I have read widely and learned from many great thinkers, even many non-Christians. But Jesus' words alone are eternal life for me.

Three Life-Changing Conversions

Several years ago, a friend told me I had experienced three great spiritual conversions. My first conversion was in 1956, when as a boy I came to *consciously* follow Jesus. Obviously I was not converted from a life of sin and rebellion. But my church background was one in which "personal conversion" was *how* you came to know Jesus. Being a young child, I had a load of questions, and I wanted answers. One evening, I felt I needed to make sure I loved Jesus. I bowed in prayer with my mother and asked Jesus to save me. I would experience this conversion model of faith many times over next two decades. In time, I realized that what I did then, and exactly how I do it now, is not the real issue. The right question was, "Do you know Jesus and do you love him?" Or to follow the teaching we see in John's Gospel, I asked: "Was I in a state of faith and the knowledge of Jesus that is eternal life?"

My second conversion came during my college years. I met many Christians with diverse beliefs. I became a new church planter while still completing graduate studies in theology and ministry. Some of my personal theology was still unsettled when I began to pastor. I had encountered a strong view of God's divine sovereignty from one of my professors. I heard the opposite view from another professor I loved. Three times a week, for a whole semester, the first professor taught about God's power and providence. But when the class ended, I was still unconvinced, believing this approach to God denied human freedom.

Over the years, I continued to question my understanding of God's nature and providence. Then, on New Year's Day 1977, I found a quiet place and poured out my heart to God. I happily embraced the insights of some of the church's greatest theologians regarding divine sovereignty and human responsibility. Strange as it might seem to some, I felt a freedom I had never known. Actually, I felt profoundly loved.

It would be an understatement to say that my life and ministry were powerfully changed in 1977. I began to preach what I saw in the Scriptures. (In hindsight, I soon began to preach more of what I read in theology books that *explained* the Bible than what I had originally seen in the Bible itself.) My preaching did not sit well with my doctrinally undefined congregation. Had I been wiser, I'm sure I could have handled this better. I am also quite sure some would have resisted the message of divine sovereignty, no matter how winsomely I presented it. Embracing human freedom *and* divine sovereignty is often done badly. Far too much harmful argumentation surrounds this subject. People in the American church do not respond easily to the idea of God reigning over all things. And those who embrace such ideas often use them to win debates for *the truth*. For these and other reasons, I do not deny what happened to me in the late 1970s. Yet as the years went on, I moved beyond these rigid ways of expressing biblical teaching.

Finally, in my forties, I became immersed in the questions behind this book: "What *is* the church? What has unity to do with Christ's mission in the world?" I sincerely wanted to understand John 17 and Ephesians 4. I confess I held a rather simplistic, even reductionistic, view of the church. I professed that the church was primarily an invisible reality that consisted of those born of God's Spirit, but I secretly doubted this exclusively "invisible" church concept because it fell short of the New Testament description of a vibrant, visible community.

Then, in May 1992, everything changed. John 17 came alive in my spirit. This change worked its way deeper and deeper into my soul, culminating in the experience I described above when the words of the creed moved me so profoundly. These events led to what my friends call my third conversion. One Sunday morning while I was preaching, the Holy Spirit took my heart to the "Lord's Prayer" recorded in the Gospel of John (17:20–23).

> My prayer is not for them alone. I pray also for those who will believe in me through their message, that all of them may be one, Father, just as you are in me and I am in you. May they also be in us so that the world may believe that you have sent me. I have given them the glory that you gave me, that they may be one as we are one—I in them and you in me—so that they may be brought to complete unity. Then the world will know that you sent me and have loved them even as you have loved me.

For me there was a special irony in being brought to these words. I had preached the Scriptures, verse by verse, for twenty-one years. I had completed a sixteen-year pastorate. For the last two-plus years of that pastorate, I had preached through John's Gospel. Then, after sixteen years, my final sermon was from John 17:20–26. The "oneness" Jesus asked the Father for became my passion.

My Second Journey: Following Jesus Into Deeper Unity

As I soaked my soul in the prayer of Jesus in John 17, my vision for the unity of the church was transformed. My love developed into a deep and growing love for Christ and the whole church as God's people. As I unpacked the insights the Holy Spirit was giving to me, I sensed two things. *First, I realized that I couldn't love what I didn't know.* I had a basic grasp of Western church history, but I knew very little about the *whole* Christian church, or what the three historic Christian churches—Catholic, Protestant, and Orthodox—believed and why. I knew about intra-Protestant disagreements and schisms, but I knew far less about the core truths shared by all Christians everywhere. I soon discovered what is called **classical Christianity**. I read materials from various churches, traditions, and theologians. I read what churches had written about themselves rather than what others had written against them. This receptive reading opened my mind in new ways. What I uncovered was nothing short of amazing. It became clear that there was so much more to learn from the whole church. But first some big walls had to fall.

Second, *I knew I couldn't be satisfied with loving a concept of the church.* So I set out to find God's people, to truly get to know people outside of my own tradition. At first this seemed a daunting task, but I began by taking one small step at a time. I made it a personal priority to meet with Christians who were different from me. Before long, I was relating to an ever-widening circle of new friends. I discovered a simple principle that has guided me ever since: *Make friendships your priority, and God can use you in ways you never imagined. True unity comes about through mutual self-giving, and this self-giving happens best in growing friendships.*

My Second Journey Leads Home

Shortly after the John 17 sermon and my encounter with the Holy Spirit in saying the creed, I began to ask God to lead me to different Christians in order to love, listen, and learn. On an airplane, I once encountered a young priest who was reading a book by the twentieth-century **Roman Catholic** theologian Hans Urs von Balthasar (1905–1988). A conversation ensued, and a new friendship was born. Another time, while speaking at Dubuque Theological Seminary, I was introduced to a group of Catholic monks. They invited me to their monastery in downstate Illinois. As a result of several visits with them, my life further changed. Out of these new relationships, and the peace and quiet of places like this monastery, fresh wind came into my soul. I saw that what united us, despite our differences, was the one Christ we knew and loved as brothers and sisters. I had no category for this kind of love, but I knew it brought an immediate sense of unity to all my relationships.

During this time, a man from a local Nazarene church asked me to participate in a public dialogue with a Catholic theologian. Nervously I said yes. I had no idea how this event would mark my life. The evening was electric. The moderator was a local Chicago TV news anchor. The place was packed. I knew what topics we would discuss. While many theological walls had begun to fall inside of me, the emotional wall of fear I felt was palpable.

I feared this intelligent, gracious priest would destroy my arguments. I think what I feared most was my old fears of ridicule, rooted in insecurity. But they proved groundless. We had an honest dialogue. We agreed on some things and disagreed on others. But my presence that evening felt to me like betrayal because of my rigid background. That night I realized I had more walls to take down, brick by painful brick.

I decided to analyze my fears. I saw that religious fear—brought about by real or perceived dangers—was harming my spiritual life. Earlier, I would have harbored doubts that some of my new friends were real Christians. While that was no longer true, I still felt as though I was betraying my calling and growing soft in my doctrinal convictions. Some people, even friends, were suggesting as much in their public attacks.

In the late 1990s, at a conference in Iowa, I began to experience an even deeper love for all God's people. The event included Methodists, Lutherans, Presbyterians, the Christian Church (Disciples of Christ), Catholics, American Baptists, Congregationalists (United Church of Christ), and Episcopalians. I had always distrusted most ministers from these groups, as they represented the more mainline (liberal) denominations. Now here I was, meeting and praying with them.

The mission I founded in 1991, ACT3, sponsored this Iowa event.[1] The conference featured five plenary speakers—Donald Bloesch, J. I. Packer, William Abraham, Carl Braaten, and me—each from very different Protestant communions. Workshops were led by both Protestants and Roman Catholics. At this conference I had my first personal encounter with an Orthodox Christian. The Baptist minister who chaired our mission met the same person and began his own journey. He would go on to become an Orthodox priest some years later. His journey radically impacted my own in incredibly positive ways. Not only do we remain the very best of friends, but his life has helped me to grow in love in profound ways.

A Prophecy About My Journey

Driving back to Illinois, a friend told me, "John, just as we now cross the Mississippi River, you have crossed a river in your own life. You can never go back to where you were or who you were before this week." Looking back, his words seem prophetic. Indeed, I had crossed a river, and there was

---

1. **ACT3** was an acronym for "Advancing the Christian Tradition in the Third Millennium." This was the name the organization chose as we processed our journey to catholicity and service to the wider church. ACT3 ended in 2019. The story of how this happened is in the last chapter.

no going back. My passion for unity was driving me forward and would soon define my entire life. I didn't have a name for what I was thinking, but now I call it missional-ecumenism. (I will unpack what this means and why it matters later.)

Sadly, I soon discovered some Christians were not interested in sharing my joy. Some of their negative responses prompted me to write articles and letters to explain what I was learning—material that became the seed that finally flowered into scores of articles and several books.

Today, my passion for the church has led me to monasteries and Methodists, to Anglicans and the Assemblies of God, to Catholics and the Orthodox, and to a growing respect for Mennonites and Moravians. It took me, an evangelical and Reformed Protestant, deeper into the words of Luther and Calvin, who left a profound mark on a large portion of the Western Christian church. To my great surprise, it propelled me back to the church fathers—to a past that is both Roman Catholic and Orthodox. In Catholicism, I discovered a community so vast that it overwhelms me in its richness, beauty, and diversity. In Orthodoxy I found an entirely different community—one that seemed so strange to me at first. Its icons, spirituality, and long liturgies were beautiful and rich. This new table of riches was beyond belief.

My Journey Home

I have often meditated on the words of John 17 over the last three decades. I now regularly recite the Apostles' Creed. I have taken up the ancient church practice of daily spiritual reading (***lectio divina***), and immersed my soul in the church fathers, both Eastern and Western. And I have learned to pray in new ways that teach me silence and contemplation. One day, reflecting on all these beneficial changes, I realized that the idea of the church I had embraced since childhood was too small. I had built so many walls around me that it would take a lifetime to tear most of them down. I am not done. The conversion continues.

Questions for Discussion and Reflection

1. What "conversions" have you experienced in your life? How have they shaped your story?
2. How do you "know" you have passed from death to life and are in union with the living Christ?

3. If you were asked to tell your own story about your faith and your church experience, how would you describe it at this point in your life?

Chapter Three

My Search for an Elusive Truth

> This unfortunate idea—that the basis of spiritual unity must stand in uniformity of doctrine—has been the poisoned spring of all the dissensions that have torn Christ's body.
>
> —John Watson

> Do not call yourselves Lutherans, call yourselves Christians. Has Luther been crucified for the world?
>
> —Martin Luther

Almost from the beginning, the nascent church struggled with disunity. The unity of Jews and Gentiles in the same fellowship was an immediate problem. Divisions over slavery and gender had to be faced to protect the life of the community (see Galatians 3:28). Paul's letters to the Corinthians bear witness to this reality: "I appeal to you, brothers and sisters, in the name of our Lord Jesus Christ, that all of you agree with one another in what you say and that there be no divisions among you, but that you be perfectly united in mind and thought" (1 Corinthians 1:10).

What is strikingly clear is the way Paul categorized this problem when he wrote about the ministry of the Holy Spirit. In a passage about life in the Spirit he concluded, "The acts of the sinful nature are obvious: sexual immorality, impurity and debauchery; idolatry and witchcraft; hatred, *discord*, jealousy, fits of rage, selfish ambition, *dissensions*, *factions* and envy;

drunkenness, orgies and the like. I warn you, as I did before, that those who live like this will not inherit the kingdom of God" (Galatians 5:19–21, italics added).

Note the words *discord*, *dissensions*, and *factions*. The modern church has been far more concerned about sexual immorality, orgies, and impurity than about disunity. When James tells us that "fights and quarrels" among Christians come from "desires that battle within you" (James 4:1–2), it becomes patently clear that disunity was a very real problem for the earliest Christians.

The New Testament Portrait

Participation in the life of the Christian community was never an optional part of following Jesus. Every Christian's life in the apostolic era was deeply rooted in the corporate life of the church, begun through one common baptism (Ephesians 4:5) and continued in their communion at the Lord's Supper (1 Corinthians 11:17–26). Running like a deep river beneath these sacraments, or signs of unity, was a sacrificial love for one another (John 13:34–35). The New Testament paints a picture of a generous, large-spirited group of people who understood the basis for their unity was their shared oneness with the risen Christ. Their life as a community was dynamic and expansive, founded on an experience of unity anchored in the Trinity—the eternal, interpersonal communion of God—and thus the New Testament sees unity as a reality to be protected.

The early church lived under what Jesus called the new covenant. He spoke most clearly about this on the night he was betrayed, drawing from Jeremiah 31. The language of the Gospels about this new arrangement, and the meal Jesus put at its center, goes all the way back to the Jewish Passover. The difference is that under the new covenant, the Spirit was poured out on all flesh so all Christian communities can join together to become the eyes and ears, hands, and feet of Jesus. This is why the earliest Christians did not look at the world, and thus at sin and evil in their neighbors, as a problem to be solved. They saw all humanity living in brokenness as an opportunity to be Jesus' mission in his love. "As the father has sent me, so I send you" (John 20:21). Our mission is *not* complicated. We are to live in the world as Jesus did, loving, serving, and sharing. When we condemn the world, or those in the world, we become radically *unlike* Jesus. John 3:17: "God did not send his Son into the world to condemn the world..."

During the apostolic era, Peter and Paul openly debated to what extent the precepts of the Jewish law should apply to Gentile converts. A generation later, the Johannine communities in Asia Minor argued over whether the interior anointing of the Spirit was a sufficient control for Christian ethics. And this was just the beginning of many doctrinal disagreements.

Division Became the Norm

Many members "abandoned the love [they] had at first" (Revelation 2:4). By the tenth century, the church looked more like a state federation than a family or community. In the West, this form paralleled the Roman patterns of hierarchy; in the East it took a less rigid form, but plainly represented a patriarchal expression of what it meant to be brothers and sisters together. By the medieval period, the church had already been tragically divided. The various invasions of Europe by "barbarians" created a division that was even more obvious when Islam became a powerful force. In 1054, several centuries of dispute and division culminated in the Great Schism, which formally separated the church into two huge, virtually unrelated branches—East and West. Then the papacy, considered to be the center of unity in the West, was moved to Avignon. The period of 1305–1377 was one that saw seven popes in quick succession in what is now France; for a time there were even two competing popes. The Catholic Church itself was divided in the fourteenth century. Eventually, disagreements and political disputes began to overwhelm the fragile church unity of the West. By the early sixteenth century, the Protestant Reformation led to a complete split in the Western church, resulting in bloody and destructive religious wars for years to come. This hastened humanism's influence on Western society as this church-inspired violence progressively pushed the church to the margins of society with every passing century.

With this history of division and disunity, it is no wonder that most American churches have a vague understanding of unity. Sadly, each of our denominational subdivisions, created by further divisions from one another, have been exported far beyond America. Aided by a guide called *Operation World*, I pray daily for the church in countries throughout the world. I am struck by how our myriad divisions have weakened the church's effectiveness in its mission. The spirit of divisiveness has spread like a virus. Many denominations and conferences have become "spreader events" where we pass this disease of disunity on to others. We have a vaccine, as we shall see, but so few trust it that our immunity remains low. Even some of our best and brightest leaders defend secondary matters; thus, our spirit remains fearful and defensive. We can no longer afford to defend the countless walls that separate us.

My thesis is simple: The walls we have constructed through theology and independent novelties are sin. How do I know? Sin is what separates us from God *and* one another. Our separation directly harms the mission of Christ. It spreads the virus of **sectarianism** and forces us to choose our friends and enemies based on whether or not we are in *complete* agreement.

How a Deeply Conservative Christian Discovered the Church

In 1992, I became the full-time president of a mission that came into existence to reform and renew the church. This mission began to embrace a deeper vision of the church through my speaking and teaching about Christian unity in many parts of the world. It eventually led to the formation of a community of Christians who embraced this deeper vision.

As I said earlier, I was born into a very conservative home and church in the American South. I vividly recall the first stirrings of the civil rights era. I attended an all-white church as a child and heard not one word about the unity of the church, nor about the burgeoning struggle for justice and civil rights. I knew there were many different kinds of churches, even in my small town of less than ten thousand people. (The Catholic church was our smallest church. All our Protestant churches were of various sizes and types, and all were marked by segregation.)

After a great public school experience I spent six years in a military prep school. I had a secure family life, where I was taught true godliness. I enrolled at the University of Alabama in 1967. Integration had just begun to impact the South. My church during those college years was (again) an all-white Baptist congregation. At the time, I thought, "I'm going to find a biblical church in Tuscaloosa." But deep down, I had doubts about what made a church *biblical*. My certainty about finding a true church was wavering. I wasn't sure how I felt about my denomination's practice of excluding other Christians from the Lord's Supper, but by late in my freshman year I was seriously questioning many things about my church.

Around this time I came in contact with Campus Crusade for Christ, a large evangelistic ministry growing rapidly on campuses across America. My life changed profoundly as I learned to personally share my faith. Looking back, I believe I was more impacted by doing mission with others as friends than I was by the witnessing itself. Through these new friends I began to experience relational unity. I even experienced the Lord's Supper in ways I'd never known—which led me to see how vital it is for all Christians. What was underscored about this key truth would later impact my journey to unity. I discovered that what was important about the Lord's Supper was Christ's presence with his people. Fighting over the outward forms various churches have adopted for serving and explaining this sacrament became less central to my life.[1]

In 1969, because of my desire to become a minister, I transferred to Wheaton College, a respected evangelical institution near Chicago. I do not recall serious conversations or teaching about Catholicism there, much less interaction with anything like moderate or progressive Protestantism. Orthodoxy remained a complete mystery. Since college, I have traveled a road less taken, but I have no regrets about this journey.

Moving to the Center of American Evangelicalism

Because of my excellent time at Wheaton College, I explored the school's historic motto: "For Christ and His Kingdom." This descriptor is rooted in nineteenth-century evangelical Christianity, a time when many Northern Christians were engaged directly with issues like abolition and the wider social values of Christ's kingdom. This exploration opened my eyes to a wider application for the gospel than just private salvation. I earned two degrees during my time at Wheaton and later had the privilege of teaching in the graduate school as an adjunct professor of mission and evangelism. My greatest joy was teaching a class built on the basic content of this book. I love the evangelical impulse of Wheaton and its kingdom mission. The school motto remains a call to my life to follow Jesus in kingdom faithfulness.

By far the greatest thing that happened to me at Wheaton was my growing encounter with Christ *through* the church. I met faculty and students from diverse backgrounds, ethnicities, cultures, and denominations. (All were Protestant, but many had very different backgrounds than my own. Today Wheaton has both Catholic and Orthodox students, but still relatively few.) My teachers agreed on basic evangelical doctrinal issues but participated in a broader dialogue about things Christians did not all agree about. For the first time, I began to think about a church *without* walls. I was invited to openly raise questions. I remember arguing with a Lutheran student until late in the night about baptism and perseverance. I fiercely

---

1. I was general editor for two books for Christians, *Understanding Four Views on the Lord's Supper* and *Understanding Four Views on Baptism*. My introductory chapter in both books lays out my journey to better understanding, and my concluding chapter seeks to narrow the debate on these two vitally important church doctrines so we can see just how much we agree on. I also show that we don't have to agree in order to keep listening more deeply. We can hold our differing views, without glossing over our differences, and still grow into deeper unity with Jesus and each other.

debated with several Calvinists who were far too fatalistic for my tastes. I lost some of my theological baggage, visited different types of local churches, and kept asking questions. Still, despite all these positive experiences, I retained a narrow view of the church protected behind safe walls.

A Pastor Who Searched

After college and graduate school, I entered the pastorate, first as a suburban church planter, and then, during the next sixteen years, as the pastor of a Baptist congregation in Wheaton. I met a lot of other ministers during my twenty-one years of pastoral ministry. In my early years in ministry, I also met a few Roman Catholic priests who became friends. (Most of the ordinary lay Catholics I met in those days sought my help in their search for a deeply personal faith in Christ.)

I still recall the first time my wife and I invited a local Catholic priest to dinner. It was the second year in my first pastorate. I was amazed at how many misconceptions I had embraced about Catholicism. I now see how this informal dialogue helped me to begin tearing down some personal walls without even realizing it. I was even more amazed when I was asked to speak at a community Thanksgiving service at the local Catholic parish. This was the mid-1970s, the early days of post-Vatican II Catholicism. Rapid changes were taking place—changes I did not fully understand at the time. My staunchest evangelical friends insisted that Vatican II changed nothing. Only later would I learn how profoundly wrong they were.

Some evangelical friends insisted Roman Catholics were members of a false church. (Of course, we evangelicals believed we were the true church.) Sadly, attempts to determine who is in a false church continue to this day. It's one reason many conservatives construct, or at least protect, their walls. Some Catholics and Protestants still treat one another with suspicion. The bigger problem, at least for me, was that evangelical Protestants didn't agree with one another. (The agreed-upon definition of **evangelical** is usually a slim list of ideas and doctrines, sometimes reduced to four common approaches to faith and practice.) In truth, we disagreed about many doctrines; e.g., our view of the inspiration of Scripture, how we define faith, and, of course, our views on baptism and the Lord's Supper. We also disagreed about church order, the doctrine of the future (the return of Christ, heaven and hell), the gifts of the Holy Spirit, atonement, the human will, and the nature of how God's grace works in salvation. The more I studied these internal evangelical debates, the longer the list grew. Something was wrong with this approach, but I still couldn't see exactly what it was.

As the charismatic movement exploded, I wondered, "How can this be? These aren't mainstream evangelicals." But I experienced the fresh wind of God personally. God used several visions and dreams to bring me into my deep pursuit of Christian unity. I suppose I needed these Spirit-given experiences because of the high walls I had constructed around my intellectual and spiritual life. Silently, I kept searching. Something seemed wrong with my narrow understanding of church, but I didn't know what to do with all my questions and fears. *Eventually, I discovered a wonderful freedom by letting go of the need to be right.* This, perhaps more than anything else, helped me tear down these personal walls.

But what gave me the greatest anxiety was not my attempt to figure it all out; the bigger problem by far was the personal ramifications of what I had experienced. Walls had fallen for me internally. I fellowshipped openly with Christians from many different Christian churches. But my past relationships in the evangelical world became a new challenge. Some people questioned whether my faith was real, even openly writing about me and my faith. For as long as I could, I tried to play it safe by not openly sharing all I was seeing and experiencing. But the walls would just not stop failing under the sheer weight of God's grace and love. I had to share this love.

Trips overseas further influenced my life. I saw the church in a whole new light when I went to India and Latin America, where I encountered contexts so unlike my own. India was the first major non-Western blow to my narrow church perspective. Latin America shook me even more profoundly, especially with its various mixtures of Catholicism, a faith practiced in ways that seemed totally foreign to my background.

By the late 1980s, the walls around my view of God's church were crumbling. In the midst of this extended season of change, the Holy Spirit moved powerfully in my heart. I sought to humble myself before clear biblical commands like these:

> This is his command: to believe in the name of his Son, Jesus Christ, and to love one another as he commanded us. (1 John 3:23)

> Dear friends, since God so loved us, we also ought to love one another. No one has ever seen God; but if we love one another, God lives in us and his love is made complete in us. (1 John 4:11–12)

> We love because he first loved us. If we say we love God yet hate a brother or sister, we are liars. For if we do not love a fellow believer, whom we have seen, we cannot love God, whom we

have not seen. And he has given us this command: Those who love God must also love one another. (1 John 4:19–21)

God was using his Word, and the witness of his diverse people, to profoundly enlarge my view of the church. A passion for unity would eventually lead me to reconsider the prayer of Jesus in John 17. This prayer would radically change my understanding of biblical oneness.

Questions for Discussion and Reflection

1. What kind of picture do you have of the New Testament church? Did unity really matter to the leaders of the early church? Why or why not?
2. Why do you think division has become the norm in the Christian church? What practical actions can we take now in the context of being so obviously divided?
3. How does your love for Christ relate to your love for his church? Try to be specific about the ways in which these two are related for you.

Chapter Four

The Jesus Prayer for Our Unity

> Although the church of Jesus Christ is found in many different places, she is one church, not many. After all, there are many rays of sunlight, but only one sun. A tree has many boughs, each slightly different from others, but all drawing their strength from one source. Many streams may flow down a hillside, but they all originate from the same spring. In exactly the same way each local congregation belongs to the one true church.
>
> —*Cyprian*

Jesus' prayer for our unity is very specific. The Son asks the Father to glorify him in his impending death and resurrection. He then prays for his immediate disciples, who will soon be formally commissioned to carry on his work. Then he prays for us, those who would believe in him through the message of the apostles. These words transformed my life, leading me into a journey of prayer and work for oneness.

> My prayer is not for them alone. I pray also for those who will believe in me through their message, that all of them may be one, Father, just as you are in me and I am in you. May they also be in us so that the world may believe that you have sent me. I have given them the glory that you gave me, that they may be one as we are one—I in them and you in me—so that they may be brought to complete unity. Then the world will know that you sent me and have loved them even as you have loved me. (John 17:20–23)

This prayer should be called "the Lord's Prayer." Only our Lord could have offered it to his Father. We cannot pray just as he did. This is also Jesus' longest and most comprehensive recorded prayer. But note that Jesus doesn't just pray for his immediate disciples. His prayer, which can be seen as three concentric circles, includes a very specific prayer for the entire church—*for all of those who will believe in him throughout the ages to follow*. In John 17:11 Jesus asks, "Holy Father, protect them [his disciples] in your name that you have given me, so that they may be one, as we are one." But he also prays for those who would come after the apostles when he says "that they may all be one [us] as we [Father and Son] are one."

A Text Badly Interpreted

I can think of few other passages of Holy Scripture (at least passages so important for the well-being of the church) for which there have been so many wrong explanations. Some teachers focus on what this text does *not* mean. Many of their interpretations appear to be reactions to what they believe are mistaken ideas. Consider a few of these:

- We should never try to unite different churches or congregations. The union of churches or denominations is not in view here. Jesus is not interested in such union/unity.

- We should never engage in serious dialogue or mission with other churches, or even other Christians, because they may well be unfaithful to the truth. We will become disobedient if we follow this course.

- There is no common mission that churches are called to engage in; thus, there is no reason to work together to embrace Christ's kingdom mission together.

- There is no concern in this prayer for the worldwide church, at least in a *visible* form, since this will lead to ecumenism, a great twentieth-century enemy of the gospel.

- We must always keep in the forefront of our practice the serious biblical warnings about compromise and false teaching (see Deuteronomy 7:1–6; 2 Corinthians 6:14; Revelation 18:4). These great truths always trump concern for visible unity.

Such fears and concerns cause some commentators to read into John 17 an idea called *invisible* unity. They argue that the invisible church, consisting of all true Christians, cannot be divided, and therefore Jesus is only praying for what already exists. This point, it seems to me, is *partially* true.

But to assume the invisible church is the "one holy catholic and apostolic church" of the Nicene Creed, or that this unseen church is the answer to Jesus' prayer, is a serious mistake. If Jesus is praying for a oneness we already possess, then this prayer has nothing to do with who we are and what we should be doing. Ask yourself a simple question: Why would Jesus pray for something that was already true? And why does he pray for us to be *brought to complete unity* if we *already* possess it?

While it is true that all who believe in Christ are one in him, it is *not* true that what he prays for here has fully come to pass. The unity Jesus prays for is far from a reality in the church. It's not even evident in most congregations, much less in the wider relationships between churches. In America, almost every congregational study since the 1980s has found the most commonly cited problem is a breakdown of church unity. The problem has only worsened with time.

Relational Unity

So what *is* Jesus praying for? *Relational unity* is the only answer that really works in the context. He is praying for a unity between persons that is rooted in their human relationships with one another. In a profound sense, the unity Jesus prays for here is *spiritual*—this is a unity of the Spirit that cannot be created or sustained by us. To be clear, I am not using *spiritual* here as a synonym for *invisible*. Confusing spiritual unity with invisible unity is the major flaw in all the arguments that use this term to explain away the relational intent of John 17.

Chapter 6 will consider a far better way to understand this unity—a way that is *both* spiritual *and* visible. For now, it is important to note that if the unity Jesus prays for is between people in relationships, then this unity can be lost to divisions, rivalries, factions, and church splits. Relational unity—even though profoundly spiritual—can be quenched and grieved through the breaking of relationships. Another reason we know this is what Jesus had in mind can be seen in the continual rivalries and debates that occurred between the twelve apostles. (This theme is common in the Gospels.)

Furthermore, Jesus is not addressing the issue of denominations (they didn't exist yet), nor is he talking about universal church councils (which had not yet taken place either). Most biblical scholars, including most modern Catholic scholars, agree with all these points.

Jesus' prayer for our relational unity means he desires that all his followers will live as he lived. In particular, his prayer points to his personal relationship with the Father. Christians believe that the second person of the Trinity, the **Logos**, was incarnated in the man Jesus. Jesus lived fully and completely as a human person. In his humanity he lived each day in total dependence on his Father. This relationship, lived by the fullness of the Holy Spirit, was one of perfect unity. This relational aspect is clearly in view in John 17.

It becomes especially clear that relational unity is the goal when Jesus prays his disciples will be "*brought* to *complete* unity" (verse 23, italics added). Consider your own relationship with Jesus. Each of us already has spiritual unity in our relationship with him through the work of the Holy Spirit. But clearly we do not experience this relational unity unless we are "brought" into it through a day-to-day interaction with Jesus.

Spiritual unity opens up a dynamic, ongoing movement toward unity—in our lives as individuals and in our relationships with one another—as we share in the divine life of the Trinity. When Christians live out their spiritual unity with Jesus, the results will be exactly what Jesus asked the Father to give us: "Then the world will know that you [the Father] sent me and have loved them even as you have loved me." When we experience this unity, the church will be a visible example of the relational and spiritual unity of the triune God.

Divide and Multiply?

Theologian Ben Witherington rightly notes that the first law of American Protestant ecclesiology seems to be, "Thou shalt divide and multiply."[1] I learned this principle in my first pastorate. My denomination desperately wanted to open new churches in Chicago. The local church I served had originally split from another nearby church. This other church had formerly been part of a third church where I had previously been a member. Confused? Simply put, here were three congregations, all within five miles of each other, in two suburban cities. In each case a new church had formed from a split due to quarreling, jealousy, and petty personal disputes. Sadly, though we were part of the same denomination, we were encouraged to separate for the sake of mission. Our buildings' signs said we were one, but in reality, the huge walls between us were palpable and real.

One day I decided to ask a denominational executive why they encouraged these church splits. He eagerly informed me that dividing churches was actually a healthy way to reach new people for Christ! I expressed my concern about schism and the obvious lack of holiness I saw in these three churches. Later I would hear this man tell other ministers that dividing

---

1. Witherington, *John's Wisdom*, 274.

churches, through any means, would multiply new churches. I was appalled, to put it mildly.

Why Does This Matter?

Jesus says his mission literally hangs on the answer to this prayer for our relational unity. John 17 makes quite clear that the world will not fully understand and experience God's love until we are "brought" into the experience of this unity. Given what we have seen throughout the history of the church, I have to wonder, "How has the church survived as a witness to God's love in the world, given our egregious schisms, constant faithlessness, and corruption?"

Historian Clyde Manschreck suggests that the message of the early Christian church was "abused, institutionalized, abandoned, [and] rationalized."[2] But we can't escape the fact the church is still here, sometimes in poor health and occasionally pulsating with power and love. Yet more often than not, the church is "lukewarm," alive and breathing but distracted from her true purpose (Revelation 3:16).

I urge every church to regularly ask, "What does Christ *really* think of our church?" An honest assessment might be troubling, but asking the question can lead to repentance and the recognition that the identity of the church is not bound up in our own sense of self-importance.

The New Testament church began with the foundation of Peter's confession of faith—the divine revelation that Jesus was the Messiah (Matthew 16:13–18). Following Jesus' death and resurrection, the power of the Holy Spirit was poured out on the earliest disciples (Acts 2). The festival of Pentecost became a birthday celebration for God's people as an empowered group of disciples emerged. They did not bear the sword or engage in the politics of Rome; they simply brought a message of God's love for all people, expressed by caring for those in need and serving one another whenever possible. Congregations grew, even in the face of intense opposition. Not even the powers of hell could stop the mission of the church.

The church has marched like a mighty army across the globe ever since. From the martyrdom of Stephen (Acts 7) through waves of slaughter brought about by Roman persecution, the church has demonstrated power in weakness. Through various attacks down through the ages, as well as twentieth-century Fascist and Communist opposition, the church—despite its problems and flaws—has continued to grow. Today, most of this growth is not happening in the Western world but in the churches of China, India,

---

2. Manschreck, *History of Christianity*, 20.

Africa, and Latin America. The church cannot be stopped, for it is *God's church*. There have been times when it seemed the light carried by Christ's church would be extinguished, but God has kept his promise to his people. His church continues to grow, even where he has administered corrective discipline (e.g., Revelation 2–3).

But what has kept the church going in the midst of all this suffering and trial? History shows that the church remained faithful not by means of a vague belief in the concept of God, but through a living and active faith in the God who is love (1 John 4:8, 16). Scripture teaches us that God's very substance and nature is love. All divine activity flows from the heart of a loving God.

This "new religion" of love was not "an external system of ritual sacrifice . . . but an internal flooding of the mind and spirit with divine love and understanding." The power of God's Spirit transformed the first believers, resulting in lives characterized by joy and peace. In addition, the early church "understood itself for what it was intended to be: *a spiritual kingdom sharing spiritual truth with a troubled world.*"[3]

God's Love in Action

Understood this way, Jesus' prayer for unity is really a prayer about God's love in action. Jesus prayed, "Then the world will know that you sent me and have *loved them even as you have loved me*" (John 17:23, italics added). The theme of God's love for the world is so common in John's writings that I see it as the special emphasis of this apostle whom Jesus loved.

Are we so comfortable with the idea that God loves us (John 3:16) that this great mystery no longer moves us? Have we become so conditioned to think of God's love for us as individuals that we fail to consider what this means for a congregation? For a city? Or for the whole world?

John taught the early church that our unity with Christ is why "we love" both God and others (1 John 4:19–21). "Above all," Peter wrote, we should "love each other deeply" (1 Peter 4:8). Early believers were urged to "make every effort to keep the unity of the Spirit through the bond of peace" (Ephesians 4:3). Love for one another was the whole point of new life in Christ.

But even before the first century drew to a close, the church began to experience the loss of this shared love (see Revelation 2:1–5). Here is a church praised for keeping faith. These Christians worked hard, persevered in their faith and dealt with false teachers. They had not grown weary as

---

3. Angel, *Yes, We Can Love*, 10.

they endured hardships and suffering. But they lacked something vital that would eventually lead to the death of their congregation—they lacked love. The church of Ephesus is a reminder that we can have sound doctrine and a great ministry, but if we lack love and are marked by divisions and quarrels, the consequences will be severe.

Jesus' prayer for unity teaches that even when we disagree on matters of doctrine or practice, we should avoid building walls between ourselves and others. We must be willing to accept those who are accepted by God. May our prayer reflect the will of Jesus, as we pray that our love will prevail by the power of the Spirit—for the unity of God's church.

How Shall We Pursue Unity: By Deeds or Ideas?

From almost the beginning of the Christian era, the church has been rightly concerned about ideas. This is quite understandable given the prevalent ideas the first Christians faced in the Greco-Roman world. Yet I believe we are warranted to ask, "Which came first, the deeds of love, or the well-developed Christian ideas that were rooted in the questions posed by ancient philosophy?"

Nineteenth-century France is a marvelous illustration of how some answered this question in the face of huge social and religious upheaval. (I have revisited this story time and again, trying to find a better way to interact with our present society roiled in deep controversy.) The reverberations of the revolution in France had led the church hierarchy to align itself with conservative causes and powers. This arrangement caused the masses of working-class people, as well as younger intellectuals who embraced the new republican spirit of liberty, to turn away from the Christian faith. During this dark period, a faithful Catholic layman and scholar named Frédéric Ozanam (1813–1853) began his life's work to tear down the walls created by the church of his time.

When Ozanam was still a student in Paris, he helped revive a discussion group called the Society of Good Studies. It became a forum for lively discussions among students. Their attention turned frequently to the gospel's social teachings. At one meeting, during a heated debate in which Ozanam and his friends were trying to prove from historical evidence alone the truth of the Catholic Church, their adversaries declared that at one time the church was a source of good but no longer. "What is your church doing now? What is she doing for the poor of Paris?" one student challenged. "Show us your works and we will believe you!"

Ozanam heard this challenge, and when he became an attorney and social advocate, he lived to answer it. He challenged the visible church to see its real mission and renounce reliance on the rich and powerful. He argued that any attempt to regain France's glory by restoring a bygone pre-revolutionary era called for a deep Christian conversion of both mind and heart. He saw the world in the way I've come to see it over the last forty years, believing the new ideologies and structures of his time were "messengers of God to test our justice and charity and to save us by our works."[4] As a consequence of these challenges, Ozanam, and a number of very bright young men, formed the charitable Society of St. Vincent de Paul.

One of the greatest challenges to the mission and unity of the church in our time is the de-Christianization of the church. Non-Christian values have gripped much of the church, on the left and the right, moving large numbers of Christians into a radicalism that promotes ideas over love. *These movements fail the gospel.* The values being promoted embrace tribalism over humanity, superiority over equality, and the heroism of victory over the willingness to sacrifice oneself for others. For me, a person like Frédéric Ozanam is an icon for a better and more-faithful way to think and live as disciples of Jesus. Ozanam's biographer says, "He valued friendships and defended his friends no matter what the cost. He was attentive to details, perhaps to the extreme. . . . He showed a great tenderness when dealing with his family. . . . He had a great reverence for his parents, and revealed his ability to sacrifice his career and his profession in order to please them."[5] In short, he modeled a path that tore down walls and built bridges.

In 1997 Pope John Paul II beatified Frédéric Ozanam, officially recognizing his powerful life of love. His life shows us what love that serves the poor, and embraces bonds of deep friendship, really means. This story provides a beautiful model of my vision for the church. Those who believe the gospel message can unite in costly love, not just by walling ourselves off by debates about good ideas but by investing ourselves together in the words *and* works of Jesus.

Questions for Discussion and Reflection

1. Why do you think we come up with so many explanations for John 17:20–23 that refuse to take seriously what our Lord actually prayed for?

---

4. Ellsberg, *Blessed Among Us*, 519.
5. Frédéric Ozanam. [not in bib]

2. How would you explain the idea of *relational unity*?
3. How does Ozanam speak to our time and the unity and mission of the church?

Chapter Five

Our Greatest Apologetic

> I believe very strongly in the principle and practice of the purity of the visible church, but I have seen churches that have fought for purity and are merely hotbeds of ugliness. No longer is there any observable, loving, personal relationship even in their own midst, let alone with other true Christians.
>
> —*Francis Schaeffer*

I can't remember when I first heard a discussion about Christian apologetics, but I do recall thinking, "Why do we need to apologize for our faith?" My ignorance of the meaning of the word contributed to my naiveté. When I realized apologetics was a branch of theology devoted to the defense of Christian doctrine, I grew more interested. I took my first apologetics class during my third year at Wheaton College under the tutelage of the late Alan Johnson. (Alan became one of my most devoted friends and was a great champion for me and for the subject of this book.) Later I would teach formal graduate courses in apologetics at Wheaton. By that time my ideas about the subject had vastly changed.

Again, apologetics is centered on the defense of the faith against anti-Christian ideas. But the really important question in the field is *how* should we do the work of apologetics. Francis Schaeffer, a highly regarded evangelical apologist during my college years, once said the greatest apologetic for real evangelism was *the oneness of Christians*. Schaeffer helped change my understanding of Christian apologetics when he said, "Love—and the unity it attests to—is *the mark* Christ gave Christians to wear before the world" (italics added).[1]

Could Schaeffer's insight be true? I believe so. It clearly reflects what Jesus taught in John 13–17 and what the Apostle John stressed in his letters.

> "A new command I give you: Love one another. As I have loved you, so you must love one another. By this everyone will know that you are my disciples, if you love one another." (John 13:34–35)

> And this is his command: to believe in the name of his son, Jesus Christ, and to love one another as he commanded us. (1 John 3:23)

> Dear friends, let us love one another, for love comes from God. Everyone who loves has been born of God and knows God. Whoever does not love does not know God, because God is love." (1 John 4:7–8)

Friedrich Nietzsche (1844–1900), a preeminent anti-Christian philosopher, once said the problem with the church is that it is "human, all too human."[2] In one way, I agree. But this "human" church is Christ's body. Complacent Christians need to be regularly reminded that they have been brought into the church by God's grace to become more and more like Christ. Our humanity is a problem, but it is also the same reality God uses to share his love with the world; after all, "The Word became flesh and made his dwelling among us" (John 1:14).

As an apologist, Francis Schaeffer clearly recognized that the church exists not just for itself but for the sake of a watching world. How we act and treat one another really matters, because our actions represent the nature and identity of God to those who do not know him. Schaeffer adds, "Anything that an individual Christian or Christian group does that fails to show the simultaneous balance of the holiness of God and the love of God presents to a watching world not a demonstration of the God who exists but a caricature of the God who exists."[3]

Let's face it: We have given the world an ugly caricature of God, and multitudes can no longer hear our good news. They actually hear us opposing their politics with strident moral pronouncements. They know we oppose their lifestyle, and they feel condemned. A plethora of recent studies

---

1. Schaeffer, *Mark of the Christian*, 35.
2. Nietzsche, *Human*.
3. Schaeffer, *Mark of the Christian*, 21.

reveals this sad fact and provides another reason for my conviction that we must labor to tear down the walls that divide us.[4]

Back to the Future

As noted in Chapter 1, the way forward for the church lies in the past—in a return to Jesus' prayer and the core idea of the kingdom of God. We need a starting point that will allow us to be clear about what really matters and why. We must know who we are and how to speak faithfully about Christ. When we have clarity on the essentials, we are free to confidently move forward into a deeper understanding of the church and our mission. Without this common ground of commitment to Christ and his kingdom, our unity will be shallow at best.

Consider this amazing prayer more carefully, for it is one of the richest, most mysterious prayers in all Scripture. The unique oneness Jesus shared with his Father was intended to spill over into the new community of Jesus' followers. John tells us that on the night before Jesus was killed, he looked beyond this little band of disciples and embraced you and me by praying for all those who would believe the apostolic message. The Spirit used the sending of these first disciples *in the same way* he used the Father's sending of the Son into the world (John 17:18). At the end of John 17, Jesus refers to heavenly realities (verse 24), yet his primary concern is the unity of all his people. In fact, twice he prays that we will be one, *just as he and the Father are one*, so we will "be brought to complete unity" (verse 23). In the ancient world, as in our own, division was common. Politics, class, wealth, gender, and religion all divided people.

The real indicator of the church's faithfulness is not successful evangelization; it is the love of Christ drawing us into this deep relationship of oneness. Christian cults prosper and grow numerically. Other religions reach and convert people, sometimes better than the Christian church. In fact, the fastest-growing religious category in America is made up of those who describe themselves as having "no religion." Any person or group, can grow numerically, but the unity Jesus prayed for cannot be manufactured. Some

---

4. See Kinnaman and Lyons, *unChristian*. Gathering the insights of Christians of many ages and traditions, the authors explain how modern Americans really see Christians. Words like *hypocritical, anti-homosexual, sheltered, too political* and *judgmental* jump out. See also Mehta, *I Sold My Soul on eBay*. The author, an atheist, describes his experience of a Sunday morning odyssey in numerous American evangelical churches and offers an eye-opening appraisal of how a non-Christian perceives the life and practice of some of our largest churches.

groups require uniformity, but true unity is always a gift to be received and lived through God's love.

The Pattern for Our Unity

The Father, Son, and Holy Spirit are one in essence (being). According to John 17, the goal of our unity is the same as that of the triune God: to reveal God's love to the world (verse 21). With this in mind, Jesus' prayer raises an important question: In what sense can our unity as Christians be compared to the unity we see in God?

It should be clear Jesus is not praying for our *essential* oneness. We already possess it, because all who know Christ participate in the divine nature (2 Peter 1:4). The oneness Jesus prayed for assumes a spiritual participation in his death and resurrection life, but he goes further to address the *functional* oneness I have referred to as *relational unity*—a oneness that is the expression of the eternal, spiritual unity of the Father and Son. During Jesus' earthly lifetime, this relational oneness was seen most clearly in his role as mediator (see John 5:19, 36; 14:10). Though the Son is co-eternal and co-equal with the Father, in the Son's incarnation he faithfully developed and expressed a relational unity with his Father every moment of his human life.

As Christians, we believe the Holy Spirit lives in us. Because he indwells us, our lives have become the unique sphere of his divine activity (John 14:12; 15:1–17). Through the direct, daily work of the Spirit in us, we experience a new vitality and freshness as we relate to one another and to God. He is truly at work in our lives, and as we grow into his love we can see the evidence of his activity working itself out through our lives. The supreme evidence of this work is revealed when we "love one another" (John 13:34–35). As those entrusted with carrying forward God's mission, our unity is rooted in this same love—which is not "an arbitrary fiat of omnipotence but rests upon a new gift. . . . the love of Christ [that] constitutes the new community."[5] Thus the life we share in him involves both human *and* divine cooperation. To experience this unity, we must live in constant dependence on God through a humble willingness to embrace his will and purposes.

---

5. Newbigin, *Light Has Come*, 176.

Love Is the Center

As we saw in chapter 4, the love of God is the greatest force in the universe. But why? "God *is* love" (1 John 4:8, italics added). The love of God is *who* God is and this eternal love is reflected in the unity of the divine life: "I and the Father are one" (John 10:30). This divine unity is also a unity of redemptive purpose (John 17:20–26). The love of God for the world is demonstrated in the giving of his Son to save the whole world from the consequences of sin (John 3:16–17). We reciprocate God's loving initiative when we offer ourselves to him in heartfelt surrender: "We love because he first loved us" (1 John 4:19).

These phrases can seem remote and sentimental if we lack the relational unity that underlies them. God's love for us, and our love for him, is meant to be visibly expressed through our actions: "Let us not love with words or tongue but with actions and in truth" (1 John 3:18). In fact, the entire will of God can be effectively summarized in two commands: We are to love God and our neighbors (Luke 10:27). Love and active obedience to God's will go hand in hand. As Jesus plainly said, "If you love me, keep my commands" (John 14:15).

Some suggest the Apostle John limits God's love to the Christian community. I disagree. But rather than argue over the details, I suggest Christ's fellowship with his disciples is the place where the love of God is to be *most openly displayed*. If "God is love," then our expressions of love within the Christian community must align with his love because we are in the same family. These familial expressions work themselves out into the wider world. His love enlarges our hearts and forms our character in community so we are free to love others, whether or not they are fellow Christians. We are to love even our enemies. Only such love can tear down all walls.

Cooperational Love

God's love is at the center of church life, and is an expression of the spiritual unity of the Trinity and our inclusion in Christ, so we are compelled to consider how we can work together in Christ's mission. Relational unity with Christ should lead us to embrace a cooperational unity with other Christians.[6] I know that word *cooperational* instantly frightens some people. Some think *cooperation* means *compromise*—that by working together we

---

6. The word *cooperation* refers to the process of working together for the same end. The end for which all Christians live is the glory of God. His glory is revealed in his love for us, and his love in us should move us toward continual cooperation with those who also love him and seek his glory.

are somehow selling out our beliefs and convictions. I find that those who approach relationships within the body of Christ with suspicion and fear generally build walls rather than bridges. When this is the case, there is little likelihood of experiencing the relational love Jesus desires us to have for one another.

What does God's love look like when we cooperate in Christ's mission? 1 Corinthians 13:4–8 gives the most magnificent description of love in all the Bible and all recorded literature. Here is my paraphrase/application of Paul's hymn of praise put into a kind of unity perspective:

> Love is patient and kind, not boastful or rude. It keeps no record of wrongs. Love hopes all things, believes all things and love never ends. This is a perfect description of God's love toward us. He puts up with all our faults and failures and never complains. He is so kind that he never tries to coerce or control us. God never boasts, because he doesn't need to impress you or me. God is never rude; he has no inner need to offend us. And he keeps no record of our wrongs. He hopes in us and believes we can strive for our potential even if we have doubts. If God is this way for and with us, then we can live our lives as an extension of his life of love in us. When we offer this kind of divine love to others, we enable them to become something beautiful for God and for others. This love leads us into the unity Jesus desires for all his people.

Let's explore three ways Christians have thought about this type of love, a love generated in us by the Spirit, who leads us into a genuinely powerful unity of cooperation. Each of these types is based on Jesus' words in John 17, and each type has a role, though they all fall short of what I believe Scripture is truly saying in John 17.

Unanimity

Unanimity assumes we should reach agreement in everything. This was the tendency of some Catholics, given their belief about the **magisterium** and the **papacy**. But this has formally changed since Vatican Council II. Professor Hans Küng, a Catholic theologian who has often criticized his church, correctly concludes:

> The unity of the church is not simply a natural unity, is not simply a moral unanimity and harmony, is not just sociological conformity and uniformity. To judge it by externals (canon law, ecclesiastical language, church administration, etc.) is to

misunderstand it completely. *The unity of the church is a spiritual entity.* It is not chiefly a unity of members among themselves, it depends finally not on itself but on the unity of God, which is efficacious through Jesus Christ in the Holy Spirit. . . . It is one and the same confession of faith in the Lord Jesus, the same hope of blessedness, the same love, which is experienced in oneness of heart, the same service of the world. The church *is* one and therefore *should be* one (italics mine).[7]

The issue of unanimity comes down to this: Can there be real disciples who understand one or more points of doctrine that seem contrary to one's own tradition? I believe a truly faithful approach—one solidly rooted in the good news of Jesus Christ (**kerygma**)—can endure different understandings on many doctrinal issues. I see it this way: We must allow for sin in other people and make room for weak or misguided Christians. In much the same way that we hold to the idea of *simul justus et peccator* (we are "simultaneously righteous and sinful"), we can embrace the corresponding idea of *simul fidelis et incredulus*—we are both believers and unbelievers at one and the same time. Belief and unbelief runs through the heart of every Christian. If we are honest, every one of us confesses, "Lord, I do believe; help me overcome my unbelief."

Uniformity

In the history of the church, *uniformity* in faith and practice has been the default approach when ritual and liturgical practices (how we worship) are made central. There is much to commend in this approach. This view, almost unknown in American Protestant churches, unites Christians around a common liturgical practice that allows the whole church to worship and practice the faith together as one. While it can lead to problems such as ritualism and traditionalism, it can also create a deep sense of unity.[8]

In the private prep school I attended, we all were required to wear a uniform. Because we all dressed the same way, I never had to think about what to wear. Some may argue this created too much uniformity, thus denying our individuality, but it had a different effect on me. It gave me a calm

---

7. Küng, *The Church*, 353–54.

8. I will say more about this, but the Orthodox Church and the Catholic Church share a deep sense of unity, even uniformity, in their liturgies and common practices. I am not criticizing this ancient practice. There is much to commend in it. However, I do not think this is the unity Jesus actually prayed for in John 17. The reasons go far beyond the scope of this book.

confidence about my appearance that allowed me to focus my energy and attention on more important matters. I remained an individual, but I was part of a group in which our unity was demonstrated through what we wore.

I do realize uniformity in the church can lead to serious problems, especially as Christ's mission takes root in various and diverse cultures. How does the gospel, a historical message given within a specific culture, adapt to new cultures? How do we "become all things to all people so that by all possible means [we] might save some" (1 Corinthians 9:22)? Later chapters will discuss how the church must become a missional community that is culturally inclusive and doctrinally guided by the gospel. Attempts to create ecclesial uniformity sometimes fail this test, especially when a particular culture or ethnicity becomes too closely identified with the truth.

Union

Union emphasizes the goal of Jesus' prayer—to bring all of us into one visible, united church. Traditionally Catholics and Orthodox Christians have believed union is essential to true unity. But this view has created a huge barrier when they try to tear down the wall that separates the historic East/West church divide, even though they have so much in common.

Nothing seemed to break the heart of the late Pope John Paul II more than the breakdown of talks about unity with the Orthodox Church. (He beautifully said the whole church—East and West—has two lungs and breathes best when both are healthy.) Part of the reason for the breakdown was the way each group understood this idea of union. The papacy, which is at the center of unity for Catholics, presents serious problems for both Orthodox and Protestant Christians. But even this wall is being slowly torn down brick by brick as recent popes have seen the papacy not primarily as an expression of power and authority, but as a "bridge" (the meaning of the word *pontiff*) to true unity. In this case, history can again serve current concerns for unity.

I frequently use the term *union* to refer to what happens when several churches unite (reconcile). In twentieth-century South India, when several walls between different Protestant churches fell, unity arose. The Church of South India was birthed through this movement. Such union takes place regularly in local communities when several churches unite to form one "new" congregation. In a global sense, we may be further from this kind of union than ever before in Christian history, yet I envision a time when unity will become a very real possibility.

Other expressions of union can be found in the common accords that have allowed certain Protestant communions to enter into ministerial relationships across their historic divides. Conservative Protestants have often feared such unions, believing they require serious doctrinal compromise. Typically, the crux of these debates has been the place and ministry of the Lord's Supper. Yet many communions, with differing views of what happens in the Lord's Supper, have transcended their differences without surrendering them. They have torn down walls—walls once seen as impossible to remove—by sharing in genuine faith and order dialogues that have borne good fruit relationally and ministerially.

Most scholars agree that very little in the New Testament resembles a central church that represents the myriad Christian churches. We find some expression of union in Acts, particularly at the Council of Jerusalem (15:1–29). Acts 15 shows how several leaders of different churches came together to reach an agreement based on a *minimal* set of conclusions aimed at preserving oneness in mission. Considering the very real danger of false teaching and doctrinal error, this agreement is stunning in terms of how far they were willing to go to ensure the gospel spread freely and the church remained undivided. Still, formal structures and plans for organizational union between churches have little to do with what we see in Acts 15. My vision of unity allows for this to happen over time, but it does not see this as our immediate or most-pressing goal.

None of these understandings of unity—unanimity, uniformity, and union—truly fit the context of the New Testament mandate for our deep unity. The aim of the early church was the mission of Christ's kingdom in the world lived by Christians who loved one another and showed love to all, even their enemies. *The purpose of their oneness was to be a visible representation of God's love.*

What Means Do We Have for Cooperation?

The Scriptures teach that Christ gives us his divine life through the gift of the Spirit—the "bond of love," according to Augustine. The earliest creeds rightly placed the doctrine of the church and its oneness in the section on the Holy Spirit.

All Christians "participate in the [mystery of the] divine nature" (2 Peter 1:3–4), thus our participation in this mystery is how we pursue our relational unity in Christ (2 Corinthians 3:18; Hebrews 12:10; 1 John 3:2). Our common participation in the divine nature means Christians should never conceive of life in community apart from Christ. All of the riches of the Godhead are found in Christ, and they are now ours through our union with him. Forgiveness, love, joy, righteousness, gentleness, and tenderness are found in him. And they are now at work in us by the Holy Spirit. This is the key to biblical unity—keeping our focus on Christ as the center.

A Model of Unity for Our Time

In 2011 I was invited to join an informal team of Catholic and Protestant missionaries in Rome. Nate Bacon, a missionary with an ecumenical order called InnerChange,[9] had followed my story for a few years and strongly felt I should join with six others to engage in conversations with scholars and practitioners of unity and spirituality. One of the most memorable stops during our time together was the Pontifical Council for Promoting Christian Unity (PCPCU). (I was disappointed that Cardinal Walter Kasper had just retired as president of the council.) We had an extensive dialogue with two Council leaders who oversaw the Vatican's work for unity in Africa and Latin America. For my purposes, this conversation proved very beneficial for my work in mission and unity.

Shortly after this visit, I began to research the history of the PCPCU. One of the great figures in the Catholic Church, who had a major role in developing its vision for unity, was Cardinal Augustin Bea, the first president of the PCPCU. On February 28, 2019, Pope Francis commemorated the fiftieth anniversary of Cardinal Bea's death, calling him "a model and a source of inspiration for ecumenical and interreligious dialogue."[10] The more I've read his story, the more I understand how the greatest apologetic works in modern life. This truth can be seen in the life of Cardinal Bea, a person who showed how "love and respect are the primary principles of dialogue." Pope Francis said Bea faced many obstacles, especially within the Catholic Church, but "though accused and maligned, he moved forward with the perseverance of one who never stops loving. . . . [Bea] was neither an optimist nor a pessimist, he was realist about the future of unity: on the one hand, conscious of the difficulties, on the other convinced of the need to respond to the heartfelt desire of the Lord that his disciples be 'one.'"[11]

I have learned a great deal from Cardinal Bea and the mission of the PCPCU. I have seen a clear way to engage in the prayerful and hard work of

---

9. InnerChange is an ecumenical order of Jesus followers whose lives are bound together by common rhythms, commitments, and values. These missionaries live among the poor and share the good news of the gospel faithfully in both words and deeds.

10. O'Kane, "Pope."

11. O'Kane, "Pope."

Christian unity. If you follow these vibrant and substantial models you will need those qualities seen in a person like Cardinal Bea: realism, perseverance, and profound hope. But most of all, you will need the love he showed, even for his opponents inside the church.

Questions for Discussion and Reflection

1. How might our unity serve as a witness to non-Christians? Can you think of an example of how this happens?
2. What does the unity of the Trinity have to do with our unity with other Christians?
3. How can our experience of oneness make our message more credible to non-Christians? How might this unity help us love our agnostic and atheist friends more effectively?

Chapter Six

Christ the Center

Only in Christ are all things in communion. He is the point of convergence for all hearts and beings and therefore the bridge and the shortest way from each to each.

—*Hans Urs von Balthasar*

If you learn anything except Christ, you learn nothing. If you learn nothing except Christ, you learn everything.

—*St. Bonaventure*

Close your eyes for a moment. Seriously, do it. Imagine hearing Jesus speak when you read his story in the four Gospels. Picture him teaching thousands of people on a grassy hillside or speaking from the bow of a boat just off the shores of the Sea of Galilee. You can almost see and hear the multitudes watching and listening to this controversial young rabbi. Jesus taught not as the professionals of his time did, but as one who had a unique authority from above. Listeners heard his stories and parables, his announcements and his warnings, and they "were amazed" (Matthew 9:33; 12:23; 15:31). We who profess to follow Jesus now need to be amazed as well.

Now envision the more relational parts of the Gospel narratives. You can readily see Jesus engaging with small groups, often with a single person. And when he engages in person-to-person dialogue, you see him asking questions that elicit surprising responses. If you pay close enough attention, you soon discover that Jesus hardly ever *answered* the questions people asked him. His common response was to ask better questions to those who questioned him.[1]

My intention in this chapter is to ask one question: *How do we keep Christ at the center of everything?* After all, Jesus is the center of his own prayer for our unity and the mission of his kingdom (John 17). It's profoundly clear in John 17 that our unity is synonymous with our being centered in Christ. If you begin here, you will be prepared to engage with some of the most difficult questions the biblical story provokes. I submit you will never take responsibility for your role in becoming an answer to Jesus' prayer for unity until you allow the Spirit of unity to fill you with the vision of oneness.

Yves Congar, the great twentieth-century Catholic theologian, expressed how we should proceed when we begin to understand unity: "The way through the door of unity is on our knees." *Are you prepared to seek Christ on your knees?* Are you ready to do your part to heal the tragic divisions of the Christian church?

Two Commitments, One Question

We have already seen that the unity between the Father and the Son forms the basis for our experience of unity with other Christians. But how is our experience of unity bound up with the success of Christ's mission? The late Roman Catholic biblical scholar Raymond E. Brown provides helpful insight on the answer to this question in his exposition of John 17:

> As in [John] 10:16, believers [evangelized by different disciples] are not one flock, but unity is prayed for. Vital contact with this future generation and all subsequent generations will not be lost, for Jesus will dwell in them. The indwelling of Jesus, the Christian's earthly share in eternal life, provides the great bond of union connecting Christians of all times with the Father. Jesus' love for them is the same as his love for his immediate disciples: a love patterned on the eternal love of the Father for the Son. (So perfect is this love that it will force even the world's

---

1. See Dias, ed., *What Did Jesus Ask?* The breadth of contributors in this book is a perfect example of ecumenical conversation. Contributors include Catholic, Orthodox, and Protestant writers as well as Pentecostals, evangelicals, and Quakers. The editor includes a reference guide that says Jesus asked 279 questions. Some are variations and repetitions of the same question, but the point is the same.

recognition!) And they too shall have a share in the eternal glory of the Son.[2]

Christian believers have lived in different nations, cultural contexts, and ethnic settings since the mid-first century. They have spoken myriad languages and worshiped the triune God in diverse ways. Yet *in Christ* they remain one people because there is only one flock and one shepherd. Expressions of this one communion vary, but Christ remains at the center when faith is alive in the promises of God. The issue of how the whole church should be visibly organized will continue to be discussed and debated, but this much is certain: We are spiritually one church, not two or three (Ephesians 4:4–6).

My understanding of biblical oneness combines two commitments that are often considered separately. The first is a commitment to work in every conceivable way to demonstrate and express our God-given oneness with other believers. This means we must have a true desire to work with Christians we know and multitudes we don't. It includes our closest friends and fellow church members as well as Christians and churches halfway around the world. I seek to practice this by praying for friends far away, friends I will never meet in this life. Whether people are a part of my church communion or another—Catholic, Protestant, or Orthodox—I know I am one with them in Christ (1 Corinthians 12:3). Growing in biblical oneness with other believers begins with a commitment to aggressively pursue specific ways to demonstrate our common love for Christ.

But my second commitment goes much further. Many Christians have been satisfied with informal person-to-person expressions of oneness. This is where I was for several decades until the Spirit got my full attention. Sadly, most American Christians see the church solely as a voluntary association for their personal benefit. Because of this profoundly individualistic mindset, we see no need to seek unity with other Christians and churches. But the pursuit of oneness means we must never shy away from every opportunity to engage in relational and co-operational unity. Though the three great historic branches of the Christian church remain formally divided, we *can* seek greater relational unity "on [our] knees." *We must never settle just for personal oneness with other individuals.* The true pursuit of biblical oneness embraces a concern for the unity of the wider church. I personally pray every day that this would become a reality between churches, locally and globally.

I am often asked, "Do you think the great divided churches will ever become one?" I respond, "Who can possibly know what God will do in the centuries ahead?" Could people from centuries past have foreseen what's

2. Brown, *The Gospel and the Epistles of John*, 86.

transpired in the last century? For nearly five hundred years, Catholics and Protestants were fierce enemies. Entire nations and families were divided. Bloody wars were fought over these differences. Following the Council of Trent in the sixteenth century, and Vatican Council I in the nineteenth, no one could have predicted what would happen in the twentieth century. What then might happen in the twenty-first or twenty-second century? Who can know what the Spirit will do as the world grows smaller and the church grows larger? What will happen in Africa, where the fast-growing Christian church and the fast-spreading religion of Islam, exist side by side? Can the church learn to love Christ *and* their Muslim neighbors?

Perhaps the most important question here relates to Christ's mission: How will God finally accomplish his purpose to save people from "every tribe and language and people and nation" (Revelation 5:9)? I see no obvious reason the church must become *organizationally* united, but I believe we will see and experience unprecedented *relational* unity. If the answer to this prayer is certain, what might happen prior to Christ's return? Will the Spirit lead us to embrace unity, bringing us closer to the final consummation? The question for us seems simple: *Will we seek the unity that God wills for the church in a future that is truly open to his guidance?*

Already we see evidence of the spread of a Spirit-given unity that defies our old categories of division. I welcome all serious interactions between churches and individuals who want to pursue the supremacy of Christ together. If Christ is truly the center, we can move toward him and find fellowship with one another in the process. The closer we get to the center, the more we are enabled to love one another!

I have frequently asked friends who work in the ministry of ecumenism what they think the long-term future of all these movements might be in, say, five hundred years. What if, for example, the Roman Catholic and Orthodox Churches found a way to enter into deep unity with one another? What if the fast-growing trans-denominational Pentecostal and charismatic expressions, in all their rich diversity, brought evangelical and mainline Protestants even more intentionally into this movement, thus uniting them even more with the Catholic and Orthodox way? Who knows? With God all things are possible.

To those who love the church, the two-commitment approach I've articulated may seem obvious, but it raises a basic question: What will *you* do with this call? This has profound practical consequences for Protestants. It means I can no longer be an anti-Catholic or remain an evangelical and Reformed Protestant who is satisfied that I can seek Christ without others. With deep conviction, I am compelled to regard both Catholics and the Catholic Church with love and warm esteem. This personal commitment to oneness has enabled me to draw great blessings from the Catholic tradition and from Catholic teaching. For me this became especially true as I developed wonderful friendships with my Catholic brothers and sisters. (The same holds true for my relationships with Orthodox Christians. I'll return to this later.)

Our Sense of Oneness Is Spiritual and Relational

For the first thousand years of its history, the church universally maintained an interest in unity, even when it seemed unattainable. However, in 1054, this outward (formal) unity was radically and tragically altered by the formal East-West Schism. Centuries later, the Protestant Reformation broke the Catholic Church's unity in Europe. The events that followed produced new visible church communions in Germany, Great Britain, the Netherlands, and Switzerland. Among Protestants, the Anabaptists and the numerous Free Church movements further divided the visible church. While both sides of the sixteenth-century debate initially tried to preserve the unity of the church, each made decisions that would eventually make this all but impossible.

As I restudied the post-Reformation era of Western church history, I discovered a virtually unknown story. Leaders on both sides found compelling reasons to attempt a restoration of unity even as the church was being divided. (The last attempt to restore some form of unity between Catholics and Protestants occurred in 1541 at the Colloquy of Regensburg. This last-ditch effort obviously failed.) For many leaders of the Reformation, especially Calvin and Luther, the division caused by the Protestant Reformation was never a *desirable* result. But as the rhetoric increased and the conflicts intensified, deeper divisions developed. Since the sixteenth century, countless church splits have only deepened the chasms between all the churches.

Still, an amazing reality points to God's ongoing work in the church. Despite these tragic schisms there remains a deep desire for unity within the hearts of many Protestants and Catholics.

> [The church] has been split by innumerable dissensions and disagreements. It has passed through many crises and vicissitudes. It has known ages of the most violent individualism as well as the most submissive collectivism. But for all the legitimate or illegitimate variety it has never lost its ultimate and indestructible unity.[3]

---

3. Bromiley, *Unity and Disunity*, 9.

The ground of this undeniable sense of oneness is found in the Bible. In the Old Testament the Israelites were chosen to bless the nations (Genesis 26:4). There were not *two* peoples but *one*. Though they were eventually divided into twelve tribes and later became two different kingdoms, Israel remained *one* chosen people descended from Abraham, the *one* man. When they left Egypt, they left as *one* people. And when God gave them his law, it was not a law for many nations and groups but a divine treasure for *one* people. Yes, they fought civil wars and turned on each other at times. Yet in the end nothing could destroy the inherent oneness Israel experienced when she remembered her divine origins and unifying covenant. When Paul urged a specific congregation to preserve the unity of God in their life together, he recalled Israel's story of failure as a warning to that church and concluded that Israel "serve[s] as an example . . . written down to instruct us, on whom the ends of the ages have come" (1 Corinthians 10:11).

The New Testament does not alter this principle of unity as a central characteristic of God's people. The church consists of people from every tribe, nation, and language, all of whom find their fundamental identity in *one* person—Jesus Christ. As I suggested earlier, this principle of the one and the many is rooted in the communal nature of God as Trinity. The ethnic ground of unity, as seen in the Old Testament covenant, has passed away. In its place, a spiritual unity grounded in the new covenant—a new unity rooted in *one* Savior, whose incarnation, death, and resurrection gave birth to *one* organism, the church (Jeremiah 31:31–34). For this reason, "the whole structure of the New Testament church, or churches, shows us that there is a strong and indissoluble sense of unity not only with the local congregation but extending to the church as a whole."[4] We should never become complacent about the disunity of God's people. In fact, we must cultivate a holy discontent about our unholy divisions and return to the covenant of love.

When Israel under the old order was brought to Messiah, the people were not destroyed but fulfilled and renewed through the gift of a new covenant. (This doesn't mean ethnic Israel has no place in the plan of God [see Romans 11] and certainly doesn't justify any form of anti-Semitism, a recurring problem throughout the history of Christianity, especially after the early second century.) What emerged from the old covenant was something in continuity with all God's intentions for his one people. The unity that was once confined to a single ethnic people is now a global spiritual reality—"a holy nation, God's special possession" (1 Peter 2:9). This new spiritual reality is inherently one since Christ is the Lord of the church. As Christians,

---

4. Bromiley, *Unity and Disunity*, 10.

our true spiritual unity is the relational oneness we experience when the Holy Spirit draws us together in Christ.

The Old Testament was the Bible of the early church. These Scriptures taught the first followers of Messiah that the temple was central to life and worship. But the New Testament writers, who preserved the apostolic teaching, taught that the one temple had now become a spiritual one. The church of God is thus made up of "living stones" built into a "spiritual house—a new temple where we collectively offer spiritual sacrifices to God (1 Peter 2:5). If Christians are to truly live out the reality of this one (spiritual) temple of God, then there is no place for rival movements. There is one "place" where we worship—the mercy seat of Christ. He is the cornerstone of the new temple, with the apostles—meaning all their teaching and witness—as the foundation. As followers of Christ, we are the building blocks ("living stones") that make up this new temple. We have been fitted together by God, the architect and builder of his church (see 1 Corinthians 3:16–17; 2 Corinthians 6:16; Ephesians 2:21–22; Hebrews 3:6).

Christ the Center

I find it helpful to think of the worldwide church as a large circle. At the center of this circle is Christ. As people on the outer edge of the circle move inward toward Christ, they grow closer and closer to one another. This Christ-centered unity is not found in manmade structures or efforts to achieve oneness. It is the fruit of our nearness to Christ. It is modeled on the unity Christ experienced with the Father. It is a *relational* unity, experienced and revealed through being in him and sharing in his mission.

Ignatius of Antioch once said, "Wherever Jesus Christ is, there is the catholic church."[5] Theologian Jürgen Moltmann adds to this idea, stating the church is present wherever "the manifestation of the Spirit" resides.[6] The British theologian P. T. Forsyth rightly contended that the unity of the church lies "not in itself but in its message, in the unity of the gospel that made the church."[7] In some sense, all these views are correct. The incarnate person of Christ, the indwelling presence of the Spirit in the hearts of believers, and the proclamation of the gospel are all *essential* characteristics of the relational unity that defines the oneness of the church.

The German martyr-theologian Dietrich Bonhoeffer has been seen as a radical who wanted to do away with the "religious elements" of the church.

---

5. Cited in Bercot, ed., *Dictionary*, 146.
6. Moltmann, *Church in the Power*, 34.
7. Forsyth, *Church and Sacraments*, 39.

But he remained a Lutheran to his final day. He rightly stressed that the *who* question—our identity—must always come before the *what* question—our practice: When I know *who* the person of Jesus is I will better understand *what* he does. Bonhoeffer's stress was always on Christ who came *before* the church, who stands at the center of the church. Bonhoeffer's famous lectures of 1933 thus bear the memorable title *Christ the Center*.

In later chapters we will see how Christ's kingdom mission is vital to our understanding of true unity. At this point it is crucial to remember that true unity always begins with this question: "Who is Jesus Christ?" Only by beginning with the person of Jesus can Christians develop a serious approach to unity, since our unity is found *in Christ alone*. Bonhoeffer was right—if we are to pursue unity, especially in the church of the future, we must begin with Christ at the center![8]

Questions for Discussion and Reflection

1. Do you believe there is only one church? If so, what does it mean to you? How does it affect your understanding of your local church and its witness?

2. If there is only one church and Jesus is Lord of that church, what should your response be to schism and division? How should you deal with personal disagreements that you have with other believers and churches?

3. How does the growth and development of the church in the non-Western nations impact you? How can the church in the West respond to these changes?

4. How can you make sure that Christ is at the center of all you are and do?

---

8. Bonhoeffer, *Christ the Center*, 60–65.

Chapter Seven

The Four Classical Marks of the Church

In the Catholic Church itself, all possible care must be taken that we hold that faith which has been believed everywhere, always, by all.

—*Vincent of Lérins*

Early Christian teaching is simple and uncluttered; it cuts through the complexities of cultured Christianity and allows what is primary and essential to surface.

—*Robert E. Webber*

Confessing faith in Christ is risky business, even in comfortable Western social spaces. I occupy my place in the world and confess what I believe. But I generally live from only one perspective—my own. I declare that what I believe is "true," at least for me. But is the Christian truth I confess also true for others? If so, how? And how did this truth I confess shape the lives of many witnesses, both ancient and modern?

The earliest Christian creeds provide a serious response to such questions. They draw their authority from Scripture *and* the lives of ancient Christian confessors who lived and died as one. The creeds became necessary because a *communal* understanding of the faith was needed to protect believers from destructive myths. Being a Christian is not merely about having certain perspective or attitudes about God and the world. It is a matter of faithful living according to a very specific vision of reality. In every age the church must confess what it believes against both heresy and paganism. But every creed or confession of faith is historically conditioned—a fact that requires continual confession and reformation. No creed is the last word, and Christians without creeds are not intrinsically non-Christians or anti-Christians. *Creeds are for Christians.* They are meant to help us affirm together what is *historically central to our shared faith.*

A **creed** (a confession, symbol, or statement of faith) expresses the *shared beliefs* of a community in the form of a statement that summarizes the core tenets of received teaching. Some New Testament scholars believe the earliest creed in Christianity can be seen in Paul's affirmation "Jesus is Lord" (Philippians 2:11). Others deem Galatians 3:28 an early confession, suggesting these words were affirmed by the first Christians at their baptism. On this point most historians have agreed: Within one generation, the earliest Christians sought to understand their confession of Jesus as Lord and their transcendent oneness in him. They confessed this individually in their baptism and corporately as statements that expressed their common beliefs. Thus, in every age the church has confessed collectively her historical faith in Jesus.

Catholic scholar Luke Timothy Johnson says one way to look at the language of these earliest creeds is to see them as a "set of critical theological concepts." Though we can never explain or define these concepts perfectly, if we deny them we will quickly distort or lose our central truths. These expressions do not give us the last word, thus we continue to plumb the depths of our shared faith. And the Spirit is clearly not limited to the words of any creed. But without them we may well remain unsure about the place and importance of the first words that we can share together.[1]

When I first began to reflect more deeply upon the Apostles' Creed, and later on the Nicene and Athanasian Creeds, I was brought face to face with a word that deeply troubled me: ***catholic***. I now believe this one word is so important that it is difficult to remain faithful to orthodoxy *and* Christian unity without somehow embracing it.[2] The reasons for its importance lie in its use by early Christians and the meaning it had in the development of the classical Christian tradition.

---

1. Johnson, *The Creed*.

2. I am not suggesting you must use the word *catholic* to be faithful to Christ, but I do believe the truth behind this word is a significant, instructive part of what it means to follow Jesus with all his people.

Anti-Catholicism

When I first began to struggle with the historical understanding of catholicity, I came to see how deeply anti-Catholic I was. Even using the word *catholic* with a small *c* disturbed me. Thinking back to my childhood, and the 1960 presidential election, I recall my pastor telling our congregation why Christians should not vote for Senator John F. Kennedy. A Kennedy presidency, he opined, would allow the papacy to have too much influence in America. I now realize I inherited a decided religious and cultural bias. Much of my struggle with the word *catholic* was the product of fear—a fear that constructed walls I didn't even know existed. To counter my fears, I dug into *why* the church chose to express its faith through these four key words in the Nicene Creed: "*one holy catholic* and *apostolic*" church. These words are traditionally called the four "marks" of the church. We'll unpack each and see what they can show us about how to better understand Christian unity.

The Church Is *One*

When we say the church is *one*, we are making a statement that is clearly consistent with apostolic testimony: "There is one body" (Ephesians 4:4). This idea of *oneness* should be taken in at least two senses. First, it implies *uniqueness*. There is nothing else like the church. This sense of a unique status can be abused when advanced as a claim of privilege over and against another group of people—e.g., when people refer to themselves as God's "*favored* people," or the "one true church throughout all history." Or, in our modern era, when some Christians assert divine judgment will come upon all who do not confess Jesus Christ as their personal savior. When this notion of uniqueness becomes too prominent, as it has in some polemics, we begin to insist salvation is found *only in our church*. Luke Johnson notes that though there is a "certain truth to the ideal of a single church, it is [nonetheless] an ideal that, when claimed as a reality, can become dangerous."[3]

I believe we can claim this ideal of uniqueness for the church in reference to our common salvation in Christ.[4] The church is made up of every-

---

3. Johnson, *The Creed*, 263. It strikes me as extremely important that the creed not be used to "exclude" but to draw us together into oneness and to draw our attention to the basic truths we hold in common. The very absence of so much that has divided Christians makes the creed appealing when seen this way.

4. The question of salvation outside of Christ is not my focus here, but there's a diverse body of Christian theology on this subject. I urge you to understand that the church has never agreed on *one simple explanation* on how far God's mercy extends in

one who "calls on the name of the Lord" (Romans 10:13; 1 Corinthians 1:2). But the uniqueness of our common identity is abused when it only refers to our narrow understanding of who belongs among God's people because "The Lord knows those who are his" (2 Timothy 2:19). We are wise to follow Paul's counsel: "Therefore do not pronounce judgment before the time, before the Lord comes" (1 Corinthians 4:5).

The second way we can understand *oneness* is as an ideal to be pursued. In this sense, the church is one because there is "one body and one Spirit . . . one hope . . . one Lord, one faith, one baptism; one God and Father of all" (Ephesians 4:4–6). Yet the oneness of the church does not negate the rich diversity of its individual members: The church's oneness is characteristic of its mission and identity as a body that unites diverse people. "Unity is not the same thing as uniformity. Indeed, the unity of the Spirit allows and even requires diversity. The diversity within the community is analogous to the trinity of persons within the one God."[5] The United States Conference of Catholic Bishops adds, "The church of the twenty-first century will be, as it has always been, a church of many cultures, languages, and traditions, yet simultaneously one, as God is one—Father, Son, and Holy Spirit—unity in diversity."[6]

The Church Is *Holy*

God's command to Israel was very clear: "Be holy, because I am holy" (Leviticus 11:45). In the context of the covenant, this was for all Israel, not just select individuals. God's holiness made him "other" thus he commanded his people to be "other" than the world around them. The New Testament strongly emphasizes this concept of corporate holiness (1 Corinthians 1:2; 6:11; Ephesians 5:26; 1 Thessalonians 4:3, 7). There is an ongoing tension in the New Testament between what we already are in Christ and what we are urged to become in actual practice (1 Corinthians 1:2; 2 Corinthians 7:1; 1 Thessalonians 3:13; 4:3). Though the church is the holy temple of God, it must also express holiness in its actual behavior, albeit imperfectly, through dependence on God's sustaining and transforming grace (1 Corinthians 6:19–20).

Holiness has been understood in two specific ways in the church—*ritually* and *morally*. Debates over ritual forms of worship have resulted

---

the life to come. Our task is to preach the good news of salvation in Christ but *without* attacking others. All are made in God's image and loved by their Creator.

5. Johnson, *The Creed*, 264.
6. United States Conference of Catholic Bishops, "Welcoming the Stranger."

in division, and debates about what constitutes proper moral practice still divide the church. How can we determine which ethical practices are normative for Christians?

> The impulse toward holiness in the church has tended toward disunity.... Some Christians insist that obedience to the pope is a betrayal of the obedience of faith that is owed only to the gospel, others that the obedience to the pope is the perfect expression of obedience to the gospel. Some Christians separate from others (or drive others out) over the time and style of baptism, the nature of the Eucharist, the need (or not) of bishops, how the Scripture is to be read, who is to be ordained, and many other "essentials."[7]

From the Montanists to the Marcionites, from the Hutterites to the Holiness Pentecostals, the biblical call to holiness has often created division. In light of the long history of division caused by different understandings of what is morally right and wrong for Christians, it's fair to ask if it's truly possible to pursue corporate holiness as a church *and* preserve unity. Recognizing the *diversity* of ways in which Christians have understood and responded to the call to holy living is a good starting point. Personally knowing Christians in very different cultures and ethnic contexts, and seeing how they have sought to be godly in ways that often resulted in suffering, can draw us even closer together in the spirit of true holiness—a holiness not based on moralism or rigid codes. But knowing that Christians have had different perspectives on what constitutes holiness doesn't settle all the problems that still threaten our unity. I am convinced there are no easy solutions. Still, we must recognize that holiness, both as a spiritual reality and as a mark of actual practice in the lives of believers, is an essential characteristic of the church.

The Church Is *Catholic*

The early creeds tell us the church is catholic.[8] Some argue this is simply another way of saying the church is universal. Some Protestant churches even replace *catholic* with *Christian* in the creed. This move away from the use of *catholic* not only weakens our understanding but is redundant. The church is *inherently* Christian. There is no other way of defining the church. The Greek word *katholikos* literally means "throughout the whole world." Luke

---

7. Johnson, *The Creed*, 264.

8. Some Protestant churches speak of three ecumenical creeds: the Apostles' Creed, the Nicene Creed, and the Athanasian Creed. These three are also called the catholic or universal creeds.

Timothy Johnson suggests the true sense of the word is nuanced by both universality and inclusiveness: "As applied in the creed to the ideal church, it means both a universality of extent and an inclusiveness that embraces differences within a larger unity."[9] While the notion of universality is true, it does not convey the fullness of what is meant by catholicity.

> The creed does not say that the church is "Roman Catholic." That term is, indeed, oxymoronic. It combines the element of universality with a highly particular adjective. The Roman Catholic tradition (the reader will remember it is my own) may believe the Roman tradition is all-encompassing, but that is simply mistaken.[10]

Recovering a proper understanding of the term *catholic* is vital to Christian unity. What is at stake is a reality that the creed has underscored for Christians for nearly two millennia. The notion of catholicity tells us the church is universal in its extent, and it embraces a unity that goes beyond local and personal differences. The word *catholic* also reminds us this community extends across the globe and through time, incorporating all of the redeemed throughout the ages.

Johnson advocates retaining the word because "the catholic church is the one that exists everywhere, rather than simply in one place. Implicitly, then, catholicity asserts the general over the particular in any argument about the nature of the church."[11] This gets at the idea of *inclusiveness*. Some of our historic denominations, as well as many smaller and more energetic modern fellowships, are non-creedal. (Some are actually quite anti-creedal.) Many such churches define themselves more by ethnicity, or by their views on how to read the Bible. Their practices about gender, partisan politics, and unique concerns about holiness also play a role in their adopting very differing ways. What they often reject, for various reasons, is a *common confession* of salvation through the grace offered in Christ. But Jesus offered table fellowship to a wide array of sinners and openly associated with all the "wrong" people. The word *catholic* can help keep us rooted in our historical and confessional past. It also can help us see that our fellowship must be rooted in those truths that are essential to the good news.

The word *catholic* also corrects Christians' tendency to speak in ways that emphasize the church's inherently spiritual unity while ignoring or minimizing the real, and often messy, church. Francis Schaeffer expressed this well: "We make a mockery of what Jesus is saying [John 13:33–35;

---

9. Johnson, *The Creed*, 269.
10. Johnson, *The Creed*, 268–69.
11. Johnson, *The Creed*, 269.

17:21] unless we understand that he is talking about something visible."[12] In our discussions about the catholic church, we must always keep in mind that the church isn't just a concept or idea—it is something that really exists—with real, fallible human beings.

The Church Is *Apostolic*

The Nicene Creed adds a fourth word about the Spirit's ministry: the church is **apostolic**. The church is intimately and historically linked with the apostles. This truth has also been primarily understood in two ways. First, to combat the ancient error of Gnosticism, church fathers such as Tertullian and Irenaeus made continuity with the apostles an essential mark of the church. Roman Catholic and Orthodox Christians came to believe a line of historical succession from the apostles to the present was necessary and evident in their respective traditions. For believers in these traditions, the apostolicity of the church means more than just the scriptural witness. Churches that embrace apostolic succession believe the apostolic teaching includes the interpretations offered by the church councils, especially those decisions formulated during the first eight centuries. Admittedly, there is no simple way of reconciling differing perspectives on what defines apostolic authority. However, much progress is being made through the serious study of the **patristic** writings. Still, there is a better way to understand *apostolic*. Luke Johnson expresses this well:

> The church in every age must be measured by the standard of the apostolic age as witnessed not by the later tradition but by direct appeal to the writings of the New Testament. Placing the contemporary church against the one depicted in the Acts of the Apostles makes clear how much the prophetic witness of the church has been compromised by its many strategies of adaptation and survival over the centuries. This is the sense of the word employed by reformers like Martin Luther, who combated the excrescences of medieval Catholicism by appealing to the teaching and practice of the New Testament. Where in the New Testament do we find pope or cardinals? Where do we find mandatory celibacy? Where do we find indulgences, or even purgatory? Where do we find the office of the Inquisition? These are powerful questions. Equally needed is the prophetic

---

12. Schaeffer, *Mark of the Christian*, 20.

call to a simpler and more radical "New Testament" lifestyle by Christians.[13]

A healthy concern for apostolicity reminds us that we need to constantly reexamine our practices and structures in light of the apostolic practice of the early church. We must continue to search the Scripture and be open to "new light."[14] This fourth mark reminds all of us, especially those who do *not* believe in apostolic succession, that we must take the historical witness of the church seriously. We need fresh reminders that our culture-specific manifestations of the church must undergo the constant critique of the Scriptures.

Still, a mistaken emphasis on apostolicity can sometimes result in denying the continuing work of the Spirit in our present age. Johnson concludes, "The prophetic voice can all too easily be just as reflexively hostile to institution and authority as authority and institution are reflexively hostile to the voice of prophecy."[15] It's a good word for all of us, whether we are creedal or not.

It seems there is a type of institutional authority that tries to drive an opinion or idea out the front door of the church yet it often allows it to enter through the back door later on. Holding on to both *living tradition* and the missionary mandate of the Christian faith will always require wisdom and courageous leadership. The church's apostolic nature reminds us every generation needs fresh reminders of our origins, while still looking for innovative ways to engage our contemporary context.

Tension and Conflict

Tension and conflict in relationships are common. We've all experienced them at times. Struggles that one married couple works through and survives may end up dividing another. Over time, I have noticed people tend to stay in relationships, and work through their differences, when they love

---

13. Johnson, *The Creed*, 274.

14. John Robinson, the pastor of the Leiden separatist community in England, from which the early Pilgrims migrated to New England, said in a farewell sermon: "For I am verily persuaded the Lord hath more truth and light yet to break forth from his holy Word." This phrase has been widely debated. Exactly what did he mean by "new light"? This much seems clear: He was calling on the people of God to seek the Spirit's guidance; thus, he was calling for a creative and faithful response to God's leading. The point is, there is a strong strand of Christian thought and practice that sees the creed not simply as the last and final word about expressing all the truth but rather as a helpful and unifying first word.

15. Johnson, *The Creed*, 275.

each other deeply and are committed to finding solutions. The love of Christ will only become mutual and beneficial when we learn to live under the cross. Christian unity is like all expressions of relational unity, with one major exception: *It is generated by the Spirit and preserved by God's grace.* This means we must die daily and live for one another.

In the church, we who claim to love Christ must be committed to staying together in our relationships with other believers. After five-plus decades of Christian ministry, having spoken and consulted with over a thousand widely different churches, I've noticed that most divisions are *not* due to our major doctrinal disagreements; they are most often the result of a breakdown in our love for one another. When our love grows cold, it isn't hard to find a "cause" that lets us "justify" breaking fellowship. More often than not, our divisions result because we lack the patience to "carry each other's burdens" and "fulfill the law of Christ" (Galatians 6:2).

The four historical marks of the church can be great reminders of a classical Christian perspective on unity. While these marks will not solve all our disagreements (we can even disagree on how to use and interpret them), they provide us a reliable historical context in which we can begin to develop a more common understanding of what it means to be the church together without all the walls we've built over the centuries.

Questions for Discussion and Reflection

1. How would you describe anti-Catholicism? Do you see this spirit in your life or in your church? What can be done to correct it?

2. In what way are the four marks important for you and your church? Do they matter to you? Why or why not? How would you teach these marks to those who do not understand them?

3. What brings about conflicts within your church? Have you ever experienced a church split or division? What could have been done to prevent it? What should you do now to prevent it from happening again?

Chapter Eight

Can Our Unity Be Restored?

Lord Jesus,
who prayed that we might all be one,
we pray to You for the unity of Christians,
according to Your will, according to Your means.
May Your Spirit enable us
to experience the suffering caused by division,
to see our sin,
and to hope beyond all hope.
Amen.

> The blessed apostle John distinguished no heresy or schism, neither did he set down any as specially separated, but he called all who had gone out from the church, and who acted in opposition to the church, antichrist.
>
> —*Cyprian*

The early church held an extremely high view of oneness and catholicity. Unity was not a sideline for these apostolic communities. Believers were continually encouraged to preserve it. This view of the centrality of unity can be heard in a communion prayer from the ***Didache***.[1] "As the

---

1. The *Didache*, also known as "The Lord's Teaching Through the Twelve Apostles to the Nations," is a brief, anonymous early Christian treatise written in common Greek,

broken bread was scattered upon the mountains, but was brought together from the ends of the earth and became one, so let thy Church be gathered together from the ends of the earth into thy kingdom." This prayer is consistent with Paul's theology of unity: "There is one body and one Spirit, just as you were called to one hope when you were called; one Lord, one faith, one baptism; one God and Father of all, who is over all and through all and in all" (Ephesians 4:4–6).

The ancient Jewish people, recipients of God's covenant promises, were continually assured that God's purpose was to use their witness to spread the knowledge of God to all the peoples of the earth (see Genesis 12:3; 17:4). The Old Testament prophets repeatedly reminded Israel that God's covenantal purpose had not been forgotten. God's universal, worldwide plan was to spread his glory throughout the whole earth. "The earth will be filled with the knowledge of the Lord as the waters cover the sea" (Isaiah 11:9).

When you read the earliest Christian writers, you immediately see how clearly they understood this idea of one divine purpose. In time, they understood that God's eternal purpose was fulfilled through Christ in the new covenant. This fulfillment of God's promise to Abraham was a major reason why they believed the church was *catholic*. Catholicity meant God's people would be scattered across the whole earth. But given all our differences, is it possible to restore a vibrant commitment to unity in a terribly divided age?

The Apostles' Creed Can Help Us

In the last chapter we saw the role of the Apostles' Creed in the post-apostolic era. This creed, which took differing forms in different locations, arranged the essential truths of the Christian faith in a natural, logical progression. In it we see how the order of divine revelation, consciously rooted in the persons of the Trinity, is carefully followed. The creed moves from God the Father and his creating to the person and work of Christ—his supernatural birth, life, death, and resurrection. Then it brings us to the person and work of the Holy Spirit—the church and the future. The great nineteenth-century Protestant theologian Philip Schaff spoke of its unique characteristics:

> It is by far the best popular summary of the Christian faith ever made within so brief a space. It still surpasses all later symbols for catechetical and liturgical purposes, especially as a profession of candidates for baptism and church membership. It is

dated by modern scholars to the first century, making it perhaps the earliest teaching document we have outside of the New Testament.

not a logical statement of abstract doctrines, but a profession of living facts and saving truths. It is a liturgical poem and an act of worship. Like the Lord's Prayer, it loses none of its charm and effect by frequent use, although, by vain and thoughtless repetition, it may be made a martyr and an empty form of words. It is intelligible and edifying to a child, and fresh and rich to the profoundest Christian scholar, who, as he advances in age, delights to go back to primitive foundations and first principles. It has the fragrance of antiquity and the inestimable weight of universal consent. It is a bond of union between all ages and sections of Christendom. It can never be superseded for popular use in church and school.[2]

Reciting the creed does not make us Christians, but it does clearly remind us of the truths of our salvation and provides an opportunity to personally and corporately affirm them. Martin Luther believed the Christian truth could not be put into a shorter and clearer statement. John Calvin, who followed the order of the Apostles' Creed as he arranged his *Institutes of the Christian Religion*, believed it was an admirable and true summary of the Christian faith. These kinds of widely embraced approbations are common in church history.

The Apostles' Creed is plainly a dynamic treasure. When we fail to utilize it as a basic guide for teaching the essentials of our faith, we ostensibly invite common forms of disunity. But the creed is *not* my personal statement of faith. It's a statement rooted in the history of confessing Christians. I actually confess more than the creed says, though I am comfortable with these words. I do not insist everyone personally uses these words to prove they follow Jesus. But having stated this important caveat, I believe those who ignore the creed, or something similar to it, are generally left to focus on the truths they prefer rather than on the essential beliefs that have been universally believed and taught by the overwhelming majority of faithful Christians.

No other document in early church history, apart from the Bible, served a greater purpose in uniting Christians in their common faith. Early Christians believed the Jewish Scriptures were "inspired by God" (2 Timothy 3:16). But before they had a recognized canon (rule) in the now-accepted books of our New Testament, the creed had already become a summary of the faith they confessed in baptism and regularly affirmed. The Apostles' Creed has the pride of place in history as well as the clarity of true simplicity. There is plenty in it that offends the sensibilities of modern culture, making

---

2. Schaff, *Creeds of Christendom*, 1:15.

it the perfect ancient-future way of establishing fidelity and affirming our unity.

In the early church, this creed provided a rather explicit response to three challenges. The first challenge was to define the experience of Jesus within and over against the shared story of Israel. The second challenge was to clarify the complex understanding of God that was embedded in the resurrection experiences. The third challenge was to correct misunderstandings of the newly emergent "Christian narrative," that was, at heart, a "story about Jesus."[3]

A Confessional Basis for True Catholicity

As I began to see the importance of the Apostles' Creed, I also saw how it could help shape our faith and practice in unity. I had been taught to believe the church should follow the Bible, never human creeds. In the church of my youth we proudly declared, "We have no creed but the Bible." (I now think this is one of the more divisive things a sincere Christian can utter, even though those who humbly say it often don't realize how divisive this response can be.) Until I began studying the creed, I didn't realize just how wrong my thinking was about essential Christianity. I had no concern for catholicity and thus remained a separated Christian. I was even proud of my *distinct* beliefs! The creed, however, gave me a place to stand with my brothers and sisters without having to surrender anything essential to core orthodoxy.

Everyone *interprets* the Bible; thus, quoting it rarely settles disagreements. *Bible verses by themselves are insufficient to create unity.* Consider that many anti-Christian cults affirm the Bible's inerrancy and authority, yet they interpret its meaning in ways that suit their own personal experience and preference. At its core, all forms of fundamentalism do grave harm to both our tradition and our legitimate community-based interpretation of Scripture: "[Fundamentalists] read [the Bible] directly and literally, ignoring the single most important fact about a sacred text, namely its meaning is not self-evident. It has a history and an authority of its own. Every religion must guard against a literal reading of its hard texts if it is not to betray God's deeper purposes."[4] Christianity is a "living tradition." It is not a faith rooted in making every biblical text into a literal mandate that we attempt to squeeze into modern forms.

---

3. Johnson, *The Creed*, 10–11.
4. Sacks, *Great Partnership*, 254.

Without community and tradition, such readings of Scripture lead to differing expressions of pride, and in turn, continual divisions. This is expressed well in Galatians 5:20, particularly the New Living Translation's rendering. Paul rightly says division is rooted in "the feeling that everyone is wrong except those in your own little group" (NLT).[5] He puts the sin of division squarely on *us*—not our doctrinal differences. In truth, we must find a way to grasp the answer to the larger question: *What is the essential revealed message of the Holy Scriptures regarding God, Jesus, and the Spirit?*

Answering this question will take us back to the Bible as our foundation of truth. But the Bible takes us to Jesus Christ, not to itself. *In every age we must discover the meaning of Scripture.* This task is ever and always new. But it is wise to incorporate the faithful witness of the ancient church in our reading of the Bible. We should ask such questions as: *What did the first Christians believe, and why did they believe it? How did they hear the gospel? Before there was a completed Bible, how did the church understand and confess the living Christ?* (Even when the church had the completed Scriptures, most Christians never had the opportunity to read them, much less study them in numerous translations while consulting scores of commentaries.)

If it helps, think about it this way: Are you the first person to read the Bible and attempt to understand it? Of course not. People before you wrestled with these same writings and expressed what they understood. They confessed what has been called "core orthodoxy." They celebrated the **"Great Tradition"** (what C. S. Lewis called "mere Christianity")—those elemental truths representing broadly the theological consensus of the first thousand years of Christian history.

My point here is simple but vital. Wisdom should lead us to listen to these early Christians *before* we try to work out some of the difficult issues we face today. In a very real sense, we must look to the past *before* we are adequately prepared to answer the challenges of the present and the future. I believe the Holy Spirit calls the church in every age to reexamine its faithfulness to God's Truth. We can recognize the blessings of modern insights and developments, but amnesia of our past reduces robust confessing faith to pop culture and leads to theologically shallow living. Karl Barth was right to remind us that Christian tradition includes the whole history of the church. But he also called the creeds and confessions our "parents."[6] We should honor them before we take up new challenges. Yes, there may be times to disagree with our parents as well. The church is always called to participate in the Truth. Jesus is the Truth!

---

5. *The First Edition of the New Living Translation*, Galatians 5:20.
6. Barth, *Church Dogmatics* 1/2, 589.

As best we can tell, the church has been using the Apostles' Creed since about 215 CE. The form we presently use is a later revision. (There were many modest revisions.) The creed's crisp, simple statements indicate how the earliest post-apostolic Christians understood the apostles' teaching. While no one claims the apostles actually wrote the creed, all agree that it bears this name because it is universally considered a faithful summary of their teaching. (Love for God, for neighbor and for one another, as well as for love for one's enemies, is the *critical truth* missing in the creed. We will address this problem later.)

When core orthodoxy, as represented by the Apostles' Creed and lived in the love of Christ, is *not* given primary importance, the result is always a church that builds walls rather than one that freely welcomes others into a growing friendship built on the risen and ascended Christ. Churches without this perspective tend to be driven by personalities and curious fads. We see strong evidence that this type of Christianity has spread around the world to millions of Christians and churches without a solid grasp of core orthodoxy.

People often tell me catholicity doesn't matter. What matters most, they argue, is sound doctrine. They reason, like good rationalists, that you get sound doctrine by a proper *scientific exegesis* of the Bible. These folks sometimes go on to insist that their church is right since they *truly* follow the Bible. Yet in many cases their church isn't even two generations old. (Incidentally, this provides one reason why really important doctrines, such as the Trinity, are not *practically* important in many American churches—they are not embraced theologically or historically.) Was everyone who taught the Bible before this group simply wrong? Or worse yet, have there been no true Christians for the past two thousand years? This way of thinking raises the question: Does catholicity really matter anymore, particularly for the American church?

How Important Is Right Doctrine?

The most common defense for separation and schism is rooted in appeals to right doctrine. We'll revisit this concern later, but consider for a moment these three observations. First, what we should believe about God *is* important. The Holy Scriptures reveal God so we can say, "God is not (this) nor (that). God is truth *and* God is love." No effort to marginalize good teaching (the word *doctrine* means "teaching") should become the norm. The health of the church matters, and sound doctrine is essential for its health. Paul writes that believers should be "nourished on the words of the faith and of the sound teaching" (1 Timothy 4:6). Second, Jesus made it abundantly clear that there are two commandments we must keep at the center of all we believe and teach.

> "You shall love the Lord your God with all your heart, and with all your soul, and with all your mind." This is the greatest and first commandment. And a second is like it: "You shall love your neighbor as yourself." On these two commandments hang all the law and the prophets. (Matthew 22:37–40)

Even if we get all our doctrine right—and we'll never get it *just* right—we must *apply* it correctly. If we violate these two commandments, we will even get our sound doctrine *wrong*. A lifetime of preaching and teaching has convinced me this is the missing element in a multitude of doctrinal debates. We easily disagree about so much, especially in a polarized context. We get angry, bitter, and defensive, then we're just a step away from rancorous, mean-spirited fighting over doctrinal differences. When this happens, both our words and actions build walls—walls that cause us to think *our* doctrinal differences are *essential* to sound faith and practice.

Finally, we must come to a better understating of *how* to appeal to Scripture and sound doctrine if we are to avoid the common divisions we too easily accept. I said earlier that the early Christians did not have the written New Testament for generations. This means when the apostles and prophets of the early church referred to Scripture, they were appealing to the writings we call the Old Testament. My friend George Koch grasps a point about this we should consider:

> The entire Old Testament is essentially a narrative story about a people, *the Jews*, and their robust, constant, joyful, rocky, rebellious, dedicated, awestruck and argumentative love affair with God. They are so familiar with Him that they will yell and wrestle with Him, even turn on their heels in fits of pique, and yet they are so profoundly in awe they will not even say His name aloud. *In the entire Old Testament there is virtually not a word of doctrine, nor a foundational philosophical proposition.*[7]

The Present American Reality

It's been said there are more than 100 different families of churches and more than 250 distinct denominational groups in the United States. According

---

7. Koch, *What We Believe*, 178, italics added.

to a 2014 report from the Center for the Study of Global Christianity at Gordon-Conwell Theological Seminary, there are 45,000 distinct Christian denominations worldwide. The same report says this number is growing at a rate of 2.4 new denominations per day![8] Some may wonder, "What's wrong with that? Aren't denominations a good thing?" Some even commend these divisions as a multiform expression of the one faith. But I find no solid biblical or historical basis for this way of thinking. Yes, the reality of denominations and church splits has led us to produce some of the largest churches in the world. And America has historically sent out more missionaries than any other nation, though this sending position has changed dramatically over the last few decades. But something about this pattern of division seems inherently wrong, especially when churches continue to separate from one another over minor issues.

Scandals and heresies dilute our witness to a watching world, and the church in America grows spiritually weaker with each passing day. In the classic best-selling devotional *My Utmost for His Highest*, the famous Oswald Chambers wrote for July 12: "The Church ceases to be a spiritual society when it is on the look-out for the development of its own organization."[9] This is precisely what has happened to so much of the American church. Until we first see the church as a "spiritual society," we will continue to make care for our organizations and programs central to our life in the church. We will continue to paint, fix, and strengthen our walls while we ignore those who live on the other side of our walls. The hymnist Samuel Stone wrote "The Church's One Foundation" (1865). A portion of one stanza paints a sadly accurate picture of the current American church:

> Though, with a scornful wonder
> Men see her sore oppressed,
> By schisms rent asunder,
> By heresies distressed.

Others are more optimistic. Sabine Baring-Gould, who wrote the hymn "Onward Christian Soldiers," included a not-so-well-known line in his hymn:

> We are not divided;
> All one body we,
> One in hope, in doctrine,
> One in charity.

---

8. Gordon-Conwell Theological Seminary's Center for the Study of Global Christianity, "Status of Global Mission."

9. Chambers, *My Utmost for His Highest*.

Not quite a portrait of the actual reality, is it? A more honest version was composed by the late Robert McAfee Brown in his book *The Spirit of Protestantism*: "We are all divided, not one body we, one lacks faith, another hope, and all lack charity."[10] Walls dividing Christians have been constructed with every imaginable form of brick and mortar but they remain walls. These are the walls of our organized religion, not the evidence of a true "spiritual society."

Divisions plague the American church. We are "rent asunder" by schism, thus we are not "all one body." But I do not think the real problem is solved by opposing our historic denominations, even though they become less and less relevant with the erosion of Christendom culture. We will consider our real problem in the next chapter.

Satan Hates a Unified Church

It's hard to miss the emphasis the apostles and the early church placed on catholicity. Quotations that reinforce this characteristic of the church can be found throughout the writings of the earliest Christians. The record of the patristic writers is clear and strong: There is only one church, scattered throughout the earth. The early church embraced, taught, and lived out the truth of the church's catholicity by staying focused on the essential mission given to them by Jesus, not by majoring on their idiosyncrasies or differences. Sadly, in the centuries that have passed, we have departed from this emphasis on catholicity. Our lack of unity may well be the greatest weakness in the church today. The modern church seems smugly satisfied with its individualistic, anti-historical understanding of the Christian faith.

When faithful pastors and church leaders begin to grasp this truth, and teach it to their congregations, I guarantee we will see something new begin to happen. At times, it will seem as if all hell has broken loose when you emphasize the unity and catholicity of all God's people. And I mean this literally! Satan hates a unified church and will do his best to oppose all who work and pray for it. His name literally reveals that he is totally committed to our division and disunity. He will use aggressive tactics, defame our character, and subject us to vicious gossip—whatever he can do to discourage and dissuade us from following Christ with other believers. Wonderful Christian people will, at least initially, not understand your passion for working with others. Many people have lived with these divisions for so long that they have no ability to see or understand why unity really matters. They have come to believe the present state of things is all we should expect.

10. Brown, *Spirit of Protestantism*, 24.

Many years ago, someone taught me a simple, important principle: If the Holy Spirit teaches you anything, he will also call you to live it. Those who recognize God's desire for unity and begin to obey his commands will need to learn how to forgive others. Why? Every effort at unity I've made over my lifetime has taught me that this passion for lived oneness will always involve misunderstanding. Sadly, this vision all but invites acrimonious criticism from several sides; e.g., one side is rooted in the doctrinal fear of unfaithfulness to traditionalism, while another involves indifference and a false irenicism. Both sides have ways of building walls and making them central. Take Jesus and his kingdom truth seriously, and make unity your goal in Christ's mission, and you are guaranteed to get hurt! We simply cannot undertake this kind of praying and teaching without the Holy Spirit's grace and power. Thank God that he gives what we need when we depend on him to direct our efforts and keep us watchful. If we are to move past the divisive spirit that has characterized the church for far too long, we will need a growing awareness of the *real causes* of disunity.

Questions for Discussion and Reflection

1. How can the Apostles' Creed help us establish a solid basis for doctrinal fidelity that allows Christians and churches to agree on core orthodoxy and pursue meaningful relationships in truth? What do you see as weaknesses in this approach? What are its strengths?

2. What problems have you encountered when Christians try to unite in relational contexts without a doctrinal foundation anchored in the early church?

3. What has the Spirit taught you about unity in a way that requires your obedience and potential suffering?

Chapter Nine

Sin Destroys Our Unity

He cannot possess the robe of Christ who rends and divides the church of Christ.

—*Cyprian*

How unhesitatingly the language of Scripture mentions human relationships as the only means of suggesting the unspeakable pleasure of [our] eternal fellowship with God.

—*Oswald Chambers*

All human desire for unity is profoundly rooted in our collective experience. We have an indescribable longing to be together, to experience our innate hunger for dignity and meaning as one. In the Christian tradition, the non-creedal Quakers contributed uniquely to the practice of this truth. Bayard Rustin (1912–1987), reared a Quaker by his grandparents, was a controversial American pioneer in social movements for civil rights and nonviolence. He once said, "We are one. And if we do not know it, we will find out the hard way."[1] This oneness touches all our relationships—including those of our family life, social life, community life, national life, and church life. It is especially true in the way we relate to our network of friends.

1. Rustin, *Quotes*.

The United Shades of Christianity in America

One of my favorite television programs is the cable series *United Shades of America*. It is a unique documentary starring the African-American comedian W. Kamau Bell. In each episode he takes a topic—say, the life of the homeless in Los Angeles, or the experience of Iranian immigrants in America—and explores the people and their culture by interviewing them where they live in community. He eats with people and listens. Bell shows how truly diverse we are as a nation. Few programs show the "shades" of our social fabric so wonderfully. Bell helps me tear down walls I sometimes have a hard time getting beyond. (I have found Bell's approach works wonders when I sit with people, eat, and ask questions.) One thing Bell stresses in every episode is that these "united shades" will either enrich us or pull us further apart.

In the United States' infancy, Thomas Jefferson, Benjamin Franklin, and John Adams proposed the new nation adopt the motto *e pluribus unum*—"out of the many, one." The idea of one nation, formed from different peoples, expresses the founders' goal to form a single nation out of a collection of states. The nation's history proves just how difficult this challenge has been. The Civil War resulted in over 650,000 deaths because we could not solve a moral and economic problem that led to separation. In so many ways, this American motto can be appropriated in seeking to understand the history of the church as well. We are a multiethnic, multigenerational people called by God to be one. Isolation and individualism remain the true enemies of God's gift of unity. But God intends for us to become *the united shades of Christianity*.

The Gift of Tension: "The Troubles"

Judaism has a teaching called "the Two Pockets." It likely came from a Polish rabbi who lived in the first half of the nineteenth century. It says everyone should have two pockets, with a slip of paper in each. On one paper should be the words: "I am but dust and ashes." The paper in the other pocket should read: "For my sake, the universe was created." Before we even begin to understand and live Christian unity, we must realize the point of these two pockets. Life involves tensions. We inherently dislike tensions. A contemporary author observes, "Our instinct is that tension is an obstruction to be overcome and fixed, preferably as quickly as possible."[2] Could it be

---

2. Williams, *Holy Disunity*, 61. Williams also gave me the story of the Polish rabbi I relate here.

many of our relational tensions might actually lead us to experience deeper unity? In recent years I've discovered these tensions can call us to serious problem-solving *without* simple solutions. They can actually become tipping points for embracing our mission of love.

Author Layton Williams relates a story of spending several extended periods in Northern Ireland, where she saw a deeply rooted historical tension that polarized and divided people. (The division there is framed by religious language and history, but it is more about inequalities and politics.) The long history of death and terrorism in Northern Ireland has been called "the Troubles." As a constant reminder of "the Troubles," the city of Belfast has a wall dividing Catholic and Protestant parts of the city. Some call it "the Peace Wall," though it's anything but. It separates and segregates.[3] These walls were meant to make it more difficult for people to resolve their tensions by killing one another. During the riots of 1969, barricades were set up around neighborhoods, formalizing sectarian geography. These barriers were eventually replaced by walls, prompting one writer to say, "These towering structures maintained some degree of calm by physically separating the city's populations, as if they were animals in a zoo."[4]

These so-called "peace walls" are a stark picture of a common response to tensions inside the church. We routinely hear, "We must learn to agree to disagree." Really? This is God's plan? Toleration is the best we can do? This has always struck me as a total cop-out. On the surface it seems appealing. We so desire unity that we have to settle our divisions by agreeing not to speak of serious concerns we face together. In my own story, this was how most white people tried to resolve uncomfortable dialogues about race and injustice. We sought peace without really tearing down our cultural and religious "peace walls." Williams is right: "Staying in a relationship doesn't mean being in agreement or even being peaceful or nice to each other. It doesn't mean relinquishing our convictions. It means staying engaged, whether you're in the same room or not."[5] My point about living with our tensions is not meant to glorify relational tensions. It means we can easily miss what God is doing if we embrace an either-or solution rather than a

---

3. The Good Friday Agreement, which ended much of the violence in Northern Ireland, was signed in 1998. It ended the conflict, acknowledged the legitimacy of the desire for a united Ireland, and declared a better future could only be achieved with the consent of a majority of the people of Northern Ireland. The agreement was a start, but the walls remain. The schoolchildren of Northern Ireland are still segregated by Catholic and Protestant histories and neighborhoods. In a very real sense, these walls must still come down if the people are to realize a lasting peace that goes far beyond the end to terrorism.

4. Keefe, *Say Nothing*, 502.

5. Williams, *Holy Disunity*, 72.

both-and response. True faith always struggles. People will experience tensions. Living faith does not settle for easy answers to all our questions. Faith is a gift. It is God's way for us to live *within* our tensions while we keep working to tear down walls that divide us.

Did the Early Church Experience Unity?

The time between CE 60 and 160 has been called the "tunnel period" of church history—a transitional period between the time of the apostles and the century after they died. In Acts, we see the early leaders of the church working to preserve unity between CE 30 and 62—the generation following the death of Jesus. This infant church shared a common core of faith evidenced by five historical realities:

- the historical person of Jesus of Nazareth
- the *koinonia* (fellowship) we see in believers after Jesus' ascension
- the basic beliefs (*kerygma*) shared by all of Jesus' followers
- the events at the Jerusalem Council as recorded in Acts 15
- the relationship among the various missions/leaders we read about in Acts

But what about the generation that followed them? The evidence is strong that during this period, the unity of the post-apostolic church was preserved—with some continued divisions, for sure. What helped maintain this unity was a basic understanding of the meaning of Jesus' life, death, and resurrection—a core message preserved in what is called the *kerygma*.[6] This became evident in the oldest teaching manual we have, the *Didache*. While tensions and disagreements between early Christian leaders were real, the testimony of history shows that a common core of belief and practice generally kept the church together.

As a young Christian, I was taught that the church was always divided and confused, at least immediately after the death of the apostles. But the historical evidence doesn't support this idea. Cults often suggest this notion when they seek to promote "new" revelations by appealing to the apostles' death. Even some conservative Christians have used this type of reasoning

---

6. In theology, *kerygma* and catechesis (teaching of central truths by a question-and-answer format) became the center of gospel proclamation. This was primarily done through oral instruction, generally given before baptism to those who have accepted Christ. *Kerygma* thus refers to the preaching of the apostles as seen in the New Testament. It seeks to center faith in the truth of Jesus and his redemption.

to argue against the positive role of historical traditions. The truth is, divisions have always threatened the church. And divisions were part of these earliest communities. Most scholars believe the Apostle John's writings (his Gospel and letters) were the last contributions to the New Testament canon. It dawned on me, some years ago, that if this is true, then the last teaching of the apostle Jesus loved shows how Christ's love could preserve Christian unity.

In his master's thesis, Stephen Staten concluded there was unity in the sub-apostolic church from CE 62 until at least 150. He points to a "discernible unity of belief" from the time following Jesus' resurrection through Peter's first proclamation at Pentecost and the clarifications at the Jerusalem Council all the way through the declarations of Ignatius and Justin. This unity of belief primarily involved the person and work of Jesus but also the practices of baptism and the Eucharist. As Christians talked with others about these experiences, they gained a "heartfelt appreciation for the Christian enterprise in other places . . . [and] a process of learning from one another and their resources enabled them to more firmly understand their common faith." They began to see themselves as one, gathering with the common objective of seeing that every level of society "had an opportunity to the same gospel and incorporation into the *ekklesia* community."[7]

We should recall that during this early period there was no standard creed and no identifiable single bishop. (Though my Catholic friends will likely disagree, many Catholic biblical scholars admit the picture I have painted above is accurate.) We do know there were *real differences of opinion* during this period. Matters such as eschatology and the question of whether Jewish Christians could continue some of their ancestral practices created divergent viewpoints. But the church steadfastly resisted division. Though there was no single doctrinal system, there was a developing unity of common beliefs. Even the developing of the role of a bishop, in the second and third centuries, was understood as a way to preserve unity.

The Seeds of Disunity Begin to Grow

One of the first accounts we have of the infant church (Acts 6:1–7) reveals a struggle over disputes that threatened the unity of the Jerusalem congregation. The actions the church took to resolve their disagreement may seem odd, but they clearly demonstrate that the apostolic leaders took seriously the threat of disunity. In John's letters we find exhortations to relentless, self-sacrificial love (1 John 1:8–11) alongside raging polemics against false

---

7. Staten, "Was There Unity?," 129–30.

teachers in the church (2:19–23). Undeniably, a real tension exists when we seek to balance these truths. Yet, even given the reality of false teachers in their midst, the early church somehow kept catholicity and purity together. One can see a kind of "compromise" (too often a dirty word) that refused doctrinal indifference while at the same time the leaders the church cultivated continued unity in mission.

In addition to the problems the Jerusalem congregation faced, there were disputes with the Judaizers, a group of people who continually challenged the core message of grace. These disputes created bitter controversies, as evidenced by Paul's letter to the Galatians (see 1:7–9; 2:1–5). Yet further schisms arose as the church began to address an even greater error, the looming threat of Gnosticism.

Both the later patristic and medieval periods of history reveal that schism eventually did divide the church. Disagreements between powerful churches and bishops became widespread. Even in the Middle Ages, where we find some positive evidence of external unity, the Eastern and Western churches formally divided in 1054, several centuries after they were practically separated by wars and misunderstandings. External forms of unity were sometimes enforced, but these divisions simply revealed a deeper problem—a widespread resistance to the mission of Christ and the work of the Holy Spirit.

Later, when the church in the East faced a serious external conflict that led to wide-scale martyrdom, the Western church refused to offer aid to their Eastern brothers and sisters. Help from the West could have saved the lives of countless besieged Eastern Christians, but division kept them apart. To this day, this lack of help is a sad mark against the church and hinders unity. Within a generation of this terrible struggle against persecution in the East, the Western church was itself torn apart by the Protestant Reformation. This movement challenged the Catholic Church to renew itself but resulted in a massive schism, leading to strife and bitterness on every side. Eventually, these various schisms resulted in the birth of several more major divisions within historical Protestantism, leading to an endless variety of new churches built around issues of the state, human personalities, liturgical developments, and doctrinal differences.

Today, millions of Christian congregations hold the same core doctrines while continuing to express distinctively different patterns of government and worship, not to mention different views about what each one believes is essential to sound faith. This sad story of disunity led the historical theologian G. W. Bromiley to conclude:

> Far from presenting a picture of unity to the world, the church seems almost to give a warning example of disunity, the very strength of faith and conviction giving depth and bitterness to the "unhappy divisions." The church may have a consciousness of its unity. But it cannot ignore the stubborn fact of its disunity. And in face of this fact its confession of unity can only seem to be a hollow mockery to itself and especially to the world.[8]

So how do we explain the story of all these factions and schisms? If unity is stamped on the DNA of every Christian and church, how then have we succeeded in repressing it? Why does Christ's prayer go unanswered? There are many healthy ways to respond to these questions. But I am sure of one thing: Idealistic dreams of unity will not bring it about. We must seek God for a fresh work of the Spirit to restore our unity. This will require a calm focus on the core of our faith and a passionate heart filled with love for others.

The Church in the World

The church is the bride of Christ. Christ gave her a mission to fulfill during this long period of betrothal (Matthew 28:19-20). Because we belong to Christ, we have been called to live out the unity of the triune God in his kingdom and mission. Christ is the center; thus we must press into him, working out our difficulties in relationships with one another. We cannot solve all our differences, but we can "make every effort to keep the unity of the Spirit through the bond of peace" (Ephesians 4:3).

Different communities of Christians do many things that fall into the category of human preferences. Diversity is not bad *per se*. We can expect that churches in many cultures and contexts will reflect widely different expressions of the one faith—and I believe these expressions can be a reason for the success of the gospel in so many diverse cultures. Unlike some non-Christian religions, we should not seek to conform Christians and cultures to only one way of expressing our shared faith. (The church has not always understood this well, and the results have often been tragic—e.g., promoting one nation's culture and/or interests as "truly Christian," the rise and spread of European colonialism, capitalism or socialism [both are economic ideologies, not biblical truths] being linked with Christ's mission, etc.)

A comparison with individual Christian experience can prove helpful. We know that each of us is called to follow Christ (1 Corinthians 1:2). We know holiness is necessary, even though we remain sinners. Sin permeates

---

8. Bromiley, *Unity and Disunity*, 17.

all we do, much like a dark stain in a fabric. We cannot escape this, but we must fight against it. The same pattern is true in every congregation.

To counteract the deadly virus of disunity in the church, we must draw upon the rich, diverse language of Scripture to understand the place of unity. It is quite evident that a major biblical theme is God's desire for the unity of all peoples. The actual announcement of this desire begins with the narrative of God creating and ruling the universe (Genesis 1–11). The Tower of Babel story, told in Genesis 11:1–9, has been terribly abused to attempt to say otherwise. When God calls Abraham, he tells him, "In you *all the families of the earth* shall be blessed" (Genesis 12:3). This story of God and the world reveals his gracious purpose. The theme of unity is actually the starting and ending point for the most significant New Testament texts on God's purpose for the world. The Scriptures give us a clear and realistic picture of both our human proclivity toward disunity and the experience of oneness that is possible through union with Christ. Paul express this storyline by writing: "May the God of steadfastness and encouragement grant you to live in harmony with one another, in accordance with Christ Jesus, so that together you may with one voice glorify the God and Father of our Lord Jesus Christ" (Romans 15:5–6).

The **Orthodox Church** has helped me understand this biblical theme much better. **Orthodoxy** teaches that we were created to enjoy intimacy with the Father, Son, and Holy Spirit. Angels were exalted beings, but they did not have this capacity. The descendants of the first human couple were designed to pursue this intimacy with God. While Adam and Eve were created as individuals, they were not created to be separate. They were made for social interaction with other persons, especially for personal transforming interaction with God together. Thus the natural dynamic of persons is always toward God *and* each other. We are relational beings! This means that without deep, growing relationships, we will always fail to fulfill our divine calling. This failure impacts all of society. Put simply, each one of us has a personal will to love God *and* our fellow human beings. Each of us can choose to go our own way or to pursue God and others. This is the real essence of our sin: *broken relationships.*

Most Western Christians think the human person is maximized by the individual pursuit of self-knowledge. We believe "the real you" is found in our heart. We think human joy is found through an inward journey. We cannot define ourselves in a healthy way when we pursue this path. What really must define us is found in our relationships with God and one another.

If we are to counteract division, we must firmly grasp that sin breaks our relational unity. But what will prove even more difficult than this recognition is whether we will make the serious effort needed to apply real solutions to our relational brokenness. This will mean living with real tensions. History has so jaded us, and sin so distorted our vision, that many of us have given up on the quest for unity. The result is a life filled with broken relationships in our marriages, families, work, neighborhoods, and churches. We can do better.

Questions for Discussion and Reflection

1. In what ways do you find that Christians desire unity but fail to pursue it?

2. How did the early church retain unity while it still grew in diversity? Can we pursue self-sacrificial love and a strong response against false teachers at the same time? How?

3. What do the "peace walls" of Northern Ireland teach you about living in the midst of conflict together? When is it right to walk away from disagreements? How can we walk away and still work for unity?

4. How does the Orthodox Church understand sin in terms of relationships? How could this help us better understand both division and unity?

Chapter Ten

Sectarianism: Our Real Enemy

> Sectarianism is seeking unity in uniformity rather than unity in diversity and expecting other Christians to comply fully with my views before I can have genuine fellowship with them.
>
> —Rex Koivisto

Some years ago, the comedian Emo Phillips wrote a joke about the divisions between Christians in America. Apparently, people find it hilarious. *Gentleman's Quarterly* ranked it the forty-fourth funniest joke of all time. (I have no idea how they decided this ranking.) *The Guardian* called it the best religious joke of all time.

> I was walking across a bridge one day, and I saw a man standing on the edge, about to jump. I ran over and said: "Stop. Don't do it."
> "Why shouldn't I?" he asked.
> "Well, there's so much to live for!"
> "Like what?"
> "Are you religious?"
> He said: "Yes."
> I said: "Me too. Are you Christian or Buddhist?"
> "Christian."
> "Me too. Are you Catholic or Protestant?"
> "Protestant."
> "Me too. Are you Episcopalian or Baptist?"
> "Baptist."

"Wow. Me too. Are you Baptist Church of God or Baptist Church of the Lord?"

"Baptist Church of God."

"Me too. Are you original Baptist Church of God, or Reformed Baptist Church of God?"

"Reformed Baptist Church of God."

"Me too. Are you Reformed Baptist Church of God, Reformation of 1879, or Reformed Baptist Church of God, Reformation of 1915?"

He said: "Reformed Baptist Church of God, Reformation of 1915."

I said: "Die, heretic scum," and pushed him off.[1]

How Schisms Broke Our Wider Unity

In earlier chapters we saw how early Christians confessed what they believed to be the central, historical facts of their faith. This allowed the community to interpret and evaluate various claims about Christ. We have also seen how the first three Christian creeds came to underscore the church's oneness by connecting the existence of the baptized community to the work of God: Father, Son, and Holy Spirit. The two earliest creeds expressed faith in two ways: *individually* (the Apostles' Creed says "I believe") and *corporately* (the Nicene Creed says "We believe"). But even with these creedal agreements, the church continued to face heresies and divisions. Creeds helped the church, but division was always at the door. Jesus plainly taught his first disciples: "I am giving you these commands so that you may love one another" (John 15:17). History shows clearly that without love, no creed can preserve unity. By the sixteenth century, division produced the most massive proliferation of differing churches in the history of Christianity. Love was all but lost to the life of commonly practiced Christian faith. As a result, division was accepted as normal Christianity. The words of the Apostle Paul were all but forgotten: "Finally, brothers and sisters . . . . put things in order, listen to my appeal, agree with one another, live in peace; and the God of love and peace will be with you" (2 Corinthians 13:11). Peace and unity became a thing of the past in much of the Christian world.

In her excellent book *Disunity in Christ*, social psychologist Christena Cleveland shows how ridiculous our current divisions are after five centuries of disagreeing and dividing the church again and again. She argues that decades of research reveal what now seems obvious: Most Christians

---

1. Phillips, "Die Heretic."

in America gravitate toward churches that are filled with people who look, talk, worship, and think like they do. Rather than doing all that conscience would allow us to do together, we settle for far less. Why? In such various social contexts, most Christians do not see or feel the darkness of their divisions.[2]

Back in the early 1970s, when I was doing my graduate education, a group of evangelical missions professors created what they called "the homogenous unit" principle of church growth, which sought to explain what makes a church grow. Simply put, the principle said, "Like attracts like." These professors told us we should make our church the kind of ministry that attracted those just like us. When I studied under several of these professors, one of them told me he had visited a well-known fundamentalist church in Indiana over the weekend. I commented on that church's blatant racism and separatism, "Doesn't this bother you?" He said no and then defended the church's extremes by saying this was the church where Archie Bunker would go. I was mortified. I was a church planter, and church growth was on my mind. I saw how this thinking was permeating church planting. Most of the questions that formed in me then are those I address in this chapter.

The sad truth is, we really are most comfortable with Christians who agree with us. The even greater tragedy is that a lot of what we agree with one another about has nothing important to contribute to our faithfulness to Jesus and his call to love our neighbors. Let's face it: We feel safer when the church is just like us in terms of race, class, and income. I mean, we can't expose our children to other children who might not live like we do. In these scenarios we might need to sing, "They will know we are Christians by our . . . political posts . . . or by our unkind and degrading memes . . . or by our name-calling . . . or by our divisive and racially charged talk . . . but surely not by our love." How then can we truly pursue unity in catholicity when the church actually exists in a myriad of radically diverse social groups? In Christ's mission, how do we regain the view of unity I am advocating?

As you've seen, I have lived much of my adult life deeply committed to advancing Christ's kingdom in Christian unity. A principal reason for my passion was vividly illustrated by a prominent Protestant theologian's reflection on the work of Christ in India. The leader of the "untouchables" in India renounced the caste system and urged his sixty million fellow untouchables to renounce the Hinduism that had been responsible for it. But he believed Christianity held no appeal to the people as an alternative to

---

2. Cleveland, *Disunity in Christ*, 33.

Hinduism. Why? "We are united in Hinduism, and we shall be divided in Christianity."[3] This argument is essentially unanswerable.

The Problem: Sectarianism

Over time I have come to believe the underlying problem in our quest for unity has a name: *sectarianism*. Gaining a better understanding of how the spirit of sectarianism has become the enemy of Christian unity can prove immensely helpful. Philip Schaff used this term to theologically express what I have in mind:

> Variety in unity and unity in variety is the law of God in nature, in history, and in his kingdom. Unity without variety is dead uniformity. There is beauty in variety. There is no harmony without many sounds, and a garden encloses all kinds of flowers. God has made no two nations, no two men or women, not even two trees or two flowers, alike. He has endowed every nation, every church, yea, every individual Christian with peculiar gifts and graces. His power, his wisdom, and his goodness are reflected in ten thousand forms.[4]

Again: We do not have to give up our theological or personal distinctions to pursue deep unity. In fact, any pursuit of unity that denies our uniqueness and diversity is not positive. Many Christians approach their differences as a choice between right and wrong, a zero-sum game with winners and losers. I believe there is a better way—the pursuit of catholic, multiethnic diversity, the kind of diversity that fosters vitality and teaches us how to seek the Truth in Jesus together. True ecumenism gives Christians a way of understanding our differences, a far better way to overcome the fear of others that cripples initiative (1 John 4:8). Costly love is the God-given way to overcome our differences and conquer paralyzing fear. Love allows me a way to understand who I am *and* who you are. It empowers us to engage in a diversity of ways through which we can express our faith in Christ together.

The opposite of sectarianism is *not* undefined Christianity. The opposite of sectarianism is *catholic unity in rich diversity*. Sectarianism derives from the Latin *secta*—"a path, a way, a method, a party or faction." I am using the word *theologically* to describe an exclusivity that thrives where

---

3. Brown, *Spirit of Protestantism*, 24.

4. Schaff, "Reunion of Christendom," 101. The term *sect* has been used sociologically to describe different types of churches. I am not using it in this way. I recognize many so-called sects that are clearly Christian. In this sense one might say the first Christians were a sect because of how they viewed their life and the world around them.

people and groups believe they have a *superior* claim to truth. Sectarians believe their church/denomination/tradition can best "represent the body of Christ, to the exclusion or minimization of other genuinely Christian groups."[5]

Everyone should believe the particular church they embrace is the "right" one for them. But problems arise when people and churches believe their brand of Christianity is *entirely* right—a way of thinking rooted in the notion that "I believe the truth, and what you believe is false." This thinking inflames our pride and promotes divisive attitudes. To avoid this deadly virus we must resist the intellectual certitude that will not allow for change and growth in one's own perspective. All truth can be viewed as truth, but it is truth seen from different human perspectives. This is *not* postmodern relativism. Absolute (final) truth is simply not attainable. Why? We are not infinite beings. I finally saw that when I thought I fully comprehended God I was mistaken.

I was particularly helped to see this problem by engaging with the teaching of the Orthodox Church. In the East, the church confesses that while Scripture does speak about God, it does not—indeed, *cannot*—say all there is to say about him. Here the stress is placed on God *condescending* to us, a condescension that reveals that the true God is unfathomably beyond us. St. Gregory Nazianzen, an early theologian in the East, put this well: "The divine nature cannot be apprehended by human reason; we cannot even represent to ourselves all its greatness."[6]

If you look up *sectarian* in your dictionary, you will find synonyms like "narrow-minded," "parochial," and "limited." In the ancient church, *sectarian* described apostates who broke away from the catholic church. In the modern sense, I am using the word to express *exclusivity*. Author and professor Rex Koivisto expresses this as clearly as any writer I know.

> The church must have a degree of diversity along with its unity. But sectarianism provokes diversity without the requisite New Testament relational unity. This kind of mutual exclusivity runs counter to the nature of the church itself. Such exclusiveness is a sectarianism of the worst sort. The Christian community envisioned in the New Testament is *one* church, a church catholic . . . and this requires *a relational unity*. That is mandated. And that requires an end to *sectarian attitudes* [italics added].[7]

---

5. Koivisto, *One Lord*, 14–15.
6. St. Gregory Nazianzen, *The Theological Orations*, 2:11.
7. Koivisto, *One Lord*, 15.

Without realizing it, I defended various forms of sectarianism until I reached my late thirties. I instinctively knew in my heart there were Christians in other churches, but I had no place in my affections for Roman Catholics, the Orthodox, or many mainline Protestants. This is why the "conversion" I experienced in my early forties was so life-changing.

I still describe myself with the terms I used as a young minister: *evangelical, Protestant, Reformed*—so long as these descriptors are used in a historical sense. But over the last thirty-plus years I have developed deep friendships with both Roman Catholics and the Orthodox. I have found deep love through growing friendships within many brands of Protestantism. I have been embraced within Pentecostalism and Anabaptism. I have even experienced a growing opportunity to become friends with some non-creedal believers who many Christians reject. A number of these brothers and sisters have become my closest friends. My sectarianism is not entirely gone, but I am starting to realize just how much my pride hinders deep unity in Jesus alone.

How Ideology Produces Sectarianism

When you become a Christian, you are not delivered from ideology. Ideology is a mindset committed to abstract ideas and battles. It possesses a magnetic appeal to engage in passionately formed views of life, politics, and theology. Often Christians do not realize they are defending an ideology they have equated with Christ's truth. Ideology gives us a sense of control so we can narrate the world.

> The ideological mind-set, formed as it is at bottom by a desire to dominate rather than illuminate, is an intruder in philosophy and the arts. It is closed in on itself and resentful of competition. Instead of cultivating the openness to new influences that mark real philosophy [theology] and art [biblical storytelling] and letting itself be exposed to the possible intellectual turmoil of fresh insight, ideology shunts inconvenient thought and imagination aside. Ideologues produce propaganda, although sometimes propaganda of a sophisticated kind. When such individuals set the tone, the intellectual and artistic life [and all true Christian fellowship for that matter] suffers.[8]

But true Christian knowledge is intrinsically humble. It re-actualizes biblical and historical truths by showing the inadequacy of various strands of

---

8. Ryn, "How Conservatives Failed," 118.

faith that seek to become an expression of the *complete* truth. The important point to grasp is that vital, dynamic, life-changing Christian faith is not received *through* human theological systems. They can never be final because Christ alone is the *object* of faith. We believe in him and spend a lifetime seeking to understand who/what we believe. The truth of living faith is found in the confessing act itself, and in living in the relational dynamic of God's love. Until Christ returns, our attempts to express Christian truth completely are severely limited. Thus, all theological truth claims must remain biblically contestable. By this the church remains truly open to the role of the Spirit. This is how the church is renewed by the Spirit.

Human systems of theology have a proper place in protecting and guiding the church. But when they become *the system of doctrine exclusively taught in the Holy Scriptures,* we run into serious problems. I have heard conservative ministers argue that a historically conditioned statement of faith is *the biblically correct system of true divinity.* But Scripture is clearly not a treatise on systematic theology. It is the unfolding story of God's people, given in multiple stories composed over many centuries. Christians believe all these stories were woven by the Spirit into one great story. When we turn this macro-story into a system of doctrinal propositions, we live as if getting the right doctrine is the same thing as living faithfully. The result is often loveless Christians and churches who believe they control the truth.

A long and established Christian tradition argues that sin profoundly affects our ability to perceive truth. We may think we have unsullied access to the truth, but sin hinders our understanding. When we receive God's grace, do we resolve this problem of knowing and seeing? The answer lies in Hebrews 11, which tells us we walk by faith and not by sight. A humble and faithful Christian life is marked by a "fear and trembling" (Philippians 2:12) that expresses a willingness to allow for this mystery. Even Calvin argued that "the knowledge of faith consists in assurance rather than in comprehension." He defined faith's knowing quality as a "solid constancy of persuasion" that results in "confidence."[9] By "confidence" Calvin did not mean intellectual certitude but personal trust and assent. This trust "is more [about] the heart than the brain."[10]

The Solution to Our Problem: *Amo, ergo sum*

At the heart of the problem we face in the West is a colossal error introduced by the philosopher René Descartes (1595–1650). He believed a deductive

9. Calvin, *Institutes*, 3.2.14–15 (vol. 1, pp. 560–61).
10. Calvin, *Institutes*, 3.2.8 (vol. 1, p. 552).

system of theology could be built on proofs like those discovered in mathematics. His approach created a category of thinking that severed faith and divine revelation from the self-attesting *Logos*, Jesus of Nazareth. This idea was expressed in Descartess' famous Latin phrase *cogito, ergo sum* ("I think, therefore I am"). For him this was the first step in demonstrating the attainability of certain knowledge.

But the truth is this: We are creatures whose knowledge is necessarily built on analogy; our knowledge is derivative. We can truly know the person of Christ—not through logic or propositions, but through an *encounter with divine revelation*. This means we should never adopt an attitude that suggests we know exactly what God knows. The approach I advocate does not embrace illogical ways of thinking but rather allows us to have a faith that *transcends* logical categories. This much better description of Christian knowing could be expressed as *amo, ergo sum* ("I love, therefore I am"). *We truly know by loving God and our brothers and sisters.*

Lesslie Newbigin provides a brilliant historical overview of how we moved from understanding ultimate reality as personal knowledge—something gained inside a relationship—to seeing it as the impersonal knowledge of facts. "Personal knowledge is impossible without risk; it cannot begin without an act of trust, and trust can be betrayed. We are here facing a fundamental decision in which we have to risk everything we have. There are no insurance policies available."[11] Newbigin says these types of thinking radically diverge in two ways. The first difference has to do with where our certainty rests. *For Christians, all certainty must rest in the person of Jesus Christ.*

> If the place where we look for ultimate truth is in a story and if (as is the case) we are still in the middle of the story, then it follows that we walk by faith and not by sight. If ultimate truth is sought in an idea, a formula, or a set of timeless laws or principles, then we do not have to recognize the possibility that something totally unexpected may happen.[12]

If our certainty rests on the faithfulness of Jesus Christ, whose gospel is revealed in his story, then we have to walk by faith. We do not live by sight or by system.

The second difference has to do with the fact that *there are two ways to understand seeing and hearing*. In the classical view, knowledge is *theoria*— "the vision of eternal truth." Based on seeing a truth, we can then put it into

---

11. Newbigin, *Proper Confidence*, 14.
12. Newbigin, *Proper Confidence*, 14.

action by *praxis*—"ways of embodying it in action."[13] In this approach, these two steps become the way we live and confess our faith. It is the way I was taught to preach and teach—a way I now realize is not healthy. I learned to preach a sermon under this method. It went something like this: "Tell them what the text says then apply it to their lives."

In the biblical view, "ultimate reality is personal . . . faith comes by hearing, and unbelief is disobedience."[14] Unbelief is not just the failure to understand a deep puzzle solved by exegesis and philosophy. Bonhoeffer got this right: "Only he who believes is obedient, and only he who is obedient believes."[15] Many Christians seem to have inherited a deeply flawed view of ultimate reality. Most would greatly benefit from rethinking how the human mind creates ideologies and uses them as a way of knowing and describing God. This view of reality builds walls everywhere. In the end, the battle is often not even about a particular doctrine but how we *express* it.

Christians who make ideology central will fight to preserve human systems and give up asking the greatest questions about the knowledge of God; instead, they will tend to confidently settle for answers rooted in powerful arguments or persuasive persons. If we are not careful, we give up serious reflection and cease to be sensitive to the complexity of divine truth. Theology can become a religious pursuit rather than a spiritual journey—a pursuit in which we idolize the human intellect and craft our own concepts of truth. The result is a virtual loss of the biblical tradition of wisdom. In this setting, knowledge is pursued not to draw our souls into the love of Christ but to get answers to questions posed by our ideology. A friend helped me understand this with a simple equation: *knowledge + compassionate servanthood = wisdom*. When we adopt an ideological approach to Christianity, we will likely travel the road to sectarianism. And when we follow this road long enough, a knock on the door of our souls may well demonstrate no one is home. When we become comfortable with a sectarian mind, our lives will be filled with arguments, and our souls will be profoundly empty of Christ's love and kindness.

Blessed Are the Peacemakers

As a result of my own sectarianism, I reduced the church to ideas. In the process I missed Jesus' will for his followers: "I give you a new commandment, that you love one another. Just as I have loved you, you also should

---

13. Newbigin, *Proper Confidence*, 14.
14. Newbigin, *Proper Confidence*, 14.
15. Bonhoeffer, *Cost of Discipleship*, 69.

love one another" (John 13:34). I utilized a personal checklist to determine who was in and out. When I came to realize this, I was filled with deep remorse. I spent more than a decade trying to sort out what it meant for me to really make love for God and my neighbors, as well as other Christians, my highest priorities. I especially had to work on Jesus' command to "love one another" because I received more flack from Christians than non-Christians. Having spoken against some of God's servants, I felt compelled by the Spirit to seek forgiveness and make restitution. I wrote personal letters to some to ask them to forgive me for the way I had abused their reputation. Almost all answered and graciously forgave me. When I began moving away from sectarianism, I found remarkable peace. I no longer had to make my personal battles into God's battles. I found I could pursue peace with other Christians in ways I never imagined.

Life-Giving Relationships and the Way Ahead

Eventually I learned I needed to surround myself with friends who would help me in my spiritual formation. I needed life-giving relationships to be a faithful Christian. I needed human help to learn how to repay good for evil. This was neither easy nor natural. When people asked me about a particular person or ministry, I began to find a positive way to bless them. This text helped me discover fresh grace: "Make every effort to live in peace with everyone and to be holy; without holiness no one will see the Lord" (Hebrews 12:14). In another context, but through words that transcend all specific contexts, Paul wrote, "Let us therefore make every effort to do what leads to peace and to mutual edification" (Romans 14:19). Was I willing to "make every effort" to seek peace?

But didn't Jesus say, "I did not come to bring peace, but a sword" (Matthew 10:34)? Clearly he did. While this saying may seem contradictory to the Bible's call to peacemaking, the idea behind this statement is that because of our love for Jesus there will be conflict between the forces of darkness and light. Christians live in the light; thus, they must know that darkness will oppose them. We cannot rest from this battle until our life is over. (This is why we speak of a Christian's physical death as entering into their rest.) Ministers are told to expose error and protect the church of Christ. I am convinced faithful ministers must teach the gospel *and* protect the church. But the question remains: How does love do *both* without stooping to sectarianism?

Questions for Discussion and Reflection

1. In what ways do the divisions of the church hinder our work among those who are not Christians? Is this a growing problem in North America? How and why?

2. Where do you see sectarianism in your own life and church? What practical steps can you take to confront and overcome it?

3. What would happen if we truly made every effort to be at peace with all people? If you have experienced a local church schism, do you believe the participants in the debate were making every effort to pursue peace? Think of other examples you are aware of.

Chapter Eleven

Why the Church Still Matters

The church is present wherever "the manifestation of the Spirit" takes place.
— *Jürgen Moltmann*

The church is the community founded by Jesus Christ
and anointed by the Holy Spirit.
—*A Concise [Roman Catholic] Dictionary of Theology*

The mere mention of the word *church* sends some Christians into emotional apoplexy. Many people I know love Jesus, but the church is another matter. Some people have been profoundly harmed by the church. In others, their experience has been dull and unfulfilling. Still others have found the church to be a religious corporation that seems irrelevant. I am sympathetic to all these reactions, but the truth is this: A careful reading of the Bible shows that a person cannot be a fully faithful Christian without being related to the church. The way each of us relates to the church will undoubtedly differ. We all go through stages in life and thus respond differently to various parts of our faith journey. I understand the process and have lived it. But the point is, Christians have an innate desire to be united with the people of God in growing relationships.

We generally identify ourselves by naming the people and events that have shaped us. As Christians, we are identified by the people we associate with in our faith. But we should *primarily* think of ourselves as members of

Christ's community. This identity means we are siblings who share in the love of God-given oneness. We may wish to downplay our family membership, but we must realize biblical salvation is never solitary. *We are saved as a people who are called to share in beloved community.* I see two traps to be avoided: (1) pseudo-pious *sentimentality*, in which we fail to see the church must have some organization; and (2) *institutionalism*, in which we fail to see the church is a living organism, not just a religious organization.

No Solitary Life

Eugene Peterson captured this biblical emphasis well: "God never makes private, secret salvation deals with people. His relationships with us are personal, true; intimate, yes; but private, no. We are a family in Christ. When we become Christians, we are among brothers and sisters in faith. No Christian is an only child."[1] The biblical portrait of the church includes descriptors like *disciples, brothers and sisters* (siblings), *the people, believers in the one Christ, saints*, etc. All these terms underscore the singularly important point that from the beginning, Christianity involved human relationships. "All actual life is encounter," said Martin Buber.[2] This idea of "encounter" stretches back to the covenant of creation—which runs through the Abrahamic, Sinaitic, and Davidic covenants. This encounter led to the new covenant (Jeremiah 31:31–34), a relationship with God written on the heart and open to all people. Christians believe this new covenant came through Jesus' life and death—salvific acts seen in the New Testament as the ultimate sacrifice of divine love. But again, *salvation is never a purely individual matter.* All the covenants involved peoples, not simply singular persons. The blessings were for *all*, and God's intent was to share them with the whole world. At Pentecost, the Holy Spirit was poured out on *all*—an outpouring without regard to ethnicity, race, or gender. While Christians, churches, and movements have often failed to live the life of the Spirit, we see in Acts a marvelous account of how the first Christians actually lived. What they did was truly radical within their culture. Their faith and practice transcended traditional walls of separation into new opportunities for growing relationships in God's love.

It has been suggested that the words of Galatians 3:28 might have been the first baptismal confession in the early church. Paul says: "There is no longer Jew or Greek, there is no longer slave or free, there is no longer male and female; for all of you are one in Christ Jesus." In this text there is a

1. Peterson, *Long Obedience*, 169.
2. Buber, *I and Thou*.

parallelism that includes three dyads. They involve a "differential of power."[3] Paul names three divisions that were common to and accepted by the world of that time: religious bigotry rooted in sectarianism, slavery, and gender/sex. This may have been an inversion of a traditional Jewish cliché, "I thank Fortune that I, a man, was not born a foreigner, a slave, or a woman." It also may be that this creed was centered on the powers that separated people. However we understand these words, this text undermined the human divisions that would have kept persons separated in the early church. The gospel called the baptized to live unity as a way to show the world what has been accomplished for those who follow Jesus into relational, transformative unity.

Such radical ideas clearly challenged the most obvious walls of the first century. An encounter with the living Christ showed believers how to overcome race by grace, gender by mutual acceptance, and status by giving honor and respect to all, rich and poor alike. Corrupt expressions of political power, so common to their time as to our own, created walls. These walls must be torn down. This happened through a shared encounter with Jesus and one another.

What Then *Is* the Church?

Many people answer with a list of things the church does. Others describe things that are *not* the church (for example, it is not a building or legal organization or social society). In its simplest form, *church* describes "the people of God." The New Testament Greek word for *church* refers to "an assembly or congregation that has been called out for a specific purpose." What makes the New Testament church distinctive is that it belongs to Jesus Christ. The English word *church* comes from the Old English *cirice* (ultimately from the Greek *kyriakos*, "of the Lord"). Thus the building where people met was sometimes called "the Lord's house"—not in the sense that God dwelled only there, but in the sense that "the Lord's people" met there.

I cannot advocate giving up the word *church*. But I strongly advocate reforming our understanding. Some popular writers dehistoricize the church and make a case for revolution, not reformation. They throw out the past. (They see all ritual as *ritualism* and all tradition as *traditionalism*.) The underlying theology behind this idea is deficient. This approach has been tried many times in history, often with grievous results, including radical sectarianism and new schism. It has led some to assert they have recovered the *true* church since they have followed the biblical blueprint.

3. Patterson, *Forgotten Creed*, 49.

(Such a blueprint, with all the details filled in, does not exist in the New Testament.) Because of the various claims different groups make about the church, we must seek to better understand this word. I conclude that the church is *the people of God*, and as God's people, the church will always need spiritual renewal. Because we are human, we will sometimes fail to carry God's love to the world, but God's grace and forgiveness remains. This is what the church is really to be about. Jesus expressed this clearly: "I give you a new commandment, that you love one another. Just as I have loved you, you also should love one another. By this everyone will know that you are my disciples, if you have love for one another" (John 13:34–35).

The American Reformed theologian John Leith expressed my central idea well: "The church exists where the Word of God is heard in faith and obeyed in love."[4] Nothing else is really necessary for the church to exist in space and time. Circa 110 CE, Ignatius of Antioch said, "Wherever Jesus Christ is, there is the catholic church"[5]—a concise statement written long before the church took on the external structure that would develop over the centuries. The church is the people of God hearing, believing, and obeying the Word of God. This understanding is inherent to the whole New Testament story. This definition promotes relational unity *without* compromising important differences. It welcomes creeds, confessions, and liturgies *without* insisting that only one visible church communion possesses the whole truth of all that God is and does in the world.

The Church Understood as the Local Congregation

In the New Testament, the term *church* is most often applied to Christians who gather in a specific place. The church is a local congregation in a particular place. This church consists of real people in real relationships. Paul's letters address specific human problems in congregations. In church, week after week, we confess our Christian faith, receive our baptism, and come to the Lord's Table together in corporate worship. So strong is this biblical emphasis that some Christians insist the local congregation is the only correct use of the word *church*. But the New Testament shows that no congregation ever existed apart from others. Simply put, the congregation is the church. One local congregation is as much the church as any other church. *But the church is also the whole of all such congregations throughout the whole earth.* So the church is both the local congregation *and* the whole people of God. (This universal emphasis is particularly clear in Ephesians.) As my friend

4. Leith, *The Church*, 21.
5. Cited in Bercot, ed., *Dictionary*, 146.

Craig Higgins correctly observes, being *the church* and being a part of *a church* are two sides of the same coin! And, he adds, there are no "Christians at large."

The Church in the City

The church is also addressed in the New Testament as existing in one city or region, such as the church in Jerusalem, Antioch, Rome, or Ephesus. As I read the New Testament, I see three dimensions of the church. The most frequent use is with reference to a local church congregation that meets in one specific place. The second use is that of the universal church, or all those who believe. But a third dimension offers incredible practical possibilities: The church was the collection of all the house churches in one city, such as in Rome, where several such gatherings are referenced (see Romans 16:3–5, 14–15). A simple reading of the text leads one to conclude that *local church* had two meanings: (1) a single congregation gathering in a certain place (a home or other building) and (2) a group of congregations in a particular city that may have met together on occasion but likely met as different congregations most of the time.

When a congregation sees itself as "the church" in a given location, to the exclusion of other congregations that meet there, it breeds isolation and sectarianism. Sadly, this seems to be the state of most churches in America. The strong emphasis of most congregations is almost entirely on their own ministry (and denomination) to the exclusion of the mission of all other local churches. It is right to acknowledge the universality of the church, but we must recover the biblical emphasis on the unity of *all Christian congregations in a particular community.*

As the church developed in the fourth and fifth centuries, it grew increasingly close to the state, leading to a system whereby each town had one church—the "parish" church. In modern society, especially in an increasingly post-Christendom context, this concept is all but dead. Our task is not to form parishes but to be the people of God in a society where we live among those who are not yet, or may never be, inside the church. Our mission is to be the church for *them*. We are to live so they will find the grace of God among us. We do this best when we recognize and love the one church in our city. If leaders and churches put this concept into practice, it would radically alter the ministry of almost every congregation I know. I will demonstrate later how some leaders are pursuing this concept in practice, sharing in a growing vision for city transformation.

The Church—Universal, Local, Invisible, Visible

By now it should be evident that early Christian believers confessed faith in the church that covered the whole earth. The universality of the church was important because it kept them from limiting it to one nationality, class, or race. Without this understanding we easily move away from mission into a protective institutional organization that can become nationalistic, racist, or misogynistic.[6] And it is important to recognize that the church is not the sum of the total number of local congregations added together to form one worldwide church made up of thousands of smaller parts. Every single church *is* a true church in its own place and at the same time every church *is* the church catholic. Catholicity is a *quality*, not an *organization*. This quality belongs to every church. The total body of believers can only be found in the universal church, yet a single congregation has every right to call itself a church, because it shares in Jesus' life and mission.

The church is both visible and invisible. As it is a spiritual reality, it must be invisible, in one sense. But this use of the word *spiritual* doesn't mean the church is opposed to the physical/material. As a spiritual totality, the catholic church is not found in one place or in one fellowship. Thus we can rightly say that the church, as the whole people of God, is invisible to our eyes. This is true regarding both the church in heaven and the whole church on earth, at least in the sense that Paul put it in 2 Timothy 2:19, "The Lord knows those who are his."

The catholic church can only be visible at one moment and in one place. "We who are alive in Christ represent in one place and time that whole which God alone sees in its completeness. The great procession of the faithful crosses the world's stage—and only such part of it as is actually crossing the stage is visible; and as it passes through the world, [it is] a 'mixed multitude.'"[7]

---

6. This is a current challenge for the church. Two great twentieth-century confessions addressed it. The first, the Declaration of Barmen, was written largely by Karl Barth and agreed upon at the Synod of Barmen in 1934. Hitler's National Socialist Movement had sought to provide justification for a new kind of Christianity rooted in the German people, racially and ethnically. In six short paragraphs, this declaration resisted the subordination of the gospel and the church to any political or social movement by stressing the submission of Christians and the church to Christ alone. The second, the Belhar Confession, was written in Afrikaans by the Dutch Reformed Mission Church in South Africa in 1986 and adopted by the Uniting Reformed Church in Southern Africa (1994) when a merged church was created. It was adopted by the Reformed Church in America (the oldest continuous denomination in the US) in 2010, becoming the first formal confessional addition to the historic three forms of unity in over 350 years.

7. Witherspoon and Kirkpatrick, *Manual of Church Doctrine*, 7.

A right understanding of invisibility reminds us that the unity of the church is ultimately God's work. The church is never an end in itself; thus, if we no longer struggle for the unity God has given, we become captive to a deficient understanding of our journey. We must actually engage in love in a growing relational unity. Our primary concern must be the visible church precisely because we are members together sharing in Christ's one love for us all.

Questions for Discussion and Reflection

1. How would you define *the church*? Is a local congregation the church? How does the idea of "the people of God" help you in your thinking abut the church?

2. For the Protestant Reformers, what was necessary for there to be a church?

3. Is the church visible or invisible? In what sense is it one, the other, or both?

Chapter Twelve

For Christ and His Kingdom

> The term "kingdom of God" might be more accurately translated "the reigning of God," affirming that the kingdom is the Lord's.
> —*Christian Word Book*

> Jesus' announcement of God's kingdom is the gold standard.
> —*N.T. Wright*

In the fall of 1968 I was happily engaged with classes and campus life at the University of Alabama. I had begun to ask a lot more serious questions about Jesus over the previous year. I found myself exploring questions about the church and Christ's mission almost daily. During the previous months I had become profoundly aware that I should prepare for a life in ministry. This led me to inquire about transferring to Wheaton College. At the time, I knew next to nothing about Wheaton. Why Wheaton? At the time, I wasn't sure I could explain it. Now, over fifty years later, I know I made the right choice. At thirteen or fourteen, I read a famous missionary biography, *Through Gates of Splendor*. I believe it led me to consider Wheaton. The idea that a school associated with this kind of faith and commitment to Christ's mission profoundly moved me.

My first inkling of a call to serve Christ and the church came as a young boy at a missions conference in North Carolina. When I was accepted at Wheaton late in the fall of 1968, I prepared to transfer the next January.

Wheaton was in a period of spiritual lethargy at the time. (The 1960s were anytime but calm.) In early 1970, Wheaton experienced what Robert Coleman aptly calls a "divine moment." This awakening helped me fully embrace a life of mission *and* intellect. Because of Wheaton, I learned how to think in a profoundly Christian sense, always with a clear-eyed focus on Christ's kingdom. As my life's call to mission and ministry took shape, I daily pondered Wheaton's motto: "For Christ and His Kingdom."

Christ and His Kingdom

The well-known author Frederick Buechner was invited to teach as a guest at Wheaton in 1985. Of his experience, he wrote:

> The famous pledge sends out highly misleading signals not only as to what Christianity is all about but also as to what Wheaton College is all about. Because of those signals I was apprehensive. . . . Whatever evangelical meant . . . it did not mean closed-minded [at Wheaton]. On the contrary I found the college as open to what was going on in the world and as generally sophisticated as any I have known. What made it different from any I have known can perhaps best be suggested by the college motto, which is more in evidence there than such mottos usually are. It is not in Latin like most of the other mottos I can think of but in English plain enough for anybody to read and understand. "For Christ and his Kingdom" is the way it goes—as plain as that.[1]

I believe Buechner got it right about Wheaton.

My own story underscores something vital to our understanding of mission and unity. The word *kingdom* jumps off the pages of Scripture, especially if you read the Gospels carefully, but is easily lost in translation. This is tragic because the word has a central role in understanding both the church and its mission. And the kingdom directly addresses the problem of disunity.

If we are to tear down the walls that divide us from one another, we must begin with a more robust understanding of "the gospel of the kingdom" (Matthew 4:23, 9:35; Mark 1:15; Luke 4:43, 8:1). After all, if Christ is the center, we should ask: *What did Christ say, what does his gospel mean, and what does this have to do with the assignment he gave to those who follow him?*

---

1. See Buechner, *Quote of the Day.*

Biblical scholars almost universally agree that *kingdom of God*, *kingdom of Christ*, and *kingdom of heaven* are synonymous. The biblical idea of the kingdom is deeply rooted in the Old Testament and powerfully developed in the coming of the Messiah in the New Testament. Properly understanding the kingdom will go a long way toward helping us avoid a divided and polarized church. It will also empower our mission when we grasp its importance to us.

In modern English, *kingdom* denotes a place. A king has a kingdom, a land and a people over which he rules. The Greek word for *kingdom* is *basileia*, and it translates to something akin to *activity*, though *reign* or *rule* are a lot closer to the original meaning. When Jesus preached, he said "the kingdom of God has come near" (Mark 1:15); thus *the kingdom of God* is what is most often associated with the preaching of the good news. The Gospels say something like this: *God is asserting his rule in the world in and through the mission of Jesus. Jesus has come to herald the truth that the God who seems to have been far away at times has now come near again and will take back his throne!*

The Old Testament Background

The Old Testament often ascribes kingly rule to God by acclaiming him as king (Psalm 47:2, 103:19, 145:13). When you read the psalms and the prophets you readily see there are two streams of hope in the Old Testament, both of which converge in the person of Messiah. The first stream is called the *prophetic*. Israel repeatedly hopes for a king who will be anointed by the Spirit to expel wickedness and injustice and bring about a reign of peace and prosperity. This hope began with David's kingship and line. Here is one expression of it, an expression we see clearly linked to Jesus in the New Testament (cf. Matthew 21:2, 5, 7):

> Rejoice greatly, O daughter Zion!
>   Shout aloud, O daughter Jerusalem!
> Lo, your king comes to you;
>   triumphant and victorious is he,
>   humble and riding on a donkey,
>   on a colt, the foal of a donkey. (Zechariah 9:9)

The second stream has been properly described as *apocalyptic*. Since earthly rulers all continually fail to bring in the kingdom, the Lord will intervene himself in the last days. We see this apocalyptic hope clearly expressed in an example fulfilled in Jesus in the New Testament (Revelation 7:17, 21:4).

> On this mountain the Lord of hosts will make for all peoples
>   a feast of rich food, a feast of well-aged wines,
> of rich food filled with marrow, of well-aged wines strained clear.
> And he will destroy on this mountain
>   the shroud that is cast over all peoples,
>   the sheet that is spread over all nations;
>   he will swallow up death forever.
> Then the Lord God will wipe away the tears from all faces,
>   and the disgrace of his people he will take away from all the earth,
>   for the Lord has spoken. (Isaiah 25:6–8; see also 40:10)

We can see both of these Old Testament streams converge in Jesus Christ, the Son of David, who was anointed for this work by the Holy Spirit. Jesus acts in Israel's stead, thus he comes preaching good news to Israel, specifically the good news of his kingdom. In these two streams we see one who comes with "might to rule . . . his arm rules for him." At the same time, this one who comes "will feed his flock like a shepherd." Here is the imagery and background for the kingdom of God motif in Jesus' preaching and person. These two streams were clearly mediated in him.

What does this good news of the kingdom mean for Israel? Abraham, and through him Israel, received a promise from God that "all the nations of the earth shall gain blessing for themselves through your offspring" (Genesis 26:4). This promise was fulfilled in the coming of Messiah Jesus who would "feed his flock like a shepherd . . . [and] gather the lambs in his arms . . . [and] and carry them in his bosom, and gently lead the mother sheep" (Isaiah 40:11).

Jesus and His Kingdom

What kind of kingdom did Jesus bring with his coming? Recall that even his disciples were confused about this even after the risen Christ had spent forty days teaching them the right answer (see Acts 1:3, 6). *Jesus brings a kingdom that doesn't follow the usual patterns of history.* It doesn't overthrow the Roman rule to establish a new religious, social, and political order. He does not establish a reign of domination or retribution. Jesus directed his hearers to the meaning of his reign with words like this: "But if it is by the finger of God that I cast out the demons, then the kingdom of God has come to you" (Luke 11:20). This is Jesus' way of saying he will deliver his people from oppression! Jesus calls all his followers to become the ambassadors of God's kingdom rule, a reign that delivers people and institutions from death and bondage (2 Corinthians 5:20) through his saving work. Luke says Jesus sent his disciples out "to proclaim the kingdom of God and to heal" (9:2). Where you see the good news bringing about healing and restoration from sin and death, you see most clearly see the kingdom breaking into our present reality. The kingdom of God also finds expression in a phrase near the end of the Nicene Creed: "[We] look for the life of the world to come." The "world to come" is the final manifestation of Christ's kingdom. There the blind will see, the captives and the oppressed will go free, and the poor will have good news brought to them (Luke 4:16–22). The kingdom of God is *more than* heaven above or life after death. *It is both the life of this world and the life of the world to come.* It is a better world, a world built on only one law: the law of love. Christ reigns through love and sacrifice, and we serve and live the gospel of his kingdom in the same way.

The kingdom Jesus brought into the world does not try to impose Christian values and beliefs on others. While it is right that we become involved in public and political service, we must realize that his kingdom does not come through establishing a Christian government or state. Borrowing and developing his thought from St. Augustine, Martin Luther rightly said there were *two kingdoms* in the world: the kingdom of God and the kingdom of the world. In the kingdom of God, Christ is Lord. In this kingdom, Christians freely embrace his rule through the gospel without any form of coercion. But in the other kingdom, God rules through earthly agents and structures. Hence, Luther believed godly princes were instituted for our human welfare. He said we are best ruled by good leaders, rulers who seek the well-being of their subjects. *But this second kingdom is not the kingdom of Christ.* When these two kingdoms are confused, Christians make a tragic mistake—one not always understood when political and social fevers run high.

Your Kingdom Come

Jesus urged all his followers to pray: "Your kingdom come." *This kingdom is our mission.* But if the kingdom is God's rule in our world, how can we explain what is presently going on? We can only conclude: "God's rule is not yet visible in the way we long for it to be."[2] This is precisely what Jesus clearly taught in many of his parables (e.g., Mark 4:30–32).

God's rule is breaking into our world day by day as Christ's reign wins decisive victories in every corner of the world. But this victory is not seen

---

2. Hill, *Lord's Prayer*, 35.

through unaided reason. Nor is it seen in the corridors of human power. We do see it coming, but only by faith. Someday we will see it come in all its fullness. Oscar Cullmann (1902–1999), a Lutheran theologian, illustrated this already-but-not-yet nature of God's reign by referring to the difference between "D-Day" and "V-Day" in World War II.[3] D-Day was June 6, 1944. On this day the Allied forces began their last major assault on Germany when they took Normandy Beach. They entered France to begin the all-out offensive that would end the entire war. But the end would only come eleven months later (May 8, 1945), after many deaths and much suffering. Victory was not complete until Germany surrendered to the Allies. Wesley Hill concludes:

> It is as though we live between two similarly momentous days. We look backward to the life, death and resurrection of Jesus as the moment when God's rule showed itself to be unconquerable—theological D-Day, we might call it. In a very real way, God's conquest of His rebellious world was achieved when His Son left the tomb behind on Easter morning. Yet suffering continues, and we go on longing for an end that isn't yet public and universal.[4]

The Lord and His Kingdom

When we hear words like "this is of first importance," we should pay very careful attention to what comes next. The first teaching Jesus gave publicly is massively important. Why did he come and what was his mission? John the Baptist answers by saying, "Repent, for the kingdom of heaven has come near" (Matthew 3:2). John's mission was to point his hearers to Jesus. Jesus pointed men and women to his kingdom.

After the inaugural events of Jesus' story—his baptism and temptation—he withdrew to the region of Galilee. There he came preaching for the first time. His message? "Repent, for the kingdom of heaven has come near" (Matthew 4:17). Jesus authenticates the forerunner's preaching by openly saying he is the one John pointed to by his unique mission in the wilderness. If you pay close attention to the unfolding story of Jesus' teaching and mission, you will quickly discover at least three different, but profoundly interrelated, meanings of the "kingdom of God."

---

3. Cullmann, *Christ and Time*, 84.
4. Hill, *Lord's Prayer*, 36.

First, the kingdom of God has drawn *near* and is already *present* in Jesus. Jesus called his disciples to follow him by embracing the message he taught in the synagogues. (Remember, he is the Messiah of Israel who came first to the Jews.) The heart of his message was the kingdom (Matthew 4:23; Luke 8:1). He sent his disciples out to heal and preach just as he did (Luke 9:2; Matthew 10:7). Jesus plainly but emphatically says, "When you enter a town and are welcomed, eat what is offered to you. Heal the sick who are there and tell them, 'The kingdom of God has come near to you'" (Luke 10:8–9). Jesus gave his followers this kingdom. "Do not be afraid, little flock, for your Father has been pleased to give you the kingdom" (Luke 12:32). Jesus regarded his followers as those who had received the good news of the kingdom, a kingdom that was radically distinct from the world.

Second, the kingdom is a *separate society*. This society is first revealed in Matthew 16, when Peter confesses that Jesus is the Messiah. Jesus replies: "Blessed are you, Simon son of Jonah, for this was not revealed to you by flesh and blood, but by my Father in heaven. And I tell you that you are Peter, and on this rock I will build my church, and the gates of Hades will not overcome it" (Matthew 16:17–18). (This is the first mention of the church in the Gospel narratives. The second, and the only other one, is in Matthew 18:15–20.) God saves individuals for the kingdom yet the kingdom creates a community, the church. The late biblical scholar George E. Ladd saw this clearly: "The kingdom of God is not the church. The apostles went about preaching the kingdom of God (Acts 8:12; 19:8; 28:23); it is impossible to substitute 'church' for 'kingdom' in such passages. However, there is an inseparable relationship. The church is the fellowship of those who have accepted God's offer of the kingdom, submitted to its rule, and entered into its blessings."[5]

Finally, the kingdom of God is *present now*, yet it will come in its *fullness* when Jesus returns. The kingdom is the eternal reign of Christ (Luke 1:33) that will be fully revealed in his second coming (Matthew 25:31–46). This is why eschatology, or final things, must always have a prominent role in the life and mission of the church. This is why the first Christians confessed the hope of Jesus' coming again with words like these in the Apostles' Creed: "On the third day he rose again from the dead. He ascended to heaven and is seated at the right hand of God the Father almighty. From there he will come to judge the living and the dead."

The repentance Jesus calls us to embrace is most clearly linked to this gospel of the kingdom. But it has been profoundly misunderstood, leading to our misunderstanding of what repentance means. True repentance

---

5. Ladd, "Kingdom," 660.

is far more than one-time sorrow or a solitary decision without communal impact. True repentance calls us to "put on a new attitude *because we recognize the compelling royal presence of God before us.* This entails a change of vision, a change of home, [and] a change of lover."[6] At this point we can see more clearly how the church has historically misunderstood the kingdom. More to the point, we can see how all three of the great Christian traditions—Protestant, Orthodox, and Catholic—have variously understood, and even misunderstood, the kingdom of God and the church.

How the Church and Kingdom Connect

All Christians, without exception, are called to live the reality of Christ's kingdom in every aspect of life—church, family, work, community. Why? God's kingdom reign is over *all* of life—personal and communal, public and private, individual and collective. Let's be honest: The prayer "your kingdom come" goes directly against the thinking of most North American Christians. We have been taught that all of life can fit into one of two categories—secular or sacred. But this dualistic separation must be resisted on the basis of both the biblical story and kingdom theology. The universal witness of Holy Scripture is that *all* creation is good. This means the spheres of education, politics, and the marketplace all belong to Christ. We should not withdraw from our neighbors or our communities. We are to be "salt" and "light." The gospel of the kingdom is not our private help-line. It is our public vocation.

The Passover plays a major role in the biblical story and the coming of Christ's kingdom. This Passover pattern can be readily seen in the early chapters of Acts. In chapter 11, we get a glimpse of the church's mission in Syrian Antioch (about 300 miles north of Jerusalem). Many people, from very different nationalities, are coming to faith in Jesus through the witness of the church there, and it was growing in number and strength. But a prophet arrives to tell the church that a great famine is coming. The mission takes a new direction as the Spirit leads the church.

During the 2020–2021 coronavirus pandemic, many Christians began to ask, "What is God saying to us in this time?" As the awful news of the global pandemic came, I went to Acts 11 because of a small book by N.T. Wright.[7] He observes:

---

6. Leiva-Merikakis, *Fire of Mercy*, 158.
7. Wright, *God and the Pandemic*, 31–32.

> What do the Antioch Jesus-followers say? They do not say either "This must be a sign that the Lord is coming back soon!" or "This must mean that we have sinned and need to repent"—or even "this will give us a great opportunity to tell the wider world that everyone is a sinner and needs to repent." Nor do [these Christians] start a blame-game, looking around at civic authorities in Syria, or the wider region, or even the Roman empire.... They asked three simple questions: Who is going to be at special risk when this happens? What can we do to help? And who[m] shall we send?[8]

Wright says some will look at this story and judge the Antiochian Christians' response "untheological." He correctly concludes: "Here we stumble upon one of the great principles of the kingdom of God—the principle that God's kingdom, inaugurated through Jesus, is all about restoring creation to the way it was meant to be. God always wanted to work in his world through loyal human beings. That is the point of being made in God's image."[9] Imagine what would happen if we actually looked at the world and made it our priority to serve others in the same way as we see in Acts 11! Such a response would clearly express what it means for the church to seek first the kingdom. The problem in the American church is that we are far too busy and prosperous. Thus the pandemic exposed our weakness *and* opened a door of great opportunity for mission.

From the story of the kingdom of God at work in the church in Acts 11, we can now see how we should engage the world afresh with the story of Jesus. We must show by word and deed God's purpose, his mission, in the world. This incredible good news declares that everyone who trusts in Jesus will be saved. But it also includes the servant work of God's people seeking to remove oppression, poverty, disease, and injustice. We will never transform the world entirely—that will only happen when Jesus returns—but we can experience unity in God-Love and bring Jesus' kingdom to the whole world.

The mission of Jesus is our calling. Kingdom life leads us to engage with all of human life. Abraham Kuyper expressed this vision powerfully: "No single piece of our mental world is to be hermetically sealed off from the rest, and there is not a square inch in the whole domain of our human existence over which Christ, who is sovereign over *all*, does not cry: 'Mine!'"[10]

---

8. Wright, *God and the Pandemic*, 31.
9. Wright, *God and the Pandemic*, 32.
10. Kuyper, "Sphere Sovereignty," 488.

From the very beginning, the church was taught to see the world as Jesus did. The early church adopted this same attitude—which we can surely call "the mind of Christ"—and prayerfully moved into every part of Jewish and Roman life, making known the good news of the kingdom by showing love and kindness and by preaching this message of repentance and faith. *Thus we can see that the kingdom established the mission.* Indeed, this is fundamentally what mission is all about. Jesus made this very clear. A week after his resurrection, when he appeared to his frightened disciples, he said, "'Peace be with you! As the Father has sent me, I am sending you.' And with that he breathed on them and said, 'Receive the Holy Spirit. If you forgive anyone's sins, their sins are forgiven; if you do not forgive them, they are not forgiven'" (John 20:21–23).

If any hymn lyrics were an unofficial school song at Wheaton College, it was the 1925 composition "May the Mind of Christ, My Savior." The words of this simple hymn are based on Paul's exhortation in Philippians 2:5. I still cannot sing these words without being deeply reminded that I have the mind of Christ; thus I can faithfully live "For Christ and His Kingdom."

> May the mind of Christ, my Savior,
> Live in me from day to day,
> By His love and power controlling
> All I do and say.
>
> May the Word of God dwell richly
> In my heart from hour to hour,
> So that all may see I triumph
> Only through His power.
>
> May the peace of God my Father
> Rule my life in everything,
> That I may be calm to comfort
> Sick and sorrowing.
>
> May the love of Jesus fill me,
> As the waters fill the sea;
> Him exalting, self abasing,
> This is victory.
>
> May I run the race before me,
> Strong and brave to face the foe,
> Looking only unto Jesus,
> As I onward go.

May His beauty rest upon me
As the lost I seek to win,
And may they forget the channel,
Seeing only Him.[11]

Conclusion

So, what does the kingdom have to do with the church? *The kingdom of God has a church.* The kingdom of Christ created the church. But be careful, the opposite is not true: *The church does not have a kingdom.* Church history is replete with examples of what happens when we get this wrong. If we grasp the significance of this important distinction, we will better understand the church, her unity, and our mission. This kingdom perspective will help us embrace the imperative of unity Jesus prayed for in John 17.

My call for tearing down walls that divide us sees unity through the gospel of the kingdom. It underscores that the redeemed are one in Christ, who is Lord of all (see Ephesians 4:3–6). When the redeemed experience unity in the one Spirit, they begin to live relationally the prayer Jesus taught us all to pray: "Your kingdom come. Your will be done, on earth as it is in heaven" (Matthew 6:10). Toward the end of the last century, many Christians from every historic church had finally come to see this proper biblical relationship between the kingdom and the church. The theological developments we've already seen are now rightly understood in the light of the kingdom. This means we must *distinguish* the church from the kingdom. *We can say this best when we affirm that the church is a living, relationally human witness to the kingdom.*

Questions for Discussion and Reflection

1. Can we pray together for the kingdom to come? What do you think will happen to the walls we've constructed out of fear and pride when we pray together as one? Discuss the role prayer can have in seeking oneness.

2. How should we understand our church's mission if the kingdom is *not* the church but rather the church exists to serve Christ's kingdom?

3. What do you think we can begin to do together because we all partake of Christ's kingdom?

11. Wilkinson, "May the Mind of Christ."

Chapter Thirteen
———

The Search for the Ideal Church

> The fact is that the differences between churches do matter. The question is not, "How can we overlook these differences?" but "How can we achieve a church which includes the many facets of the truth?" True catholicity is not obtained by overlooking differences but by accepting them and understanding them as a vital part of the nature of the church.
>
> —*Robert E. Webber*

> Ecumenism is a way of living that desires to think globally and live truthfully with differences in community.
>
> —*Fr. Tom Ryan, CSP*

Denominations are clearly not found in the Bible nor in the ancient church. It is time we all admit this obvious fact. Perhaps the only biblical analogy that comes close to our current situation is in Paul's discussion about the worldliness he saw in the church at Corinth (1 Corinthians 1–3). One could compare his language to our modern context and hear people saying, "I belong to John Calvin. I belong to Martin Luther. I belong to the pope." And we can hear nondenominational Christians adding, "I belong to Christ!" Lesslie Newbigin was correct when he argued that this type of plurality created an *intolerable scandal*. He concluded that the rhetorical questions of 1 Corinthians 1:13 flow from one overriding question: *Is Christ divided?* The right answer to Paul's question showed "how any breach in the unity of the church was in violent contradiction to the very heart of the gospel as Paul understood it."[1]

So how should we understand denominations? They are identifiable groups of believers and churches united on the basis of a common set of beliefs and practices. More often than not, these beliefs were based upon a historical reality that shaped their original formation and continued existence. But are such churches a problem or a solution? To ask the question more provocatively, should we end all Protestant denominations and just become independent Christians in independent churches? Or should we go back to Rome, whence we historically came in the sixteenth century? Or should we find our way into the Orthodox Church so we can live the ancient faith in the ideal church? If any of this were to actually happen—we are clearly imagining something beyond what we can conceive—would the results of this restructuring of Christians and congregations be good for the mission of Christ? As I have argued that relational unity is what Jesus prayed for, I think it is appropriate to delve more deeply into this issue of denominations. My hope is that this overview might help us understand our differences better in order that we may love one another more deeply. I have no desire to score points or win a debate.

The Ideal Church Misunderstood

The fact that the church is one should be understood in at least two ways. In the ancient sense, oneness referred to *uniqueness*. In this sense oneness expresses an *ideal*.[2] Early Christians rightly claimed there was one church because there was one Lord. God had chosen a vast company of persons to make up one Spirit-formed community. The imagery in the New Testament is frequently that of a temple where the worship of God is offered continually. The New Testament envisions a multitude of people from everywhere streaming into the light of God in this one spiritual temple.

The Christian community clearly does not exist for itself. As the church, we have a holy calling to "to be merciful, just as your [our] Father is merciful" (Luke 6:38). From her earliest days the church has understood that divine mercy was rooted in the Lord's undeserved, unfailing kindness.

---

1. Newbigin, *Household of God*, 70.

2. The word *ideal* lines up with the conception of what is perfect or most suitable. It also refers to what is desirable. It thus seems right to seek what is desirable and most faithful to the apostolic witness, but when the ideal means "perfect," the word has a very different meaning. I am using "ideal" as "most suitable" to practice and faith.

Mercy expresses the heart and seeks the well-being of others in tenderness. As we saw in our overview about the kingdom of God, every time the church has forgotten the calling to be merciful, she has opted for corrupt compromises with power and control. The more we are polarized from one another, the less likely that we will embrace the deep relational mercy God requires of us.

Remember, we are a servant church called to advance Christ's kingdom. As we saw, the kingdom creates the church, not vice versa. A modern biblical scholar speaks eloquently to the church's real claim to uniqueness:

> It can easily be turned from a sense of witness to the world into a claim of privilege. On this basis, the church can claim to have replaced Israel as "God's elect people"—and has done so. It can disqualify the spiritual teachings of other religions on the basis of exclusive spiritual truth—and does so. And rival versions of the church can and do fight bitterly against each other to represent the "one" church of Christ worthy of that name. Although there is a certain truth to the ideal of a single church, it is an ideal that, when claimed as a reality, can become dangerous.[3]

Thus the ideal of "one" church is worthy of the name. But when this ideal becomes "a claim of privilege," we lose the unease we should feel regarding our failure to live consistently with our message. And our claim can easily become "dangerous." Sectarian ideology and practice poison our true identity. Lesslie Newbigin's insights are surely correct:

> We do not find that our Lord first laid down a compendium of doctrine and then invited those who believed it to form an association on that basis. The personal fellowship and the doctrine were given together. . . . The divine society into which [Jesus] admitted men was more than a school of correct theology. It was a personal fellowship of those who believed in him, who had yet many things to learn which they could only learn slowly and stumblingly, but who could be trusted to be his ambassadors to the world and the foundation stones of his church because they abode in him.[4]

---

3. Johnson, *The Creed*, 263.
4. Newbigin, *Household of God*, 79.

The Ideal Church: Roman Catholicism

After the Reformation, the Catholic Church came to embrace ideas about the church that included the doctrine of *Communitas perfecta* ("perfect community"). By this development it was widely taught that the Catholic Church was a self-sufficient society that had all the necessary resources to achieve the salvation of all peoples. Following Vatican II, this doctrine, though not changed entirely, practically lost its importance to a certain extent. Under Pope Pius XII the Roman Catholic Church was primarily understood as "the mystical body of Christ."

At Vatican II (1962–65), the *Lumen gentium* ("light of the nations") decree gave a more expansive understanding of the church by speaking of non-Catholics being related to the Catholic Church. Chapter two of *Lumen gentium* speaks of the church as the "People of God." In the last session of Vatican II, the Council's decree on ecumenism, *Unitatis redintegratio* ("restoration of unity"), declared, "The Spirit of Christ has not refrained from using [separated churches and communities] as a means of salvation." This teaching has become very significant in the intervening years.

I cannot recall when I first heard this notion, but I vividly recall how I heard it. In various discussions with evangelicals who were former Catholics, I was regularly assured the Catholic Church *never changes*. Yet Vatican II profoundly changed the *structures and practices* of the church, and the Roman Catholic Church officially abandoned its previous "perfect" position and formally ended the thousand-year schism with the Orthodox Church. The Catholic Church also entered into ecumenical conversations with other churches with the honest and well-intentioned hope of establishing greater visible Christian unity. This led the church to assume observer status in the World Council of Churches, which has allowed profound participation in several important groups associated with the Council. One of the more significant contributions came though the writing and publication of the important document *Baptism, Eucharist, and Ministry* (BEM, 1982), which identifies areas of agreement between the various churches on several core teachings. The Catholic Church responded positively to BEM, though with qualifications.

These twentieth-century developments are not well understood. This has led to confusion on several sides, from both Catholics and Protestants. This, in turn, has led Christians in and out of the Catholic Church to say *nothing* significant changed at Vatican II. We cannot resolve this debate in a few hundred words, but it must be noted, at least for our purposes, that the Catholic Church was quite formally outside the rise of modern ecumenism until Vatican II. Now it is clearly a major contributor to the global movement for restoring Christian unity.

Since Vatican II, Roman Catholic theology has referred to non-Catholics as "separated brethren." This is a great improvement over the way the Catholic Church once addressed non-Catholic Christians. But Rome still claims to be *the* true (ideal) church, as the magisterium sees the ideal church in Rome's apostolicity, a reality that can be seen in both the hierarchy and structures of the church. The bishops are the apostles' successors, and the pope is Peter's successor. This understanding is connected with a valid administration of the sacraments. Because of this way of thinking, Western churches often consider their differences to be centered in matters of church order. While I believe this is true, so far as it goes, what is far more obvious is this: Our practical and familial divisions ultimately exist much more profoundly in our lack of love for one another. The Orthodox considered these divisions a matter of doctrine; thus they too spoke of other Christians, both Catholics and Protestants, as heretics.[5]

The Ideal Church: Orthodoxy

In the West we tend to think of the church in terms of what it *does* rather than what it *is*. Bringing what we've previously seen into clearer focus, the Orthodox Church understands: "Salvation is social and communal, not isolated and individualistic."[6] Orthodoxy sees the church as the mystical entity that comprises God's direct activity in the world. The Russian Orthodox theologian Sergei Bulgakov stated this clearly when he said the church is "a divine fixed quantity living in itself and comparable only with itself, as the will of God manifesting itself in the world."[7] Orthodox Christians place far

---

5. Orthodox Churches believe the Western churches broke away from the common catholic tradition. The development of doctrinal differences over the centuries was seen as unilaterally breaking the unity of the catholic church; e.g., the addition of the *filioque* to the Nicene Creed, papal centralization, infallibility, the Marian dogmas unique to Catholicism, and, in the case of Protestantism, the ordination of women. The Orthodox see all these movements as a rejection of the apostolic heritage. Orthodoxy has condemned ethnocentric reductionism as heretical. However, these churches were all shaped by very distinct cultural histories, which are a gift to the Orthodox in that they strengthen their liturgical, spiritual, and ethical traditions. But these also present a real challenge. Walls are raised between historic churches and Christians, isolating the Orthodox from other Christians. John Paul II's metaphor of the church having "two lungs," East and West, can help new conversations to begin, conversations that could allow us to dream about healing this thousand-year-old schism.

6. Ware, *How Are We Saved?*, 68.

7. Sergei Bulgakov, cited in Fairbairn, *Eastern Orthodoxy*, 23.

more stress on the divine character of the church than Protestants do. In Orthodoxy, the church is both the fullness of the life of the Holy Spirit *and* the body of Christ, understood both *spiritually* and *sacramentally*. The end result is this: Orthodoxy sees itself as the church of Jesus Christ in *historical continuity* with the earliest Christian assemblies. It may not use the word *true* precisely as it has been used in the West, but it still thinks of itself as *the* one apostolic church.

Anthony Ugolnik, a Ukrainian Orthodox priest and retired professor at a non-Orthodox university in the US, helps us understand Orthodoxy from his lifelong American perspective: "We Christians of America and Russia, simply by reaching a greater understanding of how each of us envisions and lives the gospel, can live the gospel more fully. If we cut ourselves off from that understanding, reject it, or mutilate it through our suspicion or hatred, we are turning ourselves away from God's grace."[8] I hear in Ugolnik's words a call to cultivate historical consciousness, the kind of call that recognizes we are not members of the same corporate structure but *siblings* in the same family. (This sounds a lot like the Catholic term from Vatican II: "separated brothers.")

Don't misunderstand. Ugolnik does not deny there is an **ontological** reality we should call the *true* church. He believes Orthodoxy is that reality, the one church. But he also says we should not isolate ourselves from each other as fellow Christians. We should move toward "loving association" with Christians everywhere.[9] Orthodoxy has historically said the healing of the divided church calls for a universal council to address the problems created by our divisions. Sadly, the Orthodox have been unable to convene a unified modern Orthodox council of her own patriarchates. As I pray for greater visible unity, I pray for this to happen sooner than later.

But this is not the whole story about unity and the Orthodox Church. The Orthodox have been actively involved in the modern ecumenical movement from its inception. All local Orthodox churches were invited, by an encyclical of Patriarch Joachim III of Constantinople in 1902, to engage with *both* Catholics and Protestants to seek a consensus of faith. In 1920 the Ecumenical Patriarch issued an encyclical titled *Unto the Churches of Christ Everywhere*. This hopeful document opens with one of the most significant affirmations of prayer and work for unity you will find: "Our own church holds that rapprochement between the various Christian Churches and fellowship (*koinonia*) between them is not excluded by the doctrinal differences [that] exist between them. In our opinion such a rapprochement

---

8. Ugolnik, *Illuminating Icon*, 264.
9. Ugolnik, *Illuminating Icon*, 266.

is highly desirable and necessary."[10] Many historians concur that this document set the direction for the birth of the World Council of Churches in 1948. By 1961, almost all local Orthodox churches were participating in the Council. (The Catholic Church has been actively working with the WCC for decades but is not a member.) Orthodox Christians were scattered in the years after World War I and World War II, resulting in what has been called the "Orthodox diaspora." This led to Orthodoxy moving into the West and resulted in closer contact between people and churches. It has had a remarkable impact on vital and relational ecumenism, especially in North America.

The Orthodox have always believed the Christian faith is deeply *relational*. I have been the beneficiary of this relational way of life through friendships with Orthodox Christians. This Orthodox way has helped me form relationships in which I have learned to pray for others quite different from myself. Through these friendships I have also learned to share in the spiritual gifts the Orthodox bring to the whole church. Two simple illustrations immediately come to mind: the proper use of icons and the power of the Jesus Prayer.

In my personal and theological journey, Orthodoxy has played an increasingly important role. This has come about through two primary means. First, through reading from the vast treasures of Orthodox tradition, I have learned from the Orthodox way, a way rooted profoundly in the gospel as apostolic truth *experienced in true Christian mysticism*. One of the most powerful examples of Orthodox theology in transforming my own life is the Orthodox teaching on transfiguration and salvation. (This is especially true with regard to the doctrine of **deification/christification/theosis**.) The second example of how Orthodoxy has impacted my life profoundly can be seen in my deep friendships with devout Orthodox priests who love and respect me.

"Everyone Who Calls on the Name of the Lord"

No matter how we understand our past and present differences, we can and should agree that salvation is given to "everyone who calls on the name of the Lord" (Acts 2:21). This should be our starting point. There is clearly more to say, but this must be affirmed. Our present state remains formally divided, but kingdom work is actually carried out in numerous so-called informal contexts. Many Catholic and Orthodox Christians can engage in a relational healing process with numerous Protestants if we walk in this way of faith.

10. Keleher, "Ecumenism," 173.

I see an additional way to understand oneness. Oneness is a claim about what the church is in itself—"the church is one because it lives a life of real unity."[11] This portrait is sketched by Luke in his account of the early church in Acts 2:44: "All the believers were together and had everything in common." He later writes, "All the believers were one in heart and mind" (Acts 4:32). This seems to be the same unity Paul urges in Ephesians 4:3-6. But in verses 7-12, Paul plainly says diversity is also desirable. Luke Timothy Johnson concludes: "Paul also allows for a diversity of practice in matters that are not critical to the identity of the community."[12]

The simple truth is this: *Unity is not uniformity.* I am convinced that the presence of the Holy Spirit guarantees unity *and* diversity. As believers, we share together in the relational unity of the Trinity. Paul argues this is why we should have the same way of thinking that we see expressed in Jesus' relationship with his Father. Their unity was complete! We only know incompletely: "Now we see only a reflection as in a mirror; then we shall see face to face. Now I know in part; then I shall know fully, even as I am fully known" (1 Corinthians 13:12).

So how should the unity and diversity we see within the Trinity impact our relationships? I suggest we consider more deeply how each member in the Trinity cares for the others with love. If we put it into practice, a social and relational understanding of the Trinity can profoundly impact how we treat each other.[13] The church has confessed this unique Trinitarian oneness from earliest times—but this is clearly not how we have lived. Unity has generally been institutionalized as sameness. Or it has been forced, often by the sword, as we see in the first thousand years of Christianity. History shows the church reeling from two extremes—uniformity and deviance. When uniformity goes too far, we will very likely oppress those who disagree with us; when deviance goes too far, we are likely to allow almost anything that our age deems appropriate. Unity in Christ and the truth must become our pattern. Uniformity is not healthy. But some forms of diversity must be understood as illegitimate, or else the church's mission will be harmed, and the gospel of the kingdom will become another ideology.

Many Protestant churches are wrestling mightily with questions on sexual ethics, marriage, women's ordination, and abortion. There is no end in sight for these debates. Some think these difficult questions come down to this: The modern world is driving an agenda not found in Scripture. I am

11. Johnson, *The Creed*, 263.
12. Johnson, *The Creed*, 264.
13. The ancient term for what I write about here is *perichoresis*, which refers to the indwelling, or mutual interpenetration, of the three persons of the Trinity. The term thus underscores their eternal unity.

not persuaded it is so simple. Personally, I find it very hard to embrace the tensions of these differences. It is very hard to stand between competing understandings of moral and ethical decisions and love friends who disagree. The sad fact is, churches and Christians often refuse to acknowledge those who disagree over these differences. As a result, we erect new modern walls of division. We all confess the church is holy, but we forget it is still human. I've watched contentious debates unfold over the last fifty years, and whether they originate on the "left" or "right," these extremes are being allowed to define who we love and pray for as brothers and sisters.

As a result of these deep divisions, many churches are now *defined* by being pro-this or anti-that. But if we grasp *both* unity and diversity, shouldn't we rather ask: "How does the ethical teaching of Scripture, principally rooted in the gospel of Christ, define the church's spiritual life?" Before you say the answer is easy, prayerfully consider this. Serious Christians can be found across a wide continuum of church practices and expressions of faith. Be prepared for a difficult struggle if you disagree with churches or friends and still desire to remain rooted in profound love. Can we create a safe space where food and fellowship can help you to resist these new walls that will divide us even further? In all differences, begin with God's love. Then avoid simplistic answers that lead to easy agreements or emotional rejection. One thing seems clear from Christian history: No matter how we address this range of vexing questions, there will always be areas where churches and Christians disagree. We must look for a third way, a way truly rooted in "faith, hope and love" (1 Corinthians 13:13).

Many Catholics struggle with their own church's teaching on sexuality and abortion. Catholic moral teaching is clear on both matters. The Church unambiguously opposes abortion. It unambiguously opposes sacramental gay marriage. But how should Catholic teaching on these topics be applied? How should social and political means be pursued in support of human life and marriage? Within Catholic parishes I have seen the Catholic teaching about abortion and marriage take many forms of expression. This is not surprising; we experience differing ways to be faithful. But these differing expressions of faithfulness are often allowed to relationally divide families and churches. The irony is that in Catholic and Protestant ecumenical contexts, where unity is highly valued, I've seen Catholics and Protestants continue to strive together to tear down a plethora of historic walls even as they continue to disagree about their emotionally charged differences. Something about a shared vision of unity changes *how* we disagree, even if it does not lead us into full agreement.

How then shall we live? After all, how we live is how we actually come into the fullness of our faith and life together. As important as affirming the teaching of the church is, and I've shown that it remains very important, how do we actually live oneness? This question will lead us to "make every effort to maintain the unity of the Spirit in the bond of peace" (Ephesians 4:3).

I can assure you of this: If you pursue this way of unity, you will soon come to see how every Christian family holds some beautiful pearls of great price. Discover these gems and use them to your benefit. Share them as widely as possible. (In the first half of my life, I never envisioned just how much I could learn from Catholic and Orthodox Christians.) Find these precious pearls, and use them to love Jesus more deeply and follow him into deeper unity.

The One True Church?

Time and again I have seen serious attempts for unity broken down by the absolute certitude that we know what constitutes the *true* church. About a decade ago I received a brochure inviting me to a "True Church Conference." The program was evangelical, with a strong emphasis on doctrine, theology, application, evangelism, and mentoring. The brochure said the event was sponsored by a "truth-driven association of churches." My heart sank as I realized just how far we still have to go if we want to tear down walls that divide us and ruin our mission together. This task is impossible without God's grace leading us to see ourselves with more humility.

Lesslie Newbigin offers a beautiful alternative to this search for the true church. He believed the one church never ceased to exist, even though it had been defaced and divided by sin. Like the Corinthian church, this church has not been divided into one true fellowship with a bunch of (untrue) counterfeit groups. What we really have are mutually compromised factions with continuing, legitimate ecclesiological claims on one another. Simply put, division and schism do not annihilate God's presence in the various fellowships.[14]

When we correctly understand our distinctions, we actually help preserve some of the hard-won strengths the whole church needs. (A wonderful example can be seen in the emphasis on grace that was recovered and highlighted by the Protestant Reformers.) But our resulting schisms compromised God's grace since no one group ever lived up to the full promise

---

14. Newbigin, *Reunion of the Church*, 113. This argument is made in the way Newbigin sets the stage for his magnificent book *The Household of God*. In his first chapter you can see this in "The Setting of the Subject" and in also chapter 2, "The Congregation of the Faithful."

of the whole church. As a result, our resulting factions now afflict both our internal health and external witness.

This diagnosis challenges the false opposites of our continual debates. On the one hand, we must resist the exclusivism of any single position—Roman Catholic, Orthodox, magisterial Protestant, evangelical Protestant, or "Pentecostal" (Free) Protestant—that claims for itself *the totality of grace and truth*. On the other hand, this "one church" approach resists inclusive approaches that add up the totality of various traditions to create a unity resulting in overly confident pluralism. Duke Divinity School professor Geoffrey Wainwright summed this up from his own experience: "After Newbigin, I have stopped searching for the One True Church, for he has helped me see that I already belong to it."[15] There's a great idea. Stop searching for the one true church, and love the church you actually know. *Seek to make your church stronger.* In doing so, embrace this compelling vision of deep and growing unity with Jesus and others.

Questions for Discussion and Reflection

1. How do you think a sectarian understanding of the church can use and abuse the concept of an "ideal church"? How can we think of the ideal church correctly?

2. Can we enter into serious dialogue about unity with Catholic and Orthodox believers if they believe they are the true church? What limitations are placed on our fellowship by our different views of the church?

3. Do you think we can use the biblical phrase "everyone who calls on the name of Lord" as an elemental starting point for our attempts at visible unity and missional cooperation? Why or why not?

---

15. Wainwright, *Lesslie Newbigin*, 399. For resources on this topic, see John Paul Todd's excellent website, www.e4unity.wordpress.com.

Chapter Fourteen

Healing Schism through Costly Love

Our unity is God's gift, and the way to give more visible expression to that gift will also be God's gift. But we will have to empty ourselves of our self-righteousness and let go of our power games in order to let this be God's work.

—*Thomas Ryan, CSP*

Love creates fellowship, fellowship loves unity, and unity preserves love.

—*St. Augustine*

He who wounds love does not build up the Church of God.

—*Brother Roger of Taizé*

I frequently try to imagine Jesus praying with his disciples in the Upper Room on the eve of his crucifixion. I turn this scene over and over in my mind and heart, trying to enter into the deepest mysteries of faith. Eugene Peterson painted a beautiful word-picture of the scene: "We cross the threshold of John 17 and find ourselves in a room of quiet listening.... Jesus is talking to the Father. Jesus is praying. He prays a long time. This is holy ground. We find ourselves embraced in holy listening. We are in a place of prayer, a praying presence. Our mouths are stopped. We are quiet: be still my soul."[1] This prayer is truly different. Here we are not sharing our personal requests. Here we simply wait in the powerful presence of Jesus. *Jesus is praying for us, praying that we will go deeper and deeper into divine unity.* We are being stretched far beyond our small ideas and personal projects to experience our personal involvement in the love of the relational Trinity. Because Jesus prays for us, "we are involved in everything that the Father does and the Son says and the Spirit incarnates in us."[2]

But we face a major difficulty when we try to imagine ourselves in this prayer meeting with Jesus. Peterson expressed our difficulty precisely: "[John 17] doesn't seem to have made much difference for twenty centuries now, and certainly doesn't seem to be having much of an impact on Christians at present."[3] This truth is too sadly plain. The Christian church has only occasionally grasped the meaning of our Lord's prayer. E. Stanley Jones rightly expressed the sad result: "In a divided world seeking unity, a divided church not seeking unity has little or no moral authority."[4] And if we are honest, we must admit we are not only divided by our innumerable walls of theology and prejudice, but we have limited the work of Christ's mission in the process. The watching world is often unimpressed by our faith, seeing it only as the result of blatant self-righteousness.

Can We Agree on Unity?

No one was more committed to working out the vision of what Eugene Peterson called the "John 17 Prayer Meeting" than the Apostle Paul. For Paul, unity was essential to the success of his church-planting mission. The Pauline epistles consistently reveal that our Christian witness springs from a Spirit-empowered fellowship that invites the three great unities of love, truth, and witness. Paul's letters are saturated with prayers and heartfelt admonitions designed to protect and preserve the inherent oneness of the community. Paul gave us many windows into a vision of unity that makes relationships central to the life of the church. Writing to the divided church in Corinth, the apostle underscores a point we must revisit again and again if we are to move into the heart of the John 17 Prayer Meeting.

---

1. Peterson, *Tell It Slant*, 217.
2. Peterson, *Tell It Slant*, 221.
3. Peterson, *Tell It Slant*, 223.
4. Jones, *Christ*, 102.

> Now I would remind you, brothers and sisters, of the good news that I proclaimed to you, which you in turn received, in which also you stand, through which also you are being saved, if you hold firmly to the message that I proclaimed to you—unless you have come to believe in vain. For I handed on to you as of first importance what I in turn had received: that Christ died for our sins in accordance with the scriptures, and that he was buried, and that he was raised on the third day in accordance with the scriptures. (1 Corinthians 15:1–4)

If the gospel is *primary*, one can assume that some other truths are not primary. The Catholic Church expressed this insight at Vatican II: "When comparing doctrines with one another, they [theologians] should remember that in Catholic doctrine there exists a 'hierarchy' of truths, since they vary in their relation to the fundamental Christian faith."[5] This idea of a "hierarchy of truths" can help us keep our focus on the Christian story rather than on all the different ways Christians have interpreted the Bible. We can continue to discuss, even debate, how we differ and why. But what is of "first importance" is where we must establish our priorities if we are to prayerfully labor for unity.

Over nearly three decades of intensive and focused labor for unity, I have discovered the Jesus prayer for our unity (John 17) can move the imagination and heart of the modern church. The "hierarchy of truths" principle can contribute to this renewal by teaching us how to order the mysteries of faith in working together. This idea is based on the varying ways the core Christian mysteries have been related to one another in the saving truth of Christian revelation. This approach places "first importance" on what we've seen in our earlier discussion about the Bible and the creed. It helps us keep our focus on the saving faith we share in common through the Great Tradition. And it reveals how the grace of God and the outworking of the saving mysteries of our shared salvation anchor us in hope. But more than all of these, it shows us how to "love one another" while we follow Jesus together into deeper unity. We must keep our eyes on the prize—the love of our brothers and sisters and the fellowship of the Holy Spirit.

The Church Responds to Controversy and Disagreement

One of the first major controversies the infant church faced came from within, and it threatened the church at the most fundamental level of both

---

5. *Unitatis redintegratio*, no. 11.

its message and mission. Judaizers were teaching that Gentile converts must first be circumcised to enter the fellowship of the church—a teaching based on the Jewish requirement of ritual circumcision. Paul saw this teaching as a serious error that directly impacted the church's mission, making it profoundly dangerous for the spread of Christianity among the Gentiles. There is much evidence in Paul's letters (especially Galatians) of his profound concern and strong reaction. Paul publicly challenged Peter for his seemingly ambivalent reaction to the Judaizers. Paul saw Peter's position as profoundly harmful (see Galatians 2:6–21). (The story reveals that this major dispute did not separate Peter and Paul—a reminder that serious difficulties do not have to divide us.) We see in this story that *both* unity and mission were at the center of Paul's concern.

The first church council in Christian history is recorded in Acts 15. This gathering of leaders sought to resolve the problems associated with this teaching and practice. The council laid down a few minimal food restrictions, which all Christians were urged to observe. They appear to have been adopted for two reasons: (1) so nothing would hinder the mission of the church and the faithful communication of the gospel, and (2) to protect the unity of all believers.

One cannot read Acts and the epistles carefully and not conclude the unity of all Christians was in accord with the message of Jesus and his apostles. Almost every epistle includes some appeal to churches regarding how unity must be preserved. Unity was both a presupposition *and* a goal in the New Testament, which consistently treats disunity as intolerable and unity as vital.

Fr. Bob Miller, a dear friend who has served an African-American Catholic parish on Chicago's South Side for decades, has reminded me often that our enemy (*diabolos*) hates all ecumenical prayer and the work we do together for unity. The devil has hated Christian unity from the first, tearing us apart from one another time and time again. His work is evident in the New Testament, and it has never ceased. Fr. Bob often reminds me of this reality when I grow discouraged and feel I have done so little. (*Diabolos* means the one who is a slanderer *and* divider.)

Heresy and Schism

As we've seen, modern attempts to recover unity began in earnest in the early twentieth century. This broader ecumenical pursuit has waxed and waned throughout history, but it has always been a concern of reformers and mystics. If the first such challenge to unity came from the Judaizers, it was clearly not to be the last. Other crises soon arose that required Christians to protect their unity and address challenges to the good news.

The story of seeking deeper unity raises a question many would rather avoid: *heresy*. Because of the abuse and misuse of this word, we tend to avoid it altogether. But the New Testament plainly speaks of *hairēseis* (see 1 Corinthians 11:18–19), a word transliterated into English as *heresy*. Heresy is a virtual synonym for what Paul calls *schismata*, transliterated as *schism*. Both Greek words represent our common use of the word *division*. The church in Corinth was a tragically divided congregation. Baptist theologian Steve Harmon notes there is a shade of difference in the words *hairēseis* and *schismata*. The divisions in Corinth resulted in part from heresies, a kind of teaching Paul saw as *self-chosen opinions*. The semantic range of these two words allows us to see heresies as a "choice" or an "opinion" that creates division.[6]

There are three criteria a person had to fulfill in order to be a heretic in the biblical sense. First, a heretic is someone whose account of the Christian story is so dangerously inadequate that it leads to an entirely different story than the biblical one of the Triune God. Examples abound in the early church era. One early heresy was Gnosticism. Gnostics challenged the Christ-centered message of incarnation and bodily resurrection, claiming secret insight that was not rooted in the biblical story but rather in a Platonic dualism that pitted matter/flesh against spirit/idea. Another example of heresy is in the fourth-century rise of Arianism, which taught that the Son's divinity was of a lesser order than that of the Father. It falsely said salvation could not come through the humanity of Jesus because humanity could not contribute anything to our salvation.

Second, heresy also refers to an alternative version of the Christian story taught by an authoritative teacher *inside* the church. In this case, there is a type of person who wants to be received as an authority. (Note that in Scripture, the word *heresy* is not used for teachers of non-Christian religions.) This person has specifically denied something in the category of "first things."

Lastly, a person who teaches a dangerously inadequate version of the Christian story threatens to divide the church. "Heresy is therefore not only about problematic theological ideas but about divisive behavior inside the church. Heresy is therefore as much a matter of ethics as it is of doctrine."[7]

---

6. Harmon, *Ecumenism*, 20. This is an excellent, popular (though not breezy or light) overview of ecumenism. I have consistently used this small book for years to mentor and guide men and women who feel particularly called to this work.

7. Harmon, *Ecumenism*, 20–21. I am indebted to Harmon for his clear articulation of these three criteria.

Heresy results in bad doctrine for sure. But it is not a "four-letter word" to be used for other Christians who do not believe everything we do. Heresy divides the church into tribes and parties. This means a heretic is a person who is used by *diabolos* to tear us apart. A heretic majors on building walls between Christians through pride and completely independent thinking.

Essentials and Non-Essentials?

Clearly the first Christians faced serious doctrinal threats that challenged their mission and life together. What can we then learn from how they addressed heresies? And what about the many subsequent struggles that divided Christians? Might even a cursory knowledge of these periods of heresy and division actually help us regain our unity in the present?

One of my favorite Bible commentaries, which I began reading in my college days, is Matthew Henry's massive devotional and Christ-centered work. His reflection on Psalm 122 helps me frame this matter of primary truths and unity:

> If all the disciples of Christ were of one mind, and kept the unity of the Spirit in the bond of peace, their enemies would be deprived of their chief advantages against them. But Satan's maxim always has been, to divide that he may conquer; and few Christians are sufficiently aware of his designs. Those who can do nothing else for the peace of Jerusalem, may pray for it. Let us consider all who seek the glory of the Redeemer, as our brethren and fellow-travelers, without regarding differences [that] do not affect our eternal welfare.[8]

The spirit of Henry's appeal was addressed at Vatican II by the adoption the idea of a "hierarchy of truths." Protestants developed similar patterns, though these vary from group to group.

One of the most famous maxims about relationships between Christians who disagree comes from a well-known sentence written by Peter Meiderlin, a virtually unknown Lutheran. This saying has been shortened and slightly altered to read: "In essentials unity, in non-essentials liberty, in all things charity." This sentence has appeared in almost every call to Christian unity since the seventeenth century.[9] The esteemed church historian

---

8. Henry, *Commentary*, 561.

9. Though this maxim has been attributed to various Christian authors, including St. Augustine, it first appeared in a tract under the pseudonym of Rupertus Meldenius, The author was an otherwise-unknown seventeenth-century German theologian who wrote this in 1627, at the height of the Thirty Years' War in Europe. This war between

Philip Schaff tells us of the historical context in which this statement was originally written.

> It was during the fiercest dogmatic controversies and the horrors of the Thirty Years' War that a prophetic voice whispered to future generations the watchword of Christian peacemakers, which was unheeded in a century of intolerance, and forgotten in a century of indifference, but resounds with increased force in a century of revival and re-union.[10]

The famous English Puritan Richard Baxter quoted this sentence in 1679, and declared Meiderlin the model of a true peacemaker. Now, think of the power of this sentence in the context in which it was first written. In the midst of a tragically dark moment in church history, when Christians were killing other Christians in large numbers, a lone Protestant voice was raised to express a deep desire that the walls that fostered these awful bloody divisions be torn down. Meiderlin aimed at peace and unity among all Christians, Catholic and Protestant. In so doing, he gave us a wonderful watchword that speaks to us almost four hundred years later.

But how should we understand this oft-quoted saying about essentials, non-essentials and charity? George Koch unpacks these words in very practical ways.

> An *essential* is something that is *necessary*, utterly *required* for something to be effective, true or real. You may recall this expression from mathematics: *if and only if*. That defines an essential. A *non-essential* may be profoundly important, valuable or highly regarded, but it is not *necessary*, not *required*. This is a critical distinction. *Liberty* means that we do not force others to conform to our practices or beliefs on issues that are non-essential. *Charity* means that we treat others with respect and love, even when we disagree or differ on *either* essentials or non-essentials.[11]

Discussing the application of this principle, Koch shows that some of the thorniest points of doctrinal dissent and division could be understood in a way that can actually foster unity. He writes: "First we need to realize

---

Christians was the bloodiest period of killing since the beginning of the Protestant Reformation. Meiderlin published this idea in a tract calling for peaceful toleration between the warring Christian factions. His original wording reads: "In a word, I'll say it: If we preserve unity in essentials, liberty in non-essentials, and charity in both, our affairs will be in the best position."

10. Schaff, *History*, vol. 7, 650–53.
11. Koch, *What We Believe*, 255.

that something can be essential in one context and non-essential in another. We can't just brand something 'non-essential' and believe we have it properly categorized for all times and places." Here are some clear examples of how we can apply Meiderlin's principle.

- Knowing how to navigate is not essential to being able to fly an airplane, but it is essential in getting from one continent to another.
- Knowing how to wire a light switch is not essential to using one, but it is essential to working as an electrician.
- Plain, modest dressing is essential to being Amish, but it is not essential to being a Christian.
- Ordination is essential in many denominations to be a priest or pastor, but it is not essential to teach or care for others.
- Apostolic succession is essential to the polity of a church in the apostolic tradition (Roman Catholics, Anglicans, others), but it is not essential to salvation or sanctification.
- The liturgy is essential to the worship of a "liturgical church," but it is not essential for a church to be Christian.
- Baptism by full immersion is essential to a Baptist church, but it is not essential to faith in Christ or salvation.[12]

Koch concludes:

> To the degree that any of our church concepts, doctrines, worship styles, polity and so on aid us in our sanctification, they are helpful, perhaps even important, *but if sanctification can proceed without them* [then] they are not *essential* to sanctification, and therefore not *essential* to life in Christ.[13]

How Do We Grow Into Deep Unity With Jesus?

In pursuing unity in the modern era, various programs and ideas have been tried. Some have called for a new federation of churches; a minority still believes the best answer is for everyone to join the *right* church. The problem with both of these solutions should be obvious. Because there have been so many walls constructed over time, we still have the natural tendency to settle for a kind of fellowship that stops short of true healing. Instinctively,

12. Koch, *What We Believe*, 256.
13. Koch, *What We Believe*, 257.

we know something needs to change, but we're not sure where to begin. I have already suggested we begin with the gospel of the kingdom and the mission of the church.

Twentieth-century ecumenical movements accomplished a great deal more than we realize. If nothing else, they led Christians to meet and pray with one another while they discussed subjects related to Christian faith and order. Meeting believers from other traditions, listening to them, and learning to love each other more deeply are truly good goals. This pursuit opens people up to the Holy Spirit's work in unique ways. These movements have profoundly impacted my life. Furthermore, these expressions of ecumenism have removed many of the walls I erected on a foundation of theological differences, personal animus, and amazing personal ignorance. I am reminded of the words of missiologist David Bosch: "We cannot possibly dialogue or witness to people if we resent their presence or the view they hold."[14]

Fall in Love

The only way I believe we can work out what we've seen to this point is by stressing the essentials of love and reconciliation. George Koch offers four steps we can take that will begin to take down walls of division. These steps are simple but incredibly powerful: confess and stop, tolerate, protect the other, and fall in love.[15] He appeals to Jesus' treatment of the woman caught in adultery for step one. For step two, he says we can tolerate other views, even if we strongly disagree. Only by tolerating and learning can we begin to love more deeply. We can start by learning how real toleration has worked in history. The third step brings us closer to the unity we desperately need if our schisms are to be healed. We must protect the other by giving up our conceptual fortresses and opening the windows of our minds to allow new light to dispel our darkness. We can do this by fostering self-criticism and by adopting an intentional lifestyle that seeks the good of the other. Even when we disagree, we can safeguard the other by blessing them and praying for them. The famous missionary-theologian E. Stanley Jones put this well: "Centered in Christ we gather; centered in anything else, we scatter." If we center ourselves in the love of Christ, we will gather and become Christlike. No adjective better describes Christians who long to become agents of deep unity than this: *Christlike*!

If we are to be healed, we must grasp what is truly new about our understanding of God. What do I mean by *new*? First, God is Trinity, and as

---

14. Bosch, *Transforming Mission*, 483.
15. Koch, *What We Believe*, 263–67.

Trinity he is both one *and* many. *Our God is unity in diversity.* And as three persons, God dwells in perfect love and unity. In him is no rivalry or competition. Love binds God together in eternal oneness. Thus the goal of all Christian unity is to enter into this relational unity with God who has been revealed in Jesus Christ. This is precisely why Jesus prayed: "As you, Father, are in me and I am in you, may they also be in us" (John 17:21). In the triune God we can see how unity and diversity live in a perfect relationship of eternal love. We cannot live as God lives, at least in such perfect harmony, but we can grow together and experience a deep and growing unity with Jesus that empowers us to love one another (John 13:34–35).

The second reason we must gain a *new* understanding of God lies in Jesus' will for our imitation. We are called to *imitate Jesus*; i.e., to follow in his steps (1 Peter 1:21).[16] The *new* thing Jesus revealed about God was this: He cares desperately and loves intensely. Simply put, he is involved in the whole human situation. The Greek idea of a god of detached serenity is not Christian. Jesus taught a *new* understanding of God in many places, but perhaps none more powerfully reveals this than the parable of the Good Samaritan (Luke 10:29–37). The whole point of the parable is the Samaritan's *concern*. While others passed by, the Samaritan was concerned and did something. The Gospels have a word for this concern and the action that flows from it: *love*. The biblical scholar William Barclay expressed this *new* idea of love (*agape*) very well.

> [Christian love] is an attitude to other people. It is the set of the will towards others. It is the attitude of a goodwill that cannot be altered, a desire for men's good that nothing can kill. Quite clearly, this is not simply a response of the heart; this is not an emotional reaction; this is an act of the will. In this it is not simply our heart that goes out to others; it is our whole personality. *And this is why it can be commanded and demanded of us.* It would be impossible to demand that we love people in the sense of falling in love with them. It would be impossible to demand that we love our enemies as we love those who are dearer to us than life itself. But it is possible to say to us: "You must try to be like God. You must try never to wish anything but good for others. You must try to look at every man with the eye of God, with the eyes of goodwill."[17]

---

16. The Greek word Peter uses is *hupogrammos*. It was the word for a perfect line of copperplate writing at the top of the page of a child's exercise-book, the line to be copied. This is clearly saying we are to "copy" Jesus. Paul says we should imitate God (Ephesians 5:1).

17. Barclay, *Ethics*, 34.

What all of this means is clear: Our final step toward healing our tragic divisions is to fall in love. If we do not fall in love, we will settle for cheap, emotionally based unity. Costly unity calls for costly love. This means we strive to love as Jesus loved. But what does this mean?

In every human relationship, Jesus demonstrated the love that made forgiveness and healing possible. When it comes to Christian disagreements there is no other way for us to be healed. If we love one another, we will listen, protect, and desire the best for the other. *Such love must be our ultimate goal, especially with our fellow Christians.* Jesus taught his followers that this love is the mark of true life in him: "I give you a new commandment, that you love one another. Just as I have loved you, you also should love one another. By this everyone will know that you are my disciples, if you have love for one another" (John 13:34–35). We will never come to complete agreement with other Christians in this present age. But we can be filled with costly love for our brothers and sisters and begin to tear down the walls that have made us enemies.[18] Love is the only balm that will dress our wounds and restore our unity.

"Beloved, let us love one another, because love is from God; everyone who loves is born of God and knows God" (1 John 4:7).

Questions for Discussion and Reflection

1. What are some of the walls you see that hinder our work for unity? How can we tear them down through love, dialogue, and prayer?

2. The famous saying "In essentials unity, in non-essentials liberty, in all things charity" can help us learn how to live in unity. How do you feel about this principle? What troubles you when you read it, and what gives you hope in it? How can this become a resource you might use to love other Christians who disagree with you?

3. Does this prayer and work for unity seem hard to you? Why or why not?

---

18. Armstrong, *Costly Love*. I wrote this book to extensively explore the riches of what I've written here. My purpose in this book is complementary to the earlier book.

Chapter Fifteen

Envisioning New Ways to Live as One: The "New Ecumenism"

> The movement promoting Christianity unity is not just some sort of "appendix" that is added to the Church's traditional activity. Rather, ecumenism is an organic part of her life and work, and, consequently, must pervade all that she is and does; it must be like the fruit borne by a healthy and flourishing tree which grows to its full stature.
>
> —*Pope John Paul II,* Ut Unum Sint

Some of the initial success of the twentieth century's ecumenical movement, especially prior to World War II, was eventually sidetracked. Various aspects of diversity and ideology played a huge role in this derailment. Some of these new directions were not entirely central to Christ's mission. By the 1980s the larger movement began to experience a loss of vision and energy, prompting some to speak of an ecumenical fatigue. In addition, the absence of evangelicals and Pentecostals left a hole in the movement from the beginning. This was especially obvious in those parts of the global church that were growing the most rapidly, namely in Africa and Asia. Endeavors to put real flesh on these movements of unity did move a new generation of leaders into ecumenical relationships. My story began to connect with the wider global movement during a time of new energy and vision.

As many younger leaders became the modern pioneers for obeying the imperative of the Jesus prayer for deeper unity, most pastors remained focused only on the ministry of their parish or diocese. Only a few felt any constraint to pray and work for unity. I get this response. I was a pastor. My first pastoral duty was always to my congregation. But I will never accept this myopic response as healthy. Especially not after the global pandemic that began to change everything.

The Decline of the Western Church Must Lead Us Into Unity

As Western Christianity precipitously declines, it becomes more apparent an institutional malaise will likely impact the days ahead. But I don't think the rapid decline of our influence will mean the complete loss of our mission. I believe the loss of our cultural power may lead us to recover our mission in a better-equipped church. I will explain why this is not false optimism.

First, we should take hope from the incredible story of how prayer for the recovery of unity happened in the Catholic Church. In the first half of the twentieth century, Catholics remained aloof from the modern ecumenical movement. But this completely changed at Vatican Council II (1962–1965). When the Catholic Church entered the ecumenical movement, a new energy became increasingly obvious. Relationships at every level, from regional to global, began to bear the fruit of living in oneness relationally. (Other, more formal ecumenical meetings led to new relationships, which may prove more important than the papers and formal gatherings themselves.) But the continued absence of a wider variety of churches—especially Pentecostals, evangelicals, and historic black churches—still remained apparent for the first decades that followed Vatican II.

Second, the Orthodox Church—to the surprise of even some Orthodox Christians—has continued to engage in the global movement of ecumenism. We should take hope from this development. Significant twentieth-century dialogues have included Orthodoxy, Catholicism, and Protestantism. I noted earlier that my own friendships with Orthodox priests have borne great fruit relationally. My journey into relational oneness has allowed me to envision a way forward I never saw before. Let me illustrate. One of America's most prominent Orthodox theologians, Fr. Alexander Schmemann, rightly argued, *"Christianity is not an institution with sacraments; it is a sacrament with institutions, and the sacrament is Christ!"*[1] (See chapter 6, "Christ the Center.") The Orthodox story in America supports my observation that something new is happening. A broader, and more lay-centric, movement of unity leads me to call this current period an era of *new ecumenism*.[2] After

1. Garvey, *Orthodoxy*, 111–12.
2. See Whitehead, *New Ecumenism*.

more than a hundred years of the modern global ecumenical movement, new fruit is blossoming in places previously untouched.

Finally, we have a major reason for hope in all the numerous pockets of new ecumenism to be seen in some of the most wonderful places. Many Protestants who remained on the sidelines of this movement are now engaging with it in less structural ways (relational). Remember, in the earlier period of ecumenism, most Protestants engaged with the movement on the basis of seeking answers to the questions of the missionary context: "Which Christ do you bring to us? The Baptist Christ? The Methodist Christ? The Lutheran Christ? The Roman Catholic Christ?" This type of mission field question led to the Edinburgh Missionary Conference of 1910, which came from a succession of earlier gatherings in New York (1854), Liverpool (1860), London (1878, 1888), and especially New York again (1900). The Edinburgh event is now rightly understood as the historical forerunner to the modern movement. (Ironically, only Protestants were present at Edinburgh, and there were only eighteen delegates from non-Western countries. But these few non-Western leaders had a *major* influence.)[3]

Over the last century all types of Protestants, both from the historically mainline churches and from some evangelical bodies, have begun to engage with the call for unity. The evangelical contribution to this development was in evidence at the birth of the Evangelical Alliance in 1846. At this gathering, representatives of ten nations met in London to talk about unity and common mission. The Evangelical Alliance was renamed World Evangelical Fellowship in 1951 and then became the World Evangelical Alliance in 1982. WEA exists as "a global ministry working with local churches around the world to join in common concern to live and proclaim the Good News of Jesus in their communities." Today it is an evangelical alliance of churches in 129 nations, with more than 100 international organizations. They have joined with one another "to give a worldwide identity, voice, and platform to more than 60 million evangelical Christians. Seeking holiness, justice, and renewal at every level of society—individual, family, community, and culture—God is glorified, and the nations of the earth are forever transformed."[4] (This statement, in its comprehensive vision of the kingdom, goes far beyond what many evangelicals understood about mission.) One of the most significant recent developments can be seen in the relationship between the WEA and the World Council of Churches. This could not have been imagined prior to 2000. Here the older ecumenism, which seems to be shifting under younger leadership and the fresh winds of the Spirit, is

---

3. Lossky et al., eds., *Dictionary*, 325.
4. World Evangelical Alliance, https://worldea.org.

finding relationship with the more evangelical parts of Protestantism. Add to this new movement young Catholics and Protestants, who represent new ways of being followers of Jesus, and you begin to see how many new endeavors for unity are evolving.

These new movements have already helped to tear down more walls than most realize. Here I am reminded of the counsel of my friend Fr. Thomas Baima, a seasoned and deeply committed ecumenist. Tom has told me several times: "John, remember this movement is only a baby so far as church history goes. We are still experiencing the growing pains of a relatively short history." Non-Catholics like me can benefit immensely from Fr. Baima's perspective.

But what about the evangelicals? Some are still moving in a more separatistic direction for sure. In some ways, rigidly conservative evangelicals sometimes sound more like the new fundamentalists than historic evangelicalism. Methodist scholar and evangelist William Abraham suggests evangelicals need a historically grounded *realism* about their divisions. He perceptively adds, "The radical differences in doctrine, ecclesial structures, and practice would sooner or later take center stage in the quest for unity."[5]

I am convinced the real danger for the modern ecumenical movement will eventually come from the loss of deep, life-giving commitment to mission and evangelism. In William Abraham's words, "The danger of losing sight of evangelism and the concomitant temptation to substitute secular conceptions of mission were waiting in the wings to seduce unwary ecumenists who had forgotten the birth pains of ecumenism."[6] Bishop Stephen Neil, writing with incredible clarity about the history of the ecumenical movement, explains what actually happened to modern ecumenism in the twentieth century:

> One of the chief problems of the ecumenical movement in the mid-20th century is that occasioned by the separation between its essential components. This *history* has shown at point after point the intimate connection between the missionary work of the church and the ecumenical ideal. Throughout, the word "ecumenical" has been used to designate the efforts of Christians to seek and promote unity; but it should now be plain to the reader that these efforts are not ends in themselves: the aim of Christian union [unity] is *that the world may believe*. The world includes the non-Christian world as well as Christendom. Evangelism, missionary work, the proclamation of the Gospel to

---

5. Abraham, "Church and Churches," 303.
6. Abraham, "Church and Churches," 303.

earth's remotest end, are not extras or fringes on the ecumenical movement; they are essentials without which its true nature cannot be grasped. Unhappily, in the thought of the Churches the two aspects have not always been held together.[7]

In spite of all the twists and turns in the ecumenical movement of the twentieth century, I remain hopeful about the future of God's mission and Jesus' prayer for our unity. Why? The expressions I call the *new ecumenism* in this chapter continue to grow and mature.

The Pentecostal and Charismatic Role in the "New Ecumenism"

We cannot overstate the role Pentecostal and charismatic movements will play in the global church of the twenty-first century. Historians agree that the first several decades of the modern Pentecostal movement, in the early 1900s, were characterized by isolation joined with a strong anti-ecumenical outlook. Racism also had a great deal to do with this sad story. Now, more than a century later, the tide is changing and rising. I believe there are a number of reasons; e.g., the Catholic charismatic renewal, the increasing openness of non-American ecumenical leaders to the Spirit (especially in Asia and Africa), and the numerous bilateral dialogues on the work of the Spirit and Christian formation taking place within Catholic and Pentecostal churches. Scholars of this movement agree that an ecumenical seed was present at the beginning of Pentecostalism. Now it is bearing fruit.

Today a growing number of Pentecostal and charismatic leaders believe the Holy Spirit birthed two great movements in the early twentieth century: the Pentecostal movement *and* ecumenism. I share their view because of my own study and engagement with Catholic and Pentecostal leaders. The emphasis of both these movements has beautifully intersected in an aspirational hope for the unity of believers through worldwide focus on spreading the good news of the kingdom. A Pentecostal leader has summarized well what has happened:

> After over a half century of isolated attempts to shape the church and culture, the ecumenical and Pentecostal movements are experiencing convergence in the fulfilling of their compatible missions. In a search for new life and relevance, the more traditional ecumenical institutions are respectfully courting participation and leadership for Pentecostal-Charismatic

---
7. Rouse and Neill, eds., *History*, 730–31. Emphasis in original.

churches and individuals. And increasingly, Pentecostals and Charismatics are wakening to the challenge and opportunity of ecumenical participation.[8]

I cannot overstate the role of friendships in prayer and dialogue. When focused on this unity, the relationships bear immense fruit for the new ecumenism. In my own (relatively brief) experience, a number of my friends have helped me see the beauty of this new ecumenism in their lives. These include men and women like the late Br. Jeffrey Gros, Dr. Norberto Saracco, Dr. Teresa Francesca Rossi, Dr. Cecil Robeck, Professor Matteo Calisi, Dr. Mark Nimo, and Fr. Bob Miller. Each of these friends has invested time and encouragement in my own journey in ways I doubt they even realize. Dr. Robeck is an Assemblies of God scholar and minister. Dr. Saracco is a leading pastor and theological voice in South America. The other five friends are Catholics who have contributed powerfully to various aspects of the Catholic charismatic movement. Through each of them I have experienced my own vision of the new ecumenism. This short list of friends underscores just how important true friendships have been in my own prayerful work.

One of the great needs being addressed by the new ecumenism is the fostering of *both* academic and local dialogue centered on unity *and* mission. I believe this happens when two biblical streams are directly situated in how we live the gospel through relationships. As Pentecostalism has continued to mature over the last century, it has been recovering the freshness and power of the gospel of the kingdom.

Another important contribution from these two streams converging can be seen in growing efforts to overcome our prevalent racism. Opening up the wider role of women is also being given back to the church. I am personally persuaded that the addition of the Catholic Church in this global dialogue makes the future of the Pentecostal and charismatic contributions to unity more likely. The pontificate of Pope Francis has built on the work of all four popes since John XXIII. Francis's many friendships, and his shared mission experience with Argentinian Pentecostals, has given him a unique background. These beautiful stories are more powerful than all our documents. They pulsate with the life of the Holy Spirit in believers. It seems clear that God is joining some unique persons and gifts into a beautiful movement of prayer and mission.

---

8. Cole, "Future Ecumenical Challenges," 254.

The Global Christian Forum

Another interesting and important development can be seen in the Global Christian Forum (GCF), a movement with representatives from diverse Christian churches, organizations, and traditions who meet together on an equal basis. GCF's stated desire is to foster mutual respect while addressing common challenges. Because GCF is a "forum," as opposed to having a stated desire to unite churches, it offers new opportunities for broadening and deepening encounters on our way to deeper unity. GCF strongly promotes relationships between Christian churches and traditions that have not often been in this conversation. GCF includes the Roman Catholic Church, the Orthodox Church, historic Protestant churches, and evangelical and Pentecostal churches. This is another evidence of the new ecumenism.

In the midst of the COVID-19 pandemic, Rev. Richard Howell, a member of the GCF committee, said:

> The Church and Christian NGOs have played a pivotal role in preserving life. They worked tirelessly to feed the hungry and provide other amenities of life; and still continue to be good Samaritans in whatever capacity possible. The tragic condition of millions of poor people, who worked as migrant laborers, including women and children in particular, demands an ongoing relief work for years together. It is also a fact that even now the poor are being exploited. Are the social goods only for the rich?[9]

You can readily see here that the gospel of salvation *and* unified efforts to extend the mission of Jesus' kingdom on earth are *both* strong priorities. By affirming both the proclamation of the gospel as the message of salvation and work on behalf of the poor the Global Christian Forum is advocating a missional direction that seeks to rightly prioritize the least of these (Matthew 25:31–46).

Christian Churches Together USA

Meanwhile, another fresh initiative, called Christian Churches Together (CCT) in the USA, began in September 2001. It has taken a new path towards finding and expressing unity. CCT began with a meeting of church leaders, including men and women who saw the need for fellowship, unity, and witness across the diverse expressions of Christian faith. Lamenting the absence of representatives from the Roman Catholic Church, the Pentecostal

---

9. Global Christian Forum, "Ministry During COVID-19."

and evangelical churches, and the Orthodox Church, CCT sought a new way to advance unity in America. These leaders felt they could strengthen their unity in Christ, and empower their mission, by being together without trying to resolve all their differences. Here we observe another effective model of the new ecumenism. CCT never purposed to bring about formal church union.

A personal confession is in order. I have been happily involved with CCT for well over a decade. I have spoken to a few CCT gatherings and shared my story. I find these meetings encouraging and challenging. I come away seeing the power of unity in Christ's mission clearly at work. CCT provides a context—through a gathering marked by prayer, worship, and fellowship—in which churches and leaders can develop relationships with other churches with whom they have traditionally had little contact. This is not all I personally hope for, but it is a very effective response to Jesus' prayer in John 17. (One soon discovers that none of these groups or movements is permanent. They are all provisional *and* renewal-oriented.) CCT offers the reality of face-to-face relationships that help tear down the private and corporate walls that have been built around our denominational, racial, and ethnic differences.

Christian Churches Together has been especially effective in helping leaders and churches address racial and ethnic division. Here commonalities can be better understood while shared witness happens. CCT offers a way forward that uses the best of our past ecumenical efforts by joining them with the present/future moment of the early twenty-first century. Because CCT is American, it seeks to develop a credible voice in addressing American churches about issues of life, social justice, and peace. It does so in a way that is deeply rooted in the gospel of Jesus Christ *without* using American liberal-conservative ideology as the basis for conversation. Another evidence of new ecumenism is the presence of younger leaders at CCT gatherings.

I attended a major three-day CCT gathering in Montgomery, Alabama, in the fall of 2019. The topic was racial reconciliation, powerfully led by diverse men and women of color. Our days were filled with prayers, creative learning sessions, and personal sharing in small groups. As a larger group we visited numerous historic civil rights sites, including the National Museum of Peace and Justice. The story of terrorist Jim Crow lynchings, told at the National Museum, was one of my most moving ecumenical moments. For me, a white Southerner by birth and background, this fellowship, shared with so many brothers and sisters of color, was life-changing.

Informal Movements for New Ecumenism

Most of the new ecumenism I've experienced has happened in informal ways. The Holy Spirit is drawing various Christians together for prayer, community service, and mission. I've seen scores of these movements as I've traveled across North America for decades. One such ministry that has impacted me is UniteBoston.

UniteBoston provides a shining example of a Spirit-directed relational movement. It was created to fill a need for the unity of churches and their members in greater Boston. Led by young people with a profound vision of a different future, UniteBoston set about bringing the Christian community together in missional ways. The concept behind UniteBoston developed from observations at casual summer gatherings in 2009, which led to several Christians praying for a common purpose that would address the disconnectedness felt in the Boston area. The story is one of grassroots unity that has worked very well. I have enjoyed a firsthand experience with several leaders of this movement, and I rejoice in what I've seen.

UniteBoston's story is wonderfully told in the 2020 documentary *One: Following Jesus' Call for Unity*.[10] Over the last decade, the vision for this film grew in my heart as I met many expressions of new ecumenism in the US and abroad. I came to believe a well-done documentary could tell this story and spread it through informal Spirit-infused movements. The focus of *One* is solidly rooted in the new ecumenism. It uses the visual medium to beautifully help viewers engage with great stories of kingdom mission. It includes stories from far beyond America, making this a rich resource that has been endorsed by a wide array of Christians from many different traditions.

How Do Tradition and God's New Thing Relate?

I've argued that the road to the future must go through the past. But a wrong approach to the past can hinder our prayer and work for unity. Let me explain. Christians are not living a first-generation experience. To suggest otherwise is a category mistake of considerable consequence. Yes, we are

---

10. *One: Following Jesus' Call for Unity* is a ninety-eight-minute documentary that includes scenes and stories from different global leaders. It includes contributions from dozens of people including N.T. Wright, Bishop Robert Barron, Brian McLaren, Fr. Thomas Baima, Geoff Tunnicliffe, Ruth Patterson, Kelly Fassett, Lisa Sharon Harper, Sarah Hinlicky Wilson, Fr. Demetrios Tonias, Fr. Bob Miller, Mark Nimo, Scott Brill, and Fr. Richard Rohr. You can see more and order the film at https://www.visionvideo.com/dvd/501918D/one-following-jesus-call-for-unity.

the heirs of all those who have gone before us. The church is historical, but it is ever new. So how do we embrace our past and welcome the new?

More specifically, what if the entire idea of a *definitive statement of the meaning of Christ and the church for all times* is fundamentally flawed? What if, as Robert Louis Wilken cogently argued in *The Myth of Christian Beginnings*, the idea of a "Golden Age" is flawed? What if the words of the prophet Isaiah should be taken more seriously within the church?

> "Forget the former things;
> do not dwell on the past.
> See, I am doing a new thing!
> Now it springs up; do you not perceive it?
> I am making a way in the wilderness
> and streams in the wasteland." (Isaiah 43:18–19)

Professor Wilken adds, "The faith was not purer, the Christians were no braver, the church was not one and undivided" at any point, either in the first century or since. This seems at complete cross-purposes to what I've said about the value of the creed and our tradition. Yet I believe Wilken's thesis provides a serious corrective to the *wrong use* of creeds and tradition. Like me, he sees great value in tradition. But he rightly argues that the most characteristic historical phenomena in any religious movement is *the reluctance to both embrace tradition and give place to change*.[11] Again, we are faced with a tension. But this tension can help us embrace the *new ecumenism* with real hope. Most Christians understand there have been changes in understanding and practice though the ages, but many still love the "Golden Age" mythology that will hinder unity and mission. Wilken shows us how the past, while honored, should never restrict the future of the church.

Conclusion

The church has been historically established once for all upon "upon the foundation of the apostles and prophets" (Ephesians 2:20). We have a powerful tradition. But we must always be the renewing people of God, not merely an institution for comfort and certitude. Our forefathers and foremothers have labored and shed blood so we can live this beautiful faith. But our past must become the *prelude* to our glorious future. The new ecumenism is a hopeful sign. Why? It points to a better future, one that has immense possibilities. Peter, citing the prophet Joel, says this better than any of us:

11. Wilken, *Myth*. The quotations are taken from the back cover copy of the 1971 edition and the preface of the 1980 edition.

"In the last days . . . [God says] I will pour out my Spirit upon all flesh, and your sons and your daughters shall prophesy, and your young men shall see visions, and your old men shall dream dreams" (Acts 2:17).

Questions for Discussion and Reflection

1. What do you think of the new ecumenism and some of the models we saw in this chapter?
2. How does ecumenism address our disunities rooted in race and ethnicity?
3. Does this work for unity seem hard to you? Why or why not?
4. Do you think the present moment presents a great opportunity? If so, how can we seize this moment?

Chapter Sixteen

Missional-Ecumenism

A Paradigm for Unity

The church is more than meets the eye. It is more than a set of well-managed functions. It is more than another human organization. The church lives in the world as a human enterprise, but it is also the called and redeemed people of God. It is a people of God who are created by the Spirit to live as a missionary people.

—*Craig Van Gelder*

Christian mission gives expression to the dynamic relationship between God and the world.

—*David Bosch*

The term *missional* became a veritable buzzword over the last thirty years—a most unfortunate turn of events. The truth expressed by this significant theological word now runs the risk of being co-opted by various popular uses. In reality, *missional* is rich word rooted in God's missionary purpose. Missional is not a movement but a quality, something the entire church desperately needs in the twenty-first century.

We've seen that Christ's mission is not about seizing political influence in order to rebuild a culture through moral influence. As important as adding members to the church is, recruiting new members is not our mission either. Our mission is "to participate in the reconciling love of the triune God who reaches out to a fallen world in Jesus Christ and by the power of the Holy Spirit brings strangers and enemies into God's new and abiding community."[1] This means the church must evangelize by faithfully living and sharing the good news. But our mission is deeper and broader than our evangelizing. Mission is our entire kingdom vocation! All of us are called to live the kingdom wherever God has placed us.

I'm convinced the first way we grasp the church's missionary task is to keep in mind that our mission is really God's mission *through* us. When Jesus inaugurated his kingdom he gave us his mission and Spirit to carry it out. But how do we *obey* our call to mission? First, we must *hear* Jesus and the prophets. We must have "ears to hear" (Mark 4:9, 23). When Jesus was transfigured before his disciples, the voice of his Father spoke: "This is my Son . . . listen to him!" (Matthew 17:5) The gospel of the kingdom is God's call to repentance and faith. This is why we must "strive first for the kingdom of God" (Matthew 6:33). But we must become good listeners if we are to "strive" for God's kingdom. Second, we must *obey* Jesus and follow in the way of the prophets. (We *are* a kingdom of prophets and priests!) So how exactly does Christ's kingdom come to earth? It comes through our serving and witnessing to God's reign of love, salvation, and justice. The entire Bible makes this plain: God calls us to love first. The prophet writes: "He has told you, O mortal, what is good; and what does the Lord require of you, but to do justice, and to love kindness, and to walk humbly with your God?" (Micah 6:8) There is no substitute for *hearing* and *obeying*.

The Third Lausanne Congress on World Evangelization, held in South Africa in 2010, brought together 4200 evangelical leaders from 198 countries. Its goal was *"to bring a fresh challenge to the global church to bear witness to Jesus Christ and all his teaching—in every nation, in every sphere of society, and in the realm of ideas."*[2] The written product of this gathering was the *Cape Town Commitment*, which revealed the core ideas of mission we need to grasp if we are to regain the centrality of unity and mission together. The *Cape Town* document rightly says mission is *central* to understanding the Bible. The loss of this perspective can be attributed to many challenges to the church, e.g. lukewarmness, misunderstanding of the biblical story, radical opposition to the central Christian mysteries, etc. God calls his people to share his mission. The *Cape Town Commitment* also states:

> God commands us to make known to all nations the truth of
> God's revelation and the gospel of God's saving grace through

---

1. Migliore, "Missionary God," 21.
2. *Cape Town Commitment*, 4.

Jesus Christ, calling all people to repentance, faith, baptism and obedient discipleship. God commands us to reflect his own character through compassionate care for the needy, and to demonstrate the values and the power of the kingdom of God in striving for justice and peace and in caring for God's creation.[3]

This mature expression was written by serious evangelical scholars and evangelists. It reveals something basic for our understanding of mission and unity. The gospel of the kingdom requires us to faithfully engage in proclaiming the good news *and* in demonstrating kingdom values that strive for justice, peace, and the care of all creation. They are both central to mission. Remember, my first serious engagement with the prayer of Jesus for our unity (John 17:21–24) in 1992 was developed in a context of *living and doing Christ's mission*. I hope you can now see why this vision led me to express my prayer through this hyphenated word: *missional-ecumenism*.

Embracing the Missional Church Model

A significant resurgence of interest in reconnecting the authority of Scripture with the resources of Christian tradition has fostered a bigger vision of the church. *After years of work as a church-planter and professor of missions, I am persuaded this resurgence of interest in the imperative of our unity will lose its momentum if it is not vitally linked with Christ's mission.* This link can be found in missional-ecumenism, a model that brings mission and unity back together.

Just before the turn of this century a research project, conducted by theologians deeply interested in the mission of the church, generated an important book: *Missional Church*.[4] The team of scholars who contributed to this book gave fresh solutions to many of the issues I have addressed. In the process, they coined the word *missional*. These Protestant contributors agreed with the language of Vatican II: "The pilgrim church is missionary by her very nature."[5] Here is the big idea: The church is missionary by her very nature!

When we grasp the real significance of our disunity, it will be because we understand how *the character of God and the nature of the church* are profoundly interrelated. Darrell Guder, professor of missional and ecumenical

---

3. *Cape Town*, 27–29.

4. Guder, ed., *Missional Church*. There are many books and resources on the vision of missional church, but this is the best book for casting a clear vision of the term and its correct use.

5. Second Vatican Council, "Decree on the Mission Activity of the Church."

theology at Princeton Theological Seminary, describes the choice of the word *missional*: "We needed, somehow, to find a way to talk about the fundamentally missional nature of the church without using terms freighted with all kinds of baggage."[6] But as I've noted, the word *missional* was co-opted. Evangelicals often use it to describe what they're already doing, even labeling old Christendom model programs as missional. This forces me to ask if the term *missional* church is still the best way to frame our calling.

Becoming Missionary Disciples

In his masterful apostolic exhortation *The Joy of the Gospel*, Pope Francis urges *the whole people of God* to experience "missionary transformation." He describes Christians as "missionary disciples."[7] *All of us are sent, and we are sent together.* We are sent as salt and light to be a communion of the whole—to be "missionary disciples" together. The choice of these words captures exactly what Jesus said: "As the Father has sent me, I am sending you" (John 20:21).

I have come to deeply appreciate the missiology and ecumenism of Pope Francis. His insights on mission, discipleship, and joy prompt me to repeatedly ask: "Is his term *missionary disciples* a better way to frame my missional theology than the ideas rooted in the *missio Dei*?"

"Missionary disciples" is clearly a fruitful way to understand both our corporate and personal calling. It may even resonate more deeply because it is closer to the commonly understood terminology of the New Testament. Missionary disciples *will* pursue unity because they understand that without it, the effectiveness of their entire joyful mission is undermined. If each of us is a missionary disciple, then we are *together* missionary disciples. Perhaps *missio Dei* fits better with a robust theology of the church's mission. The designation "missionary disciples" plainly helps us grasp our role in the corporate call. I conclude that both terms help us better understand what we should *be* and *do*. Thus we have two models—the **missio Dei** paradigm of my missional-ecumenism, a theological expression that captures our commission, and *missionary disciples*, Pope Francis' paradigm. Both link mission and unity in very helpful ways.

---

6. Guder, "Church as Missional Community," 114. The *Oxford English Dictionary* notes the first recorded use of the word *missional* came in 1907, but adds that the term was rarely used until recent years.

7. Pope Francis, *Joy*, 88–89.

Our Commission Is Corporate

So what's the great value of the word *missional*? After a lifetime of teaching and writing about evangelism and missions, I am persuaded that two words must be distinguished: *mission* and *missions*. *Mission* expresses the totality of the kingdom of God project. It underscores the *calling* of the whole church. Emil Brunner was right: "The church exists for mission as fire exists for burning."[8] The life-transforming reality of Christ demonstrates the presence of God now and points forward to the final consummation. *Mission* (singular) includes the *totality* of God's redemptive plan. *Missions* (plural) refers to the various enterprises we undertake to bring "into existence a Christian presence in a milieu where previously there was no such presence or where such presence was ineffective."[9] As we've seen, the kingdom of God *has a servant church*, and the servant church *has a mission*. This means all God's people have a *missionary vocation*. This understanding is at the very heart of the historical use of the term *evangelical*; the evangel is the good news, and those who bear this good news are disciples on mission!

> Just before his ascension, Jesus commissioned his disciples:
> "All authority in heaven and on earth has been given to me. Therefore go and make disciples of all nations, baptizing them in the name of the Father and of the Son and of the Holy Spirit, and teaching them to obey everything I have commanded you. And surely I am with you always, to the very end of the age." (Matthew 28:18–20)

I learned Matthew 28 as a boy. I was led to believe I needed go out and talk to everyone about the gospel. (It never dawned on me that this was not even possible.) I was specifically urged to invite people to accept Jesus as their Savior. This was done by a prayer that would give them entrance to heaven when they died. But what if this well-meant evangelizing project was essentially wrong?

Read Jesus' words and pay close attention. Ask questions, such as: *Who is being commissioned?* Matthew says Jesus "came to them." Who is the "you" Jesus promised to be with until the end of the age? (These pronouns are often read as *singular*, but they are *plural*.) Who was commissioned? Answer: *Jesus' disciples*. Finally, the apostles obeyed Jesus' command and passed his mission along to the whole church. The people of God, together as one body, were commissioned to "make disciples." The church would make disciples by "baptizing" and "teaching." These are not tasks given to

---

8. Brunner, *Word and World*, 108.
9. Newbigin, "Crosscurrents," 149.

each individual Christian so they become Lone Ranger missionaries. *This commission is given to all of us together.* We are God's mission. Thus the word *missional* captures this vital theological understanding.

What followed Jesus' ascension and the gift of the Holy Spirit at Pentecost? The powerful advance of the mission of the church. We see this eloquently described in Acts. The mission was clear: The good news of the kingdom was to be lived and preached so as to make known God's love for the whole world. The ultimate goal was to make disciples as far as the ends of the earth (Acts 1:8). "The Church . . . is set by God in the midst of the world as the sign of that to which all creation and all world history moves."[10]

Reconciling the World to God in Christ

Further, it cannot be overstated that the mission Jesus gave to his disciples is God's action. The book of Acts makes this plain. Mission is "the primal reality . . . the rest is derivative."[11] Mission is *primarily* expressed through communities who love and care for one another (John 13:34-35) and then share the same with their neighbors (Matthew 22:39; Mark 12:31; Luke 10:27). This love was designed by God to transcend all human barriers. Thus the mission Christ gave to his church continues the ministry of the ascended Jesus through *our* teaching, touching, healing, and restoring. But why? Because he promised: "I am with you always, to the very end of the age" (Matthew 28:20).

Mission is about the love of Jesus for the whole world (John 3:16-17). God's love, forgiveness, salvation, healing, justice, and compassion have come in Jesus of Nazareth. The apostles understood this and passed on the gospel through faithful *witness* (the word in Greek is *martyr*). Thus Jesus' mission still advances in our world through the gospel of the kingdom. This gospel is revealed in both word and deed. It is lived and taught. Thus God's mission brings the whole world into his kingdom!

We must never lose sight of one central truth: All faithful missionary work is derived from the cross and resurrection. After all, this is Jesus' mission. His saving acts are intended to lead us into a filial relationship of deep love for Jesus and one another. This means Christian mission either advances in the power of the Holy Spirit, or it becomes a forced religious and moralistic enterprise. For this reason, it is essential we root our understanding of mission and the church *directly* in the life and ministry of Jesus

---

10. Newbigin, *Mission and Unity*, 16-17.
11. Newbigin, *Gospel in a Pluralist Society*, 134-35.

himself! The ultimate goal of Jesus' mission is *the reconciliation of the whole world* (2 Corinthians 5:16–19).

Jürgen Moltmann says the church took its bearings from the *corpus Christianum* for centuries before the Protestant Reformation and the Reformers did not solve this problem. Only the Anabaptists rejected the notion of a Christian empire.[12] *Corpus Christianum* meant Christianity created a society, i.e., Christendom. The church previously understood itself by location and its role within society. But this changed after World War II. The disintegration of Christian influence in the West forced the church to address its new situation.

The confluence of these developments fostered a new missionary ecclesiology that challenged the old entrenched models. There were several prominent voices in this theological renewal, but none was more important than Lesslie Newbigin (1909–1998), who challenged the church to see that its identity had been shaped far more by culture than by Scripture. His life's work helped theologians and missionaries develop a comprehensively *biblical and ecumenical response* that reconnected ecclesiology and missiology. He poignantly asked: "*Does the very structure of our congregations contradict the missionary calling of the church?*"[13]

Christendom structures resulted in a wealthy, privileged, and established church. This church centered its mission inside a building in a specific geographical location. This church developed programs for what happened in its space. It followed cultural patterns that were Western and consumeristic. The purpose of church structures became established—the church existed to gather and preserve their members and influence others who would listen. Generally we reached people by inviting them into our space to watch and learn. This meant the church primarily existed to maintain itself. We were not *missio Deo* for the unreached, especially for the poor and broken. The structural realities of this Christendom model made the church inherently resistant to change. Writing in 1966, Newbigin said our church structures had become "clubs for [the] self-centered enjoyment of the benefits of the Christian religion."[14]

---

12. See Moltmann, "Unfinished Worlds." Moltmann argues that the only movement of the Reformation that was "by faith alone" was carried out by the Anabaptists.

13. Lesslie Newbigin, "Developments During 1962," quoted in Goheen, *Church and Its Vocation*, 121.

14. Newbigin, *Honest Religion*, 102–11.

The Logic of Mission

The logic of redemptive history is clear: *The kingdom of God is here. The end has arrived!* Our calling is to make this news known to the whole world. The centrality of this calling was almost entirely lost to much of the church. But what if it was recovered?

> The logic of mission is this: the true meaning of the human story has been disclosed. Because it is the truth, it must be shared universally. It cannot be a private opinion. When we share it with all peoples, we give them the opportunity to know the truth about themselves, to know who they are because they can know the same true story of which their lives are a part.[15]

The point is, *Christ's mission is for all people everywhere.* The Scripture gives us two perspectives we must hold together to keep this truth in proper balance. The first perspective is seen in the role of the Holy Spirit. The gospel of the kingdom moves from Jesus, and one geographical place in the ancient city of Jerusalem, out into ever-widening circles to the many (Acts 1:8). Thus we will never understand Jesus' mission until we see that it is the work of the Spirit moving us out into the lives of others. The second perspective is equally important. Jesus forms a community and commissions this people to go and serve the world. Pentecost followed Jesus' commission as day follows night. Mission is the Spirit's work, but mission is accomplished by the Spirit *through* us. This is why our mission is ultimately about the *missio Dei*. When we keep these two perspectives together, we rightly understand the missionary church as missional.

What to Do When Christendom Is Collapsing

By the second half of the twentieth century, the West was increasingly becoming an unchurched mission field. The ethos of a rapidly declining church has permeated all aspects of our corporate life. The Great Expansion, the decade-plus of church boom that followed the end of the war in the 1950s, ended almost imperceptibly. By the 1960s, millions of Baby Boomers finished high school, went to college, and began to leave their churches. Some returned when they had families. But their children and grandchildren have left in ever-increasing numbers. Loren Mead was right in 1991: "We are on the front edges of the greatest transformation of the church that has occurred for 1600 years. It is by far the greatest change that the church has ever

---

15. Newbigin, *Gospel in a Pluralist Society*, 125.

experienced in America; it may eventually make the transformation of the Reformation look like a ripple in a pond."[16] Less than four years later, Mead wrote an even more dire description: "[The problems facing the church go] to the roots of our institutions themselves. . . . The storm is so serious, I believe, that it marks the end of 'business as usual' for the churches."[17]

Incredibly, multitudes of church leaders still refuse to give up on Christendom. We remain anchored to our budgets and buildings, our programs and management theories. The coronavirus pandemic has revealed just how weak most of our churches really are. Because we have not thought of ourselves as a distinct people on mission, but rather as a building that houses our corporate organization, we struggle mightily to know what we should do next. The facts are starkly clear, but few seem willing to come to grips with them. We prefer to tell ourselves things will get better when they're back to normal. But young people aren't just walking away from the church—they're sprinting in the opposite direction. (Many express a deep interest in spirituality, but not religion. This fact alone should be explored with a missional understanding of our ministry.) Unlike earlier generations of dropouts, these modern "leavers" are very unlikely to seek out alternative forms of Christian community, such as home churches and small groups. When they leave the church, most of them leave the Christian faith altogether. We can't know where this might lead in the decades ahead, but the staggering truth is this: We have lost the future of the church in less than three decades.

Conclusion

Declining and dying churches face a huge challenge. They can either continue to seek answers in their Christendom models, or they can embrace a missional-ecumenical model of service rooted in ecumenism. If we embrace this latter perspective, we will need to make relationships central, not programs or buildings. Such missional friendships can lead us to follow Jesus into deeper relational unity, a unity that will transform our mission into purposeful action. This way will lead us to tear down many of the historical walls that have kept us apart. It will also lead to a re-envisioning of our churches centered in the mission of Jesus.

The simple fact is, none of the "easy fixes" promoted by Christian churches in the West address the overall dynamic of serious church decline. If we love Christ and his kingdom, we must ask: "How can we advance

---

16. Loren Mead, *The Once and Future Church*, quoted in Culpepper, *Decline*, 8.
17. Mead, *Transforming Congregations*, ix.

Christ's mission and tear down our cherished walls of division? How can we embrace the *missio Dei* with joy?" With Pope Francis we should ask: "How can we train a new generation of missionary disciples?" That's not a Catholic question. It's a catholic question. All of us need to answer it.

Questions for Discussion and Reflection

1. How would you define "missional church" in your words? How does this term change the way most of us have been taught to think about missions and missionaries?

2. If mission is an expression of the very nature of God, what are the implications of this truth for everything the church does? Have we reduced the nature of God to programs and activities rather than to being a Spirit-led people in mission?

3. What does the massive exodus of younger people mean for your church? If new programs cannot stop this leaving what should we do? Can you name specific ways to seek to address this problem?

Chapter Seventeen

Learning to Live Missional Lives

> Embracing missional-ecumenism will mean that our inter- and intra-church debates will look, and feel, less like trench warfare, in which both sides are firmly dug in to defend the territory that each sees as its heritage, and more like emigrants' discussions on shipboard that are colored by the awareness that soon they will be confronted by new tasks in an environment not identical with what they knew before.
>
> —J. I. Packer

When I began to immerse my mind and heart in John 17, especially during the 1990s, I found myself reading as much as I could on the subject of unity. I engaged in dialogue with people, churches, movements, schools, and leaders. I never imagined I could love all these unique Christians. But God had to get my undivided attention for me to love more deeply.

One day, just before speaking at a theology conference in Philadelphia, I had a vision while sitting on the church platform. I was shocked by what was shown to me in that moment. I heard God calling me to whole new direction. This private encounter made no sense to me. (I never thought of myself as a mystic or a charismatic, and this experience went far beyond my rational patterns of perception.) In the months ahead, this encounter was followed by a series of dreams in which God was calling me to the way of unity. He also showed me that this new way for my life would include many trials and rejections. At the end of this period of dreams, I had one final dream in which I saw God taking me through a wilderness. But I also saw this was not the end. After thirteen wilderness years, the beginning of an entirely new way began on March 26, 2012.

In 2011, the late Francis Cardinal George (1937–2015), Archbishop of Chicago, read my earlier book on unity. He emailed me, inviting me to his residence to talk. I then invited him to join me for an evening dialogue, and Wheaton College allowed us to use their large chapel for this unofficial event. That night, when I saw a crowd of well over 1200 people in Edman Chapel, I began to weep. This was the place where God had previously done so much in my life, and I realized I did not arrange this gathering. In my spirit I said, "This is God's doing, completely and totally." My tears were tears of profound joy! I realized that a new way had finally opened and my future would never be the same.

John R. Mott and the Rise of Missional-Ecumenism

One of the best ways to understand missional-ecumenism is to hear and see it through the life of faithful men and women. John R. Mott (1865–1955) was such a person—a father of the modern ecumenical movement. His story has inspired me again and again. In his life I found the essential storylines that helped me gain clear expression for my new vocation.

While a student at Cornell University, Mott underwent a marvelous conversion from agnosticism to deep evangelical faith after hearing an address by the famous C. T. Studd. Studd was a member of the "Cambridge Seven"—a group of English undergraduate athletes dedicated to foreign missions. Shortly after Mott's conversion, he began his life's work in global mission. Oliver Tomkins observes about Mott:

> In the cause of world evangelization, Mott was as tireless and as urgent as the apostle Paul—and as careful to follow up initial visits by continuing contact. He traveled repeatedly to Asia and Africa long before air travel made such journeying commonplace.... Mott was an example of his own dictum about arranging a visit or a conference: "Plan as if there were no such thing as prayer. Pray as if there were no such thing as planning."[1]

John Mott was not initially a champion for Christian unity. What convinced him to embrace a powerful call to promote unity was his deep passion for mission. After he founded the World Student Christian Federation, he felt a growing concern for unity. But why? He had come in contact with Eastern Orthodox churches and student movements that were confessional and

---

1. Tomkins, "John R. Mott," 704–5.

earnest to reach others with the good news. Yet these churches and young people expressed their faith in very different ways from Mott's own pietistic Methodist background. Meeting Christians from very different persuasions and ethnic backgrounds led him to make profound changes. At the World Student Christian Federation (WSCF), meeting in Nyborg in 1925, various student movements were invited to become members of this new federation. The synergy of these events led to a vital connection between interdenominational and denominational groups, which exponentially increased interest in ecumenism. Mott would go on to play a major role in the first two world conferences on Faith and Order (Lausanne in 1927 and Edinburgh in 1937).

All of this led Mott to become involved in efforts for international peace, demonstrating how the ministry of reconciliation is not limited to private/personal conversions. These efforts culminated in his reception of the Nobel Peace Prize in 1946. When the World Council of Churches held its inaugural meeting in 1948, the eighty-three-year-old Mott preached at the opening service. In his message he said: "We have entered the most exciting period in the history of the church. It will take all the statesmanship, all the churchmanship, and all the self-forgetfulness of all of us. But to those who believe in the adequacy of Christ, no doors are closed, and boundless opportunities are open."[2] I have kept this simple statement before me for almost thirty years.

So what do we make of Mott's work sixty-plus years after his death? One thing stands out: He was a visionary who deeply cared about missional-ecumenism. Through his global vision for missions and unity, his labors tore down many walls. He never lost his zeal to see people know Christ as their Lord. *He became one of the first modern Christian leaders to discover how a passion for mission could be vitally connected with prayer and work for Christian unity.* Mott's legacy lives on in organizations and in the lives of people like me who still find inspiration in his witness. Sadly, most evangelicals have never grasped Mott's vision. After his death, another generation would pass before evangelical Protestants began to play a significant role in the worldwide work for Christian unity. Far too much evangelical energy was spent on negative reactions to wider ecumenism. But these old postwar walls are now falling, even in a time of rabid partisanship and great cultural division.[3]

---

2. Tomkins, "John R. Mott," 705.

3. The shining exception can be seen in the recent work of the World Evangelical Alliance.

Lesslie Newbigin and the Theology of Missional-Ecumenism

Every great movement of the Spirit calls for fresh, thoughtful, and careful theology. No theological system is fixed for all time. Until Jesus returns, we should continue to gain deeper understanding of both divine revelation and our times. This pursuit is what theology does in service of the kingdom and mission of Christ.

We have in Lesslie Newbigin another great example of missional-ecumenism in the twentieth century. He has had more influence on my understanding of mission and ecumenism than any other person. He became my role model in the 1980s. His thought was used to open my mind and heart again and again. Bishop Newbigin, serving in South India for well over three decades, became one of the leading ecumenical theologians and practitioners in the twentieth century. Born James Edward Lesslie Newbigin in Newcastle-upon-Tyne (England), he made massive contributions to Christian thought in the areas of missions, apologetics, and ecumenism. He was trained for the Presbyterian ministry at Cambridge and then appointed by the Church of Scotland for missionary service in South India in 1936. During World War II, he helped bring about the union of several different churches into one new church—the Church of South India—inaugurated in 1947. In 1948, he participated in the first World Council of Churches meeting in Amsterdam as a practitioner with strong theological insights. (This was the same gathering where John Mott gave his aforementioned keynote address.) Newbigin would remain a strong voice for mission and orthodox theology for his entire lifetime.

In 1959, he returned to England as the secretary of the International Missionary Council. He also became the WCC's associate general secretary and director of the Commission on World Mission and Evangelism until 1965. He then returned to India and served as the bishop of the CSI until 1974. When he went finally back to the United Kingdom, he became a college lecturer, the moderator of the general assembly of the United Reformed Church, and even more remarkably, served as the pastor of a small inner-city church (1980–1988). In the last twenty years of his life, his legacy as a theologian of mission and unity was permanently solidified by a number of books. He provided a solid theological model for how to move away from the extremes of rigid liberalism and anti-ecumenical conservatism. Newbigin became the quintessential missional-ecumenist.

When I first began to read Newbigin's large corpus of thought, I was impressed by how lucid he was. He rooted the entire biblical story in God's redemptive and reconciling mission. His approach has also been most recently advanced by the well-known theologian N. T. Wright, who has written that the church must be shaped by mission, and our mission must be shaped by eschatology. The world will see the signs of Jesus' Lordship when we live as communities marked by holiness and unity—the marks of true authenticity as God's missional people.

But Newbigin was much more than a theologian and teacher. His life, much like that of Mott, modeled Christlikeness in the way he lived. Geoffrey Wainwright, who knew Newbigin well, said: "From my first meeting with him in 1963 to my last meeting with him late in 1996, the physical and mental impression he made on me was one of disciplined energy." Wainwright quotes a bishop of the Church of England: "Lesslie in the flesh was quite as alluring as Lesslie in print." Wainwright adds, "As they met him in various arenas, many people sensed that the driving force was the Holy Spirit."[4]

Let me be honest: The entire perspective of this book is shaped by Lesslie Newbigin. We all need role models, and mine is Lesslie Newbigin. When God dramatically shook my life in the early 1990s, this man inspired me for the long haul. I am sorry I never had the joy of meeting him, though several of my friends had that privilege. Newbigin was unique for sure. He was both an academician and a practitioner, an all-too-rare combination. When most of our books and efforts are forgotten, I believe his voice will remain strong. He connected mission to ecumenism in a profound but readable way that will keep these insights fresh. Why? His thought is deeply rooted in God's heart, and his life consistently revealed the truth of good theology.

Learning to Think Missionally

The goal of missional and ecumenical theology is to help the entire Christian church to rethink mission in cultures that have rejected Christendom. Traditional studies in missions, at least until the 1980s, were mostly motivational, inspirational, and promotional. The 1950s produced a serious challenge to the old colonialist assumptions about Christianity and Christendom. This challenge opened doors to new ways of thinking about mission.

Other voices in missions and theology have helped me better understand this calling. One is the late Lamin Sanneh, who was professor of Missions and World Christianity at Yale Divinity School. Sanneh says the results of these global church mega-shifts are increasingly clear:

---

4. Wainwright, *Lesslie Newbigin*, 17.

> Third-world, or "majority-world" Christians in the language of political correctness, are not burdened by a Western guilt complex, and so they have embraced the vocation of mission as a concomitant of the gospel they have embraced: The faith they received they must in turn share. . . . Their context is radically different from that of cradle Christians in the West. Christianity came to them while they had other equally plausible religious options. Choice rather than force defined their adoption of Christianity; often discrimination and persecution accompanied and followed that choice.[5]

Another powerful voice in my story is William Temple (1881–1944), the famous Archbishop of Canterbury. Temple called the reality of the multicultural global church "the great new fact of our time."[6] If this was true when he said it more than seventy-five years ago, how much more true is it today? Missional theology, which is kingdom theology rightly understood, has spawned a discussion that now challenges most of our previous paradigms—paradigms that saw mission almost entirely as extending the church into unreached areas. As we saw earlier, Pope Francis's missional vision also embraces this same theology by encouraging all churches and Christians to become "missionary disciples." Thus the word *missional* really does represent a profoundly theological and practical way to think about the church in this time of immense transition.

Professor Darrell Guder, introduced in the last chapter, taught missions and evangelism at Princeton Theological Seminary for decades. Guder admits there are "terminological confusions" associated with the word *missional*. But he reasons that what ultimately matters is not the word itself but that we craft a healthy response to the nature of Christ's church and the reality of its future.[7] Such a healthy response will help us tear down walls that keep us from love and partnership in mission.

> Rather than seeing mission as one of the necessary prongs of the church's calling, and at worst as a misguided adventure, it must be seen as the fundamental, the essential, the centering understanding of the church's purpose and action. The church that Jesus intended . . . is missional by its very nature. The church that the triune God gathers, upbuilds, and sends . . . exists to continue the service of witness."[8]

5. Imtiaz, "New Generation."
6. Cited in Lossky et al., ed., *Dictionary*, 977.
7. Guder, "Church as Missional," 114.
8. Guder, "Church as Missional," 116.

A Call for Missional Renewal That Seeks Unity

From the time I was a young minister, I believed in biblical reformation and Spirit-directed renewal. I understood reformation as the work of correcting defects in the church. I understood renewal as the work of the Holy Spirit empowering the church for God's mission. Reformation is not revolution! Jesus did not overthrow the past but revealed the future in his life and work. Revolution wastes precious human resources only to foster new forms of sectarianism. Reform movements can very easily move in this direction out of a desire to get back to the Bible and the first-century church. A healthy respect for historical theology and Christian tradition can correct this tendency. But love for the whole church will do even more. Renewal rightly captures the always abounding hope of God's "new thing" (Isaiah 43:19).

When I first grasped the message of missional-ecumenism, I began to teach leaders and churches how to embrace spiritual renewal as missional reformation. I was convinced this was the true reformation we needed, not simply a polemical engagement over the sixteenth century. My experience inside the widely disparate evangelical world caused this conviction to grow. We need a new movement of the Spirit to tear down many of our walls.

Mission and *evangelism* were virtually absent from much of the church's language by the time of medieval church—an absence that left the church destitute of a strong kingdom theology. Even the Protestant Reformation, with all its emphasis on the gospel of justification by faith alone through grace alone, did not fully rediscover this biblical emphasis. Guder concludes: "Very few theologians, in the formal sense, took mission and evangelism seriously. The question of mission is not found in the major confessional documents of Western Christendom before the early twentieth century."[9]

The modern Protestant missionary movement was often carried out by grassroots Christians. On the evangelical side, this movement almost never sprung from a deeply developed theology that took the church seriously. Eventually the modern mission movement began to understand how important theology was, especially as leaders engaged in wide-ranging dialogues about faith and order. But this marriage has never been completely harmonious. Sadly, theology and mission have not been comfortable partners. Both sides view the other with a degree of suspicion.

The problem is clear: We have not trained our pastors and leaders to teach and practice missional Christianity. As a result, most of our pastors and leaders have placed little importance on unity. It is seen by many

---

9. Guder, *Continuing Conversion*, 10.

modern leaders as an obstacle to the practical programs we employ to grow the church numerically. Who needs *other* Christians, *other* traditions, and *other* churches when you can focus on your own programs and goals and build a growing church?

This approach to evangelism and mission almost exclusively stressed the methods and practices of verbal witness. Guder rightly notes, "All assumed that the Western missionary brought the correct understanding of the gospel to the non-believing culture and needed only to figure out how to convey it accurately and persuasively."[10]

The famous theologian Karl Barth gave a lecture in 1932 in which he referred to the church as the *missio Dei* (mission of God). Barth was likely the first modern theologian to see so clearly how mission was an aspect of God's nature. Mission, he argued, was a *movement from God to the world*. The church was the *instrument* of God's mission. Simply put, there is a church *because* there is a mission. When I first encountered this way of thinking about God and our world, I began to see that our categories for mission are too small. The nature of God, who is love, and our mission, which is first God's movement in the world toward all people everywhere, are one. To divide them is a categorical mistake. This is why we must begin to teach leaders and churches to grasp "the comprehensive nature of God's mission."[11]

Further, it is here we discover a real problem. The temptation for churches, both those that are declining and those that are not, is to focus on their own survival and growth. This cuts at the heart of the gospel by reducing ministry to numerical growth and institutional preservation. It also explains why we have so many different versions of the gospel in free-market America. Indeed, if you don't like a particular American version of the gospel, you can attack someone else's gospel and make up your own. Among evangelicals this has produced endless gospel wars accompanied by huge debates, massive conferences, new organizations with narrowly defined perspectives, and best-selling "hot-button" books. Guder correctly observes: "Reductionism does not mean that what remains is wrong; it means that what remains is too little—the church did not set aside the gospel; it reduced it and made it manageable."[12] This is a lot closer to the truth than modern evangelical warriors may realize. When we reduce the gospel to manageable ideas, we demonize other Christians who we believe

---

10. Guder, *Continuing Conversion*, 19.
11. Guder, *Continuing Conversion*, 20.
12. Guder, *Continuing Conversion*, 189.

do not preach the gospel correctly. A favorite text for many such warriors is Galatians 1:6–9, a text often taken out of context and horribly misused.

A Living Modern Model: Brother Yun of China

One of the most life-changing weekends I have ever enjoyed, especially since embarking on this ecumenical journey in the 1990s, came through meeting the Chinese Christian known simply as Brother Yun. While speaking over a weekend in a California church, a young man gave me a copy of Brother Yun's book *The Heavenly Man*. It sat on a big stack by my chair for months. When I finally opened the book, I could not put it down. It is simple, non-technical, and filled with stories. I wept for several days while I read and prayed. I heard and saw in Brother Yun the same calling God had given to me. His words inspired me and gave me fresh courage and hope.

When a second book by Brother Yun, *Living Water*, was released in 2008, the publisher asked me to host him for various book-related events in Chicago. I happily accepted this invitation and planned a full slate of meetings. Our final event was a huge gathering of college students and area Christians on a Sunday evening on the Wheaton campus. The large area was packed with 700-plus people, and the evening was drenched in the Spirit's powerful presence. What touched me the most was Brother Yun's personal prophetic words directed to my soul. Without knowing my long story, he laid out what was happening in me and what would happen if I continued to trust the Lord. In case you wonder, he nailed it.

In some ways, this amazing man taught me more about Christian unity than anyone I've ever met, before or since. Brother Yun believes the solution to all of our division lies in rediscovering our true home in the love of Jesus. We discover this unity when we follow Jesus' commission *together* with the goal of discipling the nations. His simple vision is precisely my own. I have developed my own way to pursue this vision that fits with my particular gifts, but this persecuted Chinese leader helped reassure me in my calling and gave me renewed courage to live it.

> Most of our church disputes and petty infighting come when we start arguing about unimportant matters. Our eyes come off the Great Commission and we start to fight one another instead of fighting against the works of the Devil, which is the very reason Jesus Christ came into the world. The Bible plainly declares, "The reason the Son of God appeared was to destroy the devil's work" (1 John 3:8).[13]

13. Yun, *Living Water*, 141.

Questions for Discussion and Reflection

1. How does unity (ecumenism) relate to God's mission, and thus to missionary discipleship? Can you think of ways the term missional-ecumenism might help you clarify the work of unity across all of divisions?

2. Both John R. Mott and Lesslie Newbigin lived long lives, almost ninety years. How do you think they helped us "see" the twentieth century more clearly? How did their life experience impact their commitment to missional-ecumenism?

3. How did the gospel come to non-Western Christians? What about this story strikes you as helpful in embracing missional-ecumenism?

4. How do you think our becoming the first to love can actually help us to love our neighbors better?

Chapter Eighteen

Building Relational Bridges for Unity

Any concern for fresh spiritual life that is in accordance with the teaching of the New Testament must also lead to a concern for the unity of the church. Our search is not for uniformity. But it is only when we can pray together, work together, worship together, break bread together, and truly love and trust one another, that we can begin to speak of a united church, however varied its form of expression and worship may continue to be.

—David Watson

Many Americans recall a political debate about the so-called "Bridge to Nowhere." This bridge, meant to connect the Alaskan town of Ketchikan with an airport on Gravina Island, was estimated to cost $398 million. The project became the concern of the Alaskan congressional delegation, and the debate over it allowed the whole fiasco to enter our public lexicon as a perfect description of an ill-advised project, hence the phrase the "Bridge to Nowhere." This image remains a symbol of bad management, massive financial waste, and human division, resulting in wasteful partisan bickering.

My sense of church history suggests we've built a few bad bridges in our past. Such projects have often been rooted in bad ideas, financial mismanagement, and human wastefulness. Many of them were ill-conceived because they were rooted in our divisions. As I ponder an image of a bridge being built where a wall once stood, I am reminded of the dangers of another Bridge to Nowhere. When we begin to tear down walls of division, we must understand that new bridges will be needed. These new bridges must be built with the materials of a robust kingdom theology joined with the practice of a servant missional church.

The psalmist reminds us, "How good and pleasant it is when God's people live together in unity" (133:1). He portrays a vision of shared worship within a family of refreshed and consecrated people who walk in the abundance of God's divine presence. God always desires this good reality for his people.

No Time to Stand Alone: How Tension Can Lead Us to Unity

Our culture celebrates the individual. My generation was fed by personal stories of individual accomplishment. Most of us grew up thinking we attained our life goals on our own. But now a hunger for community has surfaced among young adults. Their broken, dysfunctional families reveal the loss that comes through weak and damaged relationships. The evidence is clear: We all hunger for community. "God places the lonely in families" (Psalm 68:6a, NLT).

There is a good reason for this American individualism. America was born in opposition to a foreign power. Our default reaction has inherently been to embrace individualism as a social theory that favors the personal freedom of individuals over our collective responsibility. This tendency now poses a serious threat to the fabric of democracy. (This is also a reason why Americans have historically come together when they feel they are under attack.)

Though it has made a positive contribution to democracy, individualism easily becomes a habit or principle of being self-reliant and independent. Sadly, self-reliance has created much confusion about Christian unity. Protestants inevitably think of the church as a "voluntary society." (Modern Catholics are increasingly influenced by this same American individualism.) We choose our church and then we leave it when we no longer like it. Thus we have built a labyrinth of walls to protect our fears and hostilities. These walls extend right through our lived church experience. On one side, many believe any serious consideration of Christian unity will lead to compromise; on the other, just as many believe giving serious attention to doctrinal understanding will hinder our unity. This struggle creates a powerful tension. But I've learned that this tension can become an instrument of the Spirit to lead us into missional-ecumenism.

I believe this tension can become our strength if we prayerfully engage it together. When I began to meet others who were so very different from me, I discovered that if I remained in a relationship, we both learned to love more deeply. Such tension can actually lead us to better ways of following Jesus. But why is this so important for the mission of the church? Simply put, *all forms of solitary Christianity are dangerous and irresponsible.* Christ did not come to form a people who live separately from one another.

I use the word *tension* because it best describes the mental and emotional strain we experience when we encounter persons and realities that threaten to tear us apart. A major reason we cannot handle such tension lies in a rather fatalistic view of the future. Many Christians see the days ahead as desperate and dark. The problems with this perspective are numerous, but for our purposes, I believe this view leads us to judge the present as the way the future must be. When we do this, we lose the *mystery* of our faith. Mystery? Yes. In the New Testament, mystery is a far better way to understand the future.

> Beyond all question, the *mystery* from which true godliness springs is great: He appeared in the flesh, was vindicated by the Spirit, was seen by angels, was preached among the nations, was believed on in the world, was taken up in glory. (1 Timothy 3:16)

> This *mystery* is that through the gospel the Gentiles are heirs together with Israel, members together of one body, and sharers together in the promise in Christ Jesus. (Ephesians 3:6)

> This is a profound *mystery*—but I am talking about Christ and the church. (Ephesians 5:32)

The *mystery* Paul speaks of in such texts is not like a mystery novel "whodunit." *It is more like the gradual lifting of a pervasive fog.* Until Jesus came and established the new covenant through his cross and resurrection, the idea that Jews and Gentiles could be "heirs together" and "members together of one body" was unthinkable. Thus what Jesus revealed, and Paul explained, was a mystery—a previously unknown unity could be experienced through Jesus. His life tore down the religious and cultural walls that divided people. The sharp rise in congregational and internal church conflicts in recent decades calls us to tear down many more walls. This will lead us to build bridges that go somewhere—bridges that lead us into relational Christlikeness. Here we can share our stories, meet one another, and truly learn to pray "Our Father" together.

Two Extremes

I've personally seen how broad-based calls for ecumenism frighten many conservative Christians. Such calls also don't motivate more liberal believers to engage with conservatives. For many Americans, faith has become a left-right way of thinking. This simplistic duality denies the real way of seeing the kingdom at work, and it inevitably leads to either a vaguely defined catholicity or a rigidly held fundamentalism. Both deny the robust faith life of the kingdom.

In my early conservatism, I rarely dealt with the obvious implications of the central passages of Scripture we've considered in this book, e.g., John 17 and Ephesians 4. As a result, I remained inside my sectarian mindset. I reasoned that most of those who were unlike me were liberal, maybe not even Christians. My tribe defended Scripture and engaged in numerous battles about the right way to understand the Bible. Over time, these battles became central to our identity. The denomination of my childhood, the Southern Baptist Convention, would eventually experience massive division over such struggles. Now the side that won the so-called "battle for the Bible" holds many of the same partisan political opinions that divide white conservative Christians from the rest of the church. Sadly, much of the church in America has become a "Red State" or "Blue State" expression of Christianity. These tensions have created a huge wall that must be torn down.

As I was researching the "Bridge to Nowhere," I found a photo of a California bridge built in 1936—the *original* "Bridge to Nowhere." The more I looked at this photo, the more I saw my vision on that California bridge. Today it has tables on it where you can see people gathered together. The image is a picture of missional-ecumenism. Build a bridge where we can share and listen. Learn to talk and pray together. More can be done here than almost anywhere else.

I am persuaded that the answer to our breakdown can be found in this paradigm of life together. This model adopts the images of the Bible and sees Christ's mission in the symbols of table and fellowship. In such ways we can imagine mission again as our response to physical *and* spiritual hunger (Luke 4:14–20). When we gather around a table for friend-making, we will be renewed in body and soul. All cultures recognize this human need for social interaction. True friendships will produce deep and transformative conversation. Friendships can survive, even thrive, when we remain willing to seek reconciliation. Such conversation can become the Holy Spirit's way of pushing us forward into the new ecumenism we saw in Chapter 15. Vatican II's decree on ecumenism (*Unitatis Redintegratio*) called this "spiritual ecumenism." The council said this type of ecumenism should be regarded as the *true soul of the ecumenical movement*. Spiritual ecumenism allows us to find a way into friendship and friendship can lead us to construct relational bridges of love for Christ's mission. This will lead us to do the work of missional-ecumenism.

James I. Packer: My Teacher

One of the most significant persons in my own story was the late Anglican minister-theologian James I. Packer (1926–2020). Jim and I became friends when I was a very young minister. I invited him into my home, where we began to build an uncommon friendship. (I learned over the years that Jim shared his life in a similar way with countless others.) In responding to my desire for informal mentoring through friendship, Jim showed me what real love looked like through sacrifice. He was a first-rate theologian *and* a humble man. He helped me understand ecumenism when I had little or no understanding. Jim modeled spiritual ecumenism and always demonstrated a gracious spirit joined with generous orthodoxy. He could make good arguments for unity, but he was an even better icon of the spiritual way by which deep unity in Christ's mission could be advanced. By engaging in dialogues related to missional-ecumenism, Jim helped me view apostolic tradition, and the historic church, with new eyes. Even as my own circle of friendship grew much wider, Jim never stopped encouraging me to press on in my faithfulness to Christ and his kingdom. Our phone conversations in his last years still encouraged me to trust in Christ alone.

Dr. Packer rightly concluded that in John 17, Jesus never had in mind an "all-embracing ecclesiastical organization."[1] He believed we share together in a relational oneness through which the Spirit will guide us to "see eye to eye with each other regarding God's nature, will, and work, so that a shared orthodoxy ['right belief,' as the word literally means] will take form and be firmly held among [us]."[2] As you've seen in my story, I have witnessed the power of this relational oneness firsthand for more than three decades. Here I've found the best place to build bridges and pursue mission. This approach has the advantage of *not* opposing formal ecumenical dialogue. In fact, it should welcome it precisely because it has done so much good for the unity of the church regionally and globally. At the same time, missional-ecumenism puts the right amount of stress on what Jesus taught: Personal relationships with other Christians must always come first.

1. Packer, *Christian Unity*, 5.
2. Packer, *Christian Unity*, 5–6.

Packer said the call to unity will always include "togetherness of spiritual life: togetherness that is in what Jesus called 'eternal life' and in a meditative moment in his prayer defined as knowing 'you the only true God, and Jesus Christ"— me!—'whom you sent' (John 17:3)." He explains that there are four implications of this togetherness that express what it means for us to live the mission of Jesus:

- recognizing the reality of God and the Lord Jesus Christ
- responding to the impact of the Father and the Son mediated through the apostolic word, just as living things in this world respond to physical stimulation
- the inner change that Jesus described to Nicodemus as being born again of water and the Spirit (John 3:3–7), whereby Jesus dying for sins and drawing us to himself becomes the central focus of our life (3:14–21)
- the imparting by God of energy to stand against the world and the Devil and to spread the gospel message (17:14–16, 20)

Dr. Packer sums it up: "This supernatural Christlikeness results from Christ himself being in us, united to each one in a way that sustains the divine life in the human soul and binds us all to each other through the binding of each one to the other."[3] Here is the major lesson I learned from Packer. The work of prayer and trust is rooted in supernatural Christlikeness. It is not a program or a series of steps to follow. It is a life infused with the Spirit's power and love.

Packer's understanding of unity included "a togetherness of active love: a love that is motivated and animated by knowledge of the redemptive, life-transforming love of God to us (John 17:23, 26). Such an active love works diligently, in the spirit of gospel reconciliation, to honor and exalt *everyone* who loves the Lord Jesus Christ."[4] The good sense of Dr. Packer's argument should be obvious. N. T. Wright sees the same truth and concludes that relational love between Christians created "a community, of a sort previously unimagined."[5] I see in these observations a spiritual reality the modern church desperately needs. We have tried almost everything under the sun to build and grow our churches. Yet very little of our labor has produced the lasting fruit of costly love. But could it really be this simple? Can life together, in the love of Christ, actually lead us into a community-based oneness that makes the gospel attractive to outsiders? It surely did in

3. Packer, *Christian Unity*, 6.
4. Packer, *Christian Unity*, 6.
5. Wright, *Interpreting Paul*, 111.

the first churches we read about in the New Testament. They had at least as many problems as us, but they lived as those baptized into the one body.

Packer affirmed this same conclusion. He sounded the correct note when he said our togetherness should be centered in mission. "When the incarnate Son was on earth, the Father and he, the sender and the sent, were, as we would put it nowadays, on mission together.... The Son's post-resurrection commissioning of his disciples... involves all Christians in the mission, one way or another." He concludes, "We are called to be one, united and cooperating, in actively spreading the gospel, in and under Christ as mission leader."[6]

But what about the sacraments, church orders for gospel ministry, church forms, and ecclesial organizations? Packer said belief in apostolic succession through bishops is theologically and historically commendable, yet, "We [must] note that no form of church organization is mentioned, and we infer that organization will only be relevant to Christian unity insofar as it expresses and furthers the ones in Christ that we have described."[7] Packer's greatest strength is here: His ecumenism was joined with his commitment to a deeply spiritual and practical faith that was non-pejorative and non-political. His perspective lines up beautifully with Pope John Paul II's conviction that "what unites us is much greater than what divides us."[8] Clearly this is also Pope Francis's conviction, as we saw in his lovely description of the church as "missionary disciples."

The points that leaders (e.g., Jim Packer, Pope Francis, N.T. Wright) have made about the calling and discipleship of the whole people of God align with the conclusions I have reached. For this reason I remain supportive of every attempt to express true Christian unity in formal *and* informal ways. I have given my full support to a wide range of ecumenical practices and formal agreements because together all of these efforts contribute to our lived oneness. As an ordained minister in the Reformed Church in America, I have continually discovered new ways of practicing unity with other Protestant churches through our *Formula of Agreement*. This agreement between several historic churches establishes full communion with each other. This full communion between diverse churches has allowed me to preach and serve sacramentally in a wide range of churches.[9] (I am an

---

6. Packer, *Christian Unity*, 6.
7. Packer, *Christian Unity*, 7.
8. John Paul II, *Ut Unum Sint*.
9. This historic agreement between four Reformation churches allows full communion between members and full ministry recognition for ordained leaders.

active part of a local Lutheran church, where I have found freedom to use my gifts to be an immense blessing.)

My wide experience in ecumenism has taught me that we must continue to find new ways to foster the spirit passed on to us by leaders like John Mott and Lesslie Newbigin—the same spirit now passed on to me by Jim Packer, N.T. Wright, and Pope Francis in the twenty-first century. These men (and the many women who have shared this same vision) have demonstrated the ecumenical movement is a work of grace rooted in friendships. All these witnesses have lived missional-ecumenism, an ecumenism rooted in mission, holiness, and prayer. They have practiced Paul's admonition to "encourage one another and build up each other" (1 Thessalonians 5:11) by showing us the way to teach *and* practice Christian unity.

But as important as all our formal efforts for unity have been, the primary progress must still come in the trenches of shared everyday life—person to person, school to school, congregation to congregation, movement to movement, and yes, sometimes, denomination to denomination. This point was driven home to me on a morning I spent with Dr. Mary Tanner at the Anglican Center in Rome. The esteemed scholar and global ecumenist asked me about my personal vision for unity. When I explained that I called this vision "missional-ecumenism," she memorably said, "John, after a lifetime of work in formal and informal ecumenism, giving lectures, drafting agreements, and attending global gatherings, I think you are right about the *real* need. If the Spirit comes upon this work then we shall see a fire consume all our labors into a great renewal of life and mission."

Real progress is being made in various human relationships, within families and communities, as well as in our cities and towns. All Christians have a role to play in this movement of God's Spirit. This is where I believe the great evangelical principle we saw earlier will show itself again, a principle displayed in kingdom movements for renewal that have taken place in all three of the great Christian churches. This renewal of the Holy Spirit thrusts us out into the world around us and brings about healthy ecumenism. True revivals have always broken down barriers. We noted earlier an example of this point in the early Pentecostal movement in America in the early 1900s. The first wave of this renewal included a call to unity which was sadly lost because of racial and class prejudice that protected old walls.

A Different Answer

In my vocation, I have experienced a growing movement of convergence that seeks the unity of the whole church by learning from one another through shared involvement in Christ's mission. I see this movement of love stretching out into every religious practice and person we encounter, even to non-Christians, if we rightly understand our faith and respect them for theirs. Such a movement should not lead Christians to abandon their unique aspects of faith, rooted in the incarnation and resurrection of Jesus. But we must hear afresh the apostle's words: "Contribute to the needs of the saints; extend hospitality to strangers" (Romans 15:13). The "stranger" in our midst is most often an alien or an immigrant. If we adopt a me-first attitude, rooted in our personal security, we miss the mission God has given us. Serving the most disadvantaged is always a direct path into missional-ecumenism, which has the eyes and ears to see and hear the words of Jesus calling us together. "I was hungry and you gave me food, I was thirsty and you gave me something to drink, I was a stranger and you welcomed me, I was naked and you gave me clothing, I was sick and you took care of me, I was in prison and you visited me'" (Matthew 25:35–36). This is the call that led the Catholic Church to express the "preferential option for the poor."[10]

We must also learn to practice good listening through the type of love that extends beyond our own borders. This too can be part of what I call missional-ecumenism. (Much like Pope Francis, I have *not* given away the mission of Jesus but rather understood it in a more encompassing way that aligns with the story of oneness from Genesis through Revelation. The kingdom of God is simply not limited to our church or churches.) I see at least seven common elements that are powerfully converging in modern ecumenism. Through such a powerful convergence, missional-ecumenism is creating a new life-giving river of grace that knits together our various theological contributions into a richer and deeper ecumenical tapestry. These seven elements are:

1. A *restored commitment to the sacraments*, especially to regular celebrations at the Lord's Table. Neither the charismatic nor evangelical streams of Christianity have stressed this commitment, but evidence abounds that this is changing.

2. An *increased appetite to know more about the early church*. For many Christians there has been a huge gap between the pages of their Bible

---

10. The "preferential option for the poor" is a phrase that refers to the biblical imperative to care for the poor and the powerless. This phrase was first articulated by Fr. Pedro Arrupe, a Jesuit, in 1968, and emphasized in 1979, by both bishops and Pope John Paul II, at the Puebla Conference in Mexico. It is now a mainstream idea in Catholicism and has been embraced widely by many churches and Christians. Pope Francis, being from South America, has advanced it widely in the church.

and the modern church. The search for common roots has brought them to a deeper interest in the Catholic and Orthodox Churches.

3. An *obvious open expression of love for the whole church and a real desire to see the church become one*. This growing regard for catholicity is more evident now than at any time in my six decades of life. Prayer for unity drives this expression, but conferences, seminars, retreats, and shared witnessing experiences fuel it.

4. The *blending of the practices of worship, devotion, and prayer from all three streams*, even as churches approach this convergence from different emphases. Most congregations clearly reveal a particular expression of the church that regulates their life together. What is changing is that the convergence of several streams is drawing churches together while they retain their distinctive base. At the same time, they are opening themselves up to the strengths of other churches they never knew.

5. An *interest in integrating more liturgical depth and structure with spontaneity and freedom in the Holy Spirit*. Charismatic Christians are finding exciting treasures in liturgy, and liturgical Christians are finding deep joy in praise and new songs.

6. A *greater involvement of sign and symbol in worship through aids such as crosses, Christian art, icons, and clerical vestments*. Some evangelicals and charismatics are skeptical about these streams, but this movement does not involve one stream as much as a convergence of several wonderful streams that can only help each church to mature.

7. A *continuing commitment to personal salvation, solid biblical teaching, and the work and ministry of the Holy Spirit*. The rich, vital heritage of the Protestant Reformation is not being abandoned but is being accessed in unheard-of ways as thousands of convergence-model Christians and churches embrace these key elements of vital biblical Christianity.

Conclusion

The late David Watson wrote more than three decades ago: "Among many Christian leaders there is the deep conviction that it is only by concentrating on the fundamentals of our faith, supremely the cross of Christ and the renewal of the Holy Spirit that any real experience of unity will be a serious possibility."[11] I believe Watson was spot on! He has also helped me picture how this unity may advance. He suggested that when we travel by air and first lift off the ground, the walls, hedges, and buildings all look very large. But the higher we rise, the smaller they seem to become. In the same way, Watson said, "When the power of the Holy Spirit lifts us up together into the conscious realization of the presence of Jesus, the barriers between us become unimportant. Seated with Christ in the heavenly places, the difference between Christians can often seem petty and marginal."[12] Indeed, the better our perspective on missional-ecumenism, the sooner we will see more walls come down. And the sooner we begin to build bridges, the stronger will be our work for Christ and his kingdom!

Questions for Discussion and Reflection

1. How do you understand the two extremes we face in dealing with ecumenism? How should you address these tensions in your church and life while you also respect the conscience of those who do not agree? Can you be a true peacemaker?

2. Do you believe America is increasingly post-Christian? Why or why not? How should the church respond to the loss of our privileges in society? What does this loss mean for your mission?

3. How would you explain the term *ecumenical theology*? How could a theology of ecumenism be produced? Is it desirable to do so?

---

11. Watson, *I Believe*, 346.
12. Watson, *I Believe*, 347.

Chapter Nineteen

Models of Missional-Ecumenism

> The church exists for mission as fire exists for burning.
> —*Emil Brunner*

> One reason the church is failing today is that it has so many members who are not kingdom-of-God men and women! They may be active in the church program—regular at worship, involved in the administration of the religious establishment—but they lack kingdom-of-God qualities.
> —*Richard Halverson*

When missional-ecumenism takes root in a single soul, a local church, a group of area churches, or a specific community of Christians from varied backgrounds, what will this vision look like? How can a pastor, a city-focused mission leader, or a single humble Christian, with or without public gifts, help others pursue the kingdom of God through this vision of missional-ecumenism? I've found the best way to answer is through stories. Stories have a distinct advantage over arguments. They also have the emotional power of life itself. They provide living examples that nurture both courage and faith. In this penultimate chapter, I will encourage you to adopt a lifestyle of missional-ecumenism by sharing some stories that reveal how this vision is working in very diverse contexts.

Evangelism and Missional-Ecumenism: Alpha

Perhaps no single church-based mission has touched more Catholics and Protestants *together* than the internationally well-known Alpha course—an eleven-week experience that explores the implications of Christianity in a relaxed, thought-provoking atmosphere. Millions of people in 169 countries have attended an Alpha course. It has been translated into 112 different languages. Alpha courses have been taught in churches, prisons, universities, and military bases. Alpha began as a church-based outreach at Holy Trinity Church (Brompton, England), an Anglican charismatic parish. The goal of the original course was to explore the meaning of life in a stress-free, relational atmosphere. (There's that key word once again: *relational*.)

Alpha courses are run all around the globe. Everyone is welcome. It works in cafés, churches, universities, homes—you name it. No two Alphas look exactly the same, but they have three key things in common: food, a very warm relational talk and really good conversation. This strategy works well in almost every social and religious context because the emphasis is on the simple, central truths about the Jesus story and relationships. Rooted in core orthodoxy and clearly built on missionary discipleship, Alpha demonstrates what missional-ecumenism looks like.

Alpha participants have included bishops and archbishops from North America, Africa, and Asia—even the head of the Coptic Church in North Africa. One Middle Eastern delegate to a recent gathering said, "We are seeing history in the making here. Not for many centuries have Christians of every denomination come together around one piece of Christian teaching in this way." I wholeheartedly agree. Alpha beautifully models the fruitful way of making disciples by telling the story of Jesus and sharing it in ways that effectively tear down walls of division. Alpha does not seek to remake or tear down the church but to share Jesus, and by setting a table where the gospel is shared relationally. Whenever I meet a Catholic or mainline Protestant congregation alive with the Spirit, seeing people come to vibrant living faith (whether for the first time or by being renewed in the Spirit), I almost always discover that Alpha has been there.[1]

Missional Prayer and Ecumenism

There are so many prayer movements worldwide, it's hard to keep up with this phenomenon. Prayer movements exist in cities and towns all across

---

1. A good introduction and explanation of Alpha USA is available at https://alphausa.org.

North America and are often centered on the mission of Christ. The famous Baptist missionary William Carey, the "father of modern missions," said, "One of the first, and most important of these duties which are incumbent upon us, is fervent and *united* prayer" (italics mine).[2] One of the most impactful written contributions to the global prayer movement is called *Operation World*, a resource available online and as a book. In the introduction to the 2010 edition, which I have used for over a decade, the editor writes: "We do not merely pray about the many points featured [in this book], we pray toward something, and that something is magnificent—the fulfillment of the Father's purposes and His kingdom come."[3] *Operation World* urges intercessors to understand the global disunity of the church by continually reminding readers to pray for the healing of our divisions. By using this resource morning by morning, I have seen time and time again how disunity hinders Christ's mission in countries around the world. This book makes it abundantly clear that when we fervently pray for the advance of Christ's mission, we must pray and work for Christian unity. When mission and unity come together, the character of God will lead us to earnestly pray and work for the end of oppression, hunger, poverty, and war. When we enter into prayer in the Spirit, we see that our stewardship of the whole earth is God's will. And when we pray, we begin to long that all who are at enmity will experience peace. We will work and pray to see his kingdom come, his will be done, on earth as in heaven. Planting new churches is good, but it is not the end of the kingdom mission. The late John R. W. Stott expressed the true goal:

> Here lies the supreme missionary motivation. It is neither obedience to the Great Commission; nor compassion for the lost, nor excitement over the gospel, but zeal (even "jealousy") for the honor of Christ's name . . . no incentive is stronger than the longing that Christ should be given the honor that is due to His Name.[4]

When you think about this, you realize it is truly a mystery that God allows his glory to be placed in our hands for the blessing of the entire world. Given our foolish and sinful missteps, spanning twenty centuries of Christian history, who has not thought about giving up on the church? But God has never given up on the church. He calls us to repent, but he never rejects his people, even when they miserably fail. Why? He loves the body of Christ, betrothed as a bride for his own Son.

2. Carey, *Enquiry*, 77.
3. Mandryk, *Operation World*, xxiii.
4. Mandryk, *Operation World*, xiii.

The global prayer movements I've shared in over the last twenty-five years have shaped concerns about racial reconciliation, community development, compassionate care for the suffering, pastors' prayer networks, and various forms of servant evangelism. Though much of this prayer movement in America has been evangelical, more and more Catholics and other Protestants are getting involved. I see an expanding fire in our midst. (This fire may have begun with the rise of the Moravians in the fifteen century, decades before the Protestant Reformation.)[5] Most major American cities have a significant ministry of intercessory prayer, even though most Christians do not even know these ecumenical prayer meetings exist.

The Global Week of Prayer for Christian Unity

Another prayer movement that expresses missional-ecumenism is the Week of Prayer for Christian Unity. This movement for unity began in 1908, through the work of Fr. Paul Wattson, a Catholic priest. It eventually became an international ecumenical observance and is now kept annually. It is an octave, meaning it lasts eight days. The history of this prayer movement is remarkable when you realize just how much has happened over the last one-hundred-plus years. Abbé Paul Couturier (Lyons, France), rightly called "the father of spiritual ecumenism," had a slightly different approach to this week of prayer. Wattson had a more traditional view of the end goal of ecumenical activity: the union of the church. But Couturier advocated prayer "for the unity of the Church as Christ wills it, and in accordance with the means he wills."[6] His focus enabled Christians with differing views of the papal ministry to join in prayer. In 1935, Couturier proposed naming this observance "Universal Week of Prayer for Christian Unity." The Catholic Church adopted the proposal in 1966, shortly after Vatican II. Couturier's message influenced a Trappist nun, Blessed Maria Gabriella of Unity, to embrace a sacrificial devotion to the cause of unity. Her vision was adopted by popes since that time, and when the World Council of Churches was established in 1948, it became a leading vehicle for promoting this prayer octave. Now most Orthodox churches—as well as Anglican, Baptist, Lutheran, Methodist, Reformed, Presbyterian, Independent, and United—cooperate in it. Today the theme, Scripture texts, logos, study guides and liturgical suggestions are all jointly prepared by Catholics and member churches of the WCC. Until 2010, I didn't know this movement existed. Now, having

---

5. An excellent historical summary of the vision and mission of the Moravians can be found at https://www.moravian.org/2018/07/a-brief-history-of-the-moravian-church.

6. Week of Prayer.

participated in many events related to the Week of Prayer for Christian Unity in many parts of America, I have witnessed its immense potential for missional-ecumenism. It annually plants a seed that allows more and more people to meet and pray and witness firsthand what unity looks like.

John Paul II urged Christians to "grow ever more in united common prayer around Christ" so we could pursue the ecumenism God is directing. He wrote, "If they meet more often and more regularly before Christ in prayer, they will be able to gain the courage to face all the painful human reality of their divisions," adding, "It is true that we are not yet in full communion. And yet, despite our divisions, we are on the way toward full unity, that unity which marked the apostolic church at its birth and which we sincerely seek. Our common prayer, inspired by faith, is proof of this."[7] His desire is being met by a growing response to the vision of missional-ecumenism.

Make no mistake about this: Movements of prayer for Christian unity have played a huge role over the last century. I believe these movements will have an even more central role in restoring our unity in the years ahead. Prayer is potent and powerful. In prayer we experience what we could not know otherwise.

Living in Ecumenical Community: Taizé

The Taizé Community is an ecumenical monastic order located in a small town in Burgundy, France. Founded in 1940 by Brother Roger Schütz, a Reformed Protestant minister, it was originally a sanctuary for World War II refugees. Both Catholics and Protestants have shared life and ministry together at Taizé for nearly seventy years. Taizé's ecumenism is experienced in both prayers and liturgical music in many languages, as well as through Eastern Orthodox icons and chants. Taizé never wanted to be a movement so much as a place, where young people could be encouraged and then return to their local churches and communities to pursue a "pilgrimage of trust on earth."[8] Many Americans know of Taizé only because of its music, but it is used to serve the wider vision of unity in Christ's kingdom mission.

Jason Brian Santos's book *A Community Called Taizé* tells the story of this unique mission that has become a focal point for millions of young people around the world.[9] Taizé has become a living ecumenical icon by modeling peace and reconciliation. Here popes and evangelicals have drawn

---

7. John Paul II, *Ut Unum Sint*, sections 22, 23.
8. Taizé, "Pilgrimage."
9. Santos, *A Community Called Taizé*.

strength in prayer and worship through life together. When John Paul II died, Brother Roger was an honored participant in his funeral service, even receiving the Eucharist from his dear friend Cardinal Joseph Ratzinger days before Ratzinger became Pope Benedict XVI.

The Focolare: A Global Movement for Oneness and Love

A little over a decade ago I conducted an afternoon dialogue on unity in Philadelphia. I will never forget the event, for two reasons. First, only two people attended. (I've done some small events, but I cannot recall expecting at least ten and having only two!) Second, the two who did come included a Catholic sister, with an obvious desire to hear more about unity, and Gerald Stover, an Anabaptist lay leader who is profoundly committed to the work of ecumenism. That afternoon, as we listened to one another, this brother asked me, "Have you ever heard of the Focolare?" I had no idea what he was referring to but was interested. A few days later he had introduced me to the Focolare Movement in Chicago. This introduction became a turning point in my life.

Focolare is an international movement that promotes unity and universal brotherhood, both in the Catholic Church and beyond. (It includes Christians from many denominations and has a calling to share unity with people from non-Christian traditions as well.) Founded in 1943 in Trent, Italy, the site of the famous Council of Trent, the Focolare movement now operates in 180 nations and has over 140,000 members. Officially named the "Work of Mary," the organization's common name, "Focolare," means "hearth" or "family fireside" in Italian.[10]

During the difficult days of World War II, the city of Trent was routinely strafed by bombing. A young elementary-school teacher named Chiara Lubich saw how God's love was the only antidote for times when life was crumbling around her. While reading her copy of the Gospels, often in bomb shelters during air raids, Chiara had an encounter with God and entered deeply into Jesus' desire (John 17:21): "that they all may be one." A small group of women initially shared her vision while helping those in the shelters and streets. The number of these Christian servants began to grow. In 1948, a journalist who was also a member of Parliament and a pioneer in ecumenism joined the Focolare, bringing what has been described as "the ideal of social unity." Another cofounder was a sympathetic priest whose

---

10. The history and development of Focolare USA can be found at https://www.focolare.org/usa.

theological background helped bolster the young movement. His work led to the founding of New City Press in 1964. The Focolare spread to other parts of Italy. In time, a Lutheran pastor in Germany contacted Chiara, asking her to share the vision of John 17:21 among Lutherans. This led her to visit other parts of Europe, her first taste of ecumenism outside the Catholic Church. This little movement eventually spread worldwide: South America (1958), North America (1961), Africa (1963), Asia (1966), and Australia (1967).

The president of the Focolare Movement, according to its constitution, will always be a lay woman. (There are many similar movements supported by the Catholic Church, including the aforementioned charismatic movement.) The movement respects men but powerfully embraces women and their gifts of leadership. The chief goals of the Focolare are to cooperate in the consolidation of unity in the Christian world, with individuals and groups, movements, and associations; to contribute to full communion with Christians in different churches; and to work towards the universal brother/sisterhood of all peoples, regardless of their religious beliefs.

When I returned to Chicago, after my visit in Philadelphia, I was introduced to my friend Tom Masters, a committed Catholic member of the Focolare. Tom invited me to share a meal in the home of several unmarried men who lived in community. This evening fellowship was unforgettable. These brothers expressed profound interest in both me and my story. As if it were yesterday I recall being openly loved in a remarkable way. This evening felt like "home" after thirteen years in a spiritual desert. At the time I believed God still had a role for me in this vision of unity in mission, but I was unclear how it would work out. (My dream of being restored to fruitful public ministry had yet to be fulfilled.) Tom eventually joined the board of my mission ACT3. I began to attend Focolare gatherings, large and small, in Chicago and beyond. They all emphasized experiencing oneness in fellowship with "Jesus forsaken." I drank deeply from these wells of relational unity that had been dug by the work of this amazing movement. I learned, I questioned, and I engaged in warm, non-judgmental dialogue through growing friendships.

The Luminosa Award for Unity[11] is periodically given to institutions or individuals that the Focolare recognizes as having made a significant contribution to the building of universal brotherhood through their work in ecumenism, inter-religious dialogue, or any other aspect of social life. In 2014, to my complete surprise, I was invited to come to Hyde Park, New

---

11. For a description of the award, see https://www.focolare.org/mariapolisluminosa/award-for-unity.

York, to receive the award. To say the least, I never imagined such an honor when I first "heard" the words of Jesus in John 17:21 many decades ago. As I look back over this story, I realize my life would never have been empowered by such deep, prayerful friendship had I not met men and women who were actually living a unique model of missional-ecumenism. The course of my life has truly been altered by the love and friendship of the Focolare.

Evangelicals and Catholics Together: Practicing Unity for Evangelism

No ecumenical endeavor has brought about as much interest among American evangelicals, at least over the past several decades, as the cause of Evangelicals and Catholics Together. ECT is the fulfillment of the dream of two well-known American leaders, Charles W. Colson (1931–2012) and Father Richard John Neuhaus (1936–2009). I believe ECT accomplished more for informal ecumenism and Christ's mission than most realize. While it prompted negative reactions from well-known evangelicals, it also served as a model for the very things I've written about.[12] My initial reaction to ECT was negative. I saw it through the lens of a narrowly conceived sixteenth-century framework. But this movement compelled me to reexamine both my attitudes and actions, and I underwent one of the more painful changes in my personal life. Not only did several of my good friends play a huge role in the direction of the ECT project, but Jim Packer became a major contributor to the theological statements. I was eventually drawn into a series of private meetings with several of the leading figures in this movement. I believe God used these friends to help me learn how to listen with an open and teachable spirit. Thus my embracing of ECT's work came about because relational, spiritual ecumenism allowed me to love, listen, and learn. But my involvement cost me numerous relationships and significant financial support.

One night in Virginia, over a meal with six leaders, I asked Chuck Colson: "What did you want to accomplish with this ecumenical effort?" He calmly replied, "I want to see doors opened for Christ's mission to make disciples, especially in Latin America." (The original idea, before the ECT documents even came about, was to convene a symposium to discuss the growing rivalry between Catholics and evangelicals in Latin America.) Colson said he wanted to preach Christ where he had not been able to do so, in

---

12. "Evangelicals and Catholics Together." This is the original ECT document. Several more have been published since, but this was the foundation upon which they were all built.

order to show what God's love for all could look like. It may make no difference to his critics, but one fact is now abundantly clear: Hundreds of Latin American prisons that were closed to joint gospel mission have now been opened to the witness of Catholics and Protestants evangelizing together. I believe history will look on these developments with more favor than the critics could have imagined.[13]

Gospel Call: A Gift to Churches Praying for Unity

One of the first things I realized as I embraced my growing vision of Christian unity was the need to personally engage in public efforts for Christian unity. I was often afforded a unique opportunity to experience new life-changing friendships as I tore down more and more of my personal walls. During a church renewal conference in Birmingham, Alabama, I met the late Jeffrey Gros (1938–2013). When Jeff moved to Chicago in 2011 we began to meet. He taught me how I could engage with Catholics effectively in life-changing ways. (He literally *coached* me on how to best dialogue with Francis Cardinal George before we did a large public discussion on the Wheaton College campus.) Perhaps the most wonderful thing Jeff did for me, however, was to introduce me to his longtime friend, Fr. Thomas Ryan, CSP.

Tom Ryan, whose work is cited several times above, has personally invested so much into my story, especially through a mission appropriately named "Gospel Call." Through our work together I learned firsthand the powerful effect of serving churches in ways that can lead them to tear down walls that traditionally separate us.

Gospel Call is a four-day event hosted by three or more congregations, anywhere in the U.S. and Canada. This mission invites Christians to *experience* unity. Gospel Call's purpose statement says this well: "Provide(s) Christian believers with an opportunity to discover, experience, and express our unity in Christ. The overarching objective of this event is to respond to the gospel call to reconciliation with God and one another."

---

13. Colson said, "When all is said and done, and my life is viewed in perspective, ECT is likely to be the most significant project I invested my time and capital into. It has been well worth the struggle, and I think we have yet to see the great things God will do with it" (quoted in Aitken, *Charles W. Colson*, 388). Because of Colson's commitment to ECT, his Prison Fellowship ministry lost $1.5 million. Radio stations dropped his broadcasts. All over the Bible Belt, churches and pastors protested Prison Fellowship. Aitken calls the response to Colson "evangelical hostility"—a description I know to be apt, as I was in the middle of the response and also engaged in private conversations with Colson following the first wave of attacks. His gracious response to opposition, and genuine love for Christian unity, endeared him to me as a strong role model. I gladly acknowledge my debt to him.

As Tom and I led Gospel Call meetings we preached sermons *together* from the same text. This shared preaching experience was unique and life-changing. Most of those who attended our public evening meetings had never seen a Protestant minister and a Catholic priest preach the gospel side-by-side. We saw the grace of God at work in fresh ways as we shared life with others. This mission prompts me to pray for new expressions of this vision of unity at work. Tom and I would love to teach others how to do this kind of work together even though we have both retired from leading this particular effort.[14]

Conclusion

It was not easy for me to decide on these few stories. (I could share so many more.) I have limited my stories to churches and movements begun in North America or Europe. I am aware of multitudes of similar stories that demonstrate missional-ecumenism. In each of these stories one can see the DNA of missional-ecumenism. My goal is to feed your imagination so you will begin to pray and engage in this beautiful, life-changing work of receptive mission-centered ecumenism. But why? Aslan is on the move!

Questions for Discussion and Reflection

1. As you reflect on these stories of missional-ecumenism, prayerfully ponder how they can inform your own story. What kind of missional ventures might stir a vision for Christ's kingdom in your community? In your own local congregation? In your organization?

2. How can missional-ecumenism be encouraged while you remain faithful to what your church/mission/school believes are the non-negotiables? What needs to be changed? What should not be changed?

3. Where should you begin pursuing this vision in terms of your own leadership and service? Take one of the models you've read and consider how it might help you in the work of unity. Why did you choose this model, and what particularly did you learn that you can put into practice?

---

14. Tom Ryan is the founder-director of the Paulist North American Office for Ecumenical and Interfaith Relations. http://www.tomryancsp.org/gospelcall.htm

Chapter Twenty

Costly Love, Costly Unity

*Our faith in God should play a unifying role among believers.
This may seem obvious, but all too often we forget it or ignore it.*

—*Jimmy Carter*

My experience of missional-ecumenism has been a journey of the heart. But don't misunderstand. My intellect has been fully engaged with Scripture and tradition at every point. This path allows me to embrace what can be called *ecumenical theology*. But my heart holds first place because "out of the heart" the issues of life are addressed (Proverbs 4:23).

A growing commitment to ecumenical theology has allowed me to engage with the living theology of the entire church, past *and* present. I discovered that no theological system holds all the truth. None can express the beauty of Christ to the heart. The more I have understood this vision I call missional-ecumenism, the more I see life as a "long obedience in the same direction."[1] But one thing remains clear: Love has guided my obedience at every turn. Indeed, love alone has led me to tear down many walls of division and follow Jesus into a deep, heartfelt unity. The Apostle John summarizes this clearly when he writes: "So we have known and believe the love that God has for us. God is love, and those who abide in love abide in God, and God abides in them" (1 John 4:17).

---

1. Peterson, *Long Obedience.*

Begin at the Beginning

All true spiritual progress begins here: God is love. If God is love, there is no other way to *know* the truth but *through* love. This is mystery, yet it is not complicated: When we "abide in love [we] abide in God, and God abides in [us]." What became increasingly clear to me was this: We don't know what we don't know! In fact, we generally don't even know the right questions to ask until we are seized by God's love. When God called me through dreams to devote my entire life to unity, it was divine love alone that led me. Again and again I discovered that when you are the first to love, you will be enabled to know more. Blaise Pascal grasped this: "The heart has its reasons which reason knows not . . . We know the truth not only by the reason, but by the heart."[2]

In the rich history of Christianity, the way of love was often found in a desert. I went to a desert place in my private life in order to hear God speak. I learned to pray and wait in my desert. During those thirteen years I realized silence allowed me to receive God's love. I saw clearly that I was a needy, affirmation-seeking minister. But God wanted me to trust his love. By love alone I could finally stop feeding my considerable ego, or false self. During those years I sought men and women sent by God to the desert. One of my frequent companions was an Italian Catholic named Carlo Carretto (1910–1988), a dynamic activist in Catholic Action, a lay movement. In the midst of a busy life, and at the mid-life age of forty-four, he was called by God to *literally* go into the Saharan desert in Algeria. God spoke to him in a dream: "Leave everything and come with me into the desert. It is not your acts and deeds that I want. I want your prayer, your love." Carretto's calling profoundly resonates with my own. My desert was not literal, but it often felt that way. As a result of his years alone, Carretto came to a mature view of true spirituality: "Love is the synthesis of contemplation and action, the meeting point between heaven and earth, between God and humanity."[3] Through love you can enter into a deeper unity with Jesus and come to know him as God-Love.[4]

Metropolitan Bishop Kallistos Ware (Orthodox) expresses what I learned about God during those quiet years. "It is not the task of Christianity to provide easy answers to every question, but to make us progressively

---

2. Blaise Pascal Quotes.

3. Carretto, *Letter*, xvii.

4. The term "God-Love" is my favorite way to express God and his divine being. The term seems to have originated with several, but I learned it from Chiara Lubich, the founder of Focolare. See my book *Costly Love* for a full description of how this term can help us move more intentionally into the heart of God.

aware of a mystery."[5] Repeatedly I found myself lost in the sheer mystery and wonder of God-Love. The story of the great theologian and translator St. Jerome also helped me over the years. In a dream Jerome also heard God accuse him of being more Ciceronian than Christian. Upon waking, Jerome decided to break with the world and devote himself entirely to the knowledge of God. He retreated from his activism. (He kept his considerable library, showing again that one does not have to forego their intellect to discover God-Love.) Jerome, like Carretto, went into a literal wilderness. He had grown disgusted with the luxury and greed of Rome; thus he established a monastery to show the church the way back to truth wedded to love. In his desert Jerome was filled with God-Love.

The Reformed Tradition

When I first embraced the Reformed tradition as a twenty-six-year-old pastor, I did so out of an experience of love. I had met God anew and felt baptized in the wonder of his perfect love for me. But before long I lost the context of this love experience because I got sidetracked in my new tradition. Like far too many who choose this path, I thought of John Calvin as the great defender of the "five points." (Of course Calvin never wrote the "five points," and his theology was far more about the knowledge of God and divine love than about mastering systematic doctrinal ideas.) When I think of Calvin now, I picture his greatest contribution through the symbol of his life's work: the "Heart-in-Hand." This image is the picture of a heart offered to God in the palm of one's hand. It represents the love for God that leads one to offer their entire life to him. (Ironically enough, at least for many Calvinists, Christian groups like the Amish and the Shakers have adopted this very symbol to express their love and commitment to charity. That is precisely *how* ecumenical theology works!) This lovely Reformed symbol of Calvin's teaching transcends the *unique* aspects of his theology by simply saying: Love comes first, last and always!

My journey to unity eventually allowed me to embrace the marrow of John Calvin's theology without using it as an axe to divide fellow believers. As a Reformed minister of word and sacrament, I now see this same truth in a multitude of traditions, including the thought of a twentieth-century Catholic reformer like Romano Guardini: "None of the great things in human life life spring from the intellect; every one of them issues from the heart and its love."[6] Calvin would say *amen!*

5. Ware, *Orthodox Way*, 14.
6. Guardini, Quotes.

The Center of Ecumenical Theology: "God Is Love"

Calvin was profoundly indebted to St. Augustine for a great deal of his understanding of God and grace. It is not surprising, then, that St. Augustine gave love first place in his massively rich theology. He said: "Love creates fellowship, fellowship loves unity, and unity preserves love."[7] This is my missional-ecumenism. In Augustine we clearly encounter one of the greatest theological minds in Christianity. He says we must know love and then become love. When we truly begin to love, we grow into deeper unity. This unity prompts a love that will help us properly tear down our walls of separation. Then and only then will our unity be restored!

> We are one in the Spirit, we are one in the Lord
> We are one in the Spirit, we are one in the Lord
> And we pray that our unity will one day be restored
> And they'll know we are Christians by our love, by our love
> Yeah they'll know we are Christians by our love.

The biblical writers consistently focused on love. They urge us to love God *because* he "first loved us" (1 John 4:19). Further, they show us how God's love calls us to love our neighbors (Matthew 22:37–39) and our enemies (Matthew 5:43–48). Tragically, the Christian tradition has frequently lost this focus. But a careful reading of historical sources reveals how the church's greatest thinkers have often recovered the centrality of love. Some of my favorite companions, men and women who have helped me discover this love, include people like St. Augustine, Duns Scotus, Bernard of Clairvaux, Francis of Assisi, Thomas Aquinas, Julian of Norwich, John of the Cross, Martin Luther, John Calvin, Francis de Sales, Søren Kierkegaard, Thérèse of Lisieux, P. T. Forsyth, Dietrich Bonhoeffer, Henri Nouwen, Dallas Willard, Eugene Peterson, Alexander Schmemann, Kallistos Ware, Karl Rahner, and Richard Rohr. (This is a short list of those I've drawn this truth from, but it reveals the breadth of theological writing that will feed your need to center your life in love.)

So why has this recovery of love happened time and time again throughout Christian history? Simply put, men and women came to believe the central emphasis of Scripture is love. *I have come to believe this recurring theme warrants us to place love at the center of all theology.*

> It matters whether love or something else lies at the heart of our understanding of Christian belief. Seen in relationship to love then all our convictions and practices take on their proper meaning. And love provides us with a standard we can use to

---

7. Cited in Bray, ed., *Ancient Christian Commentary*, 93.

assess what we teach—a standard that is central to the Christian tradition, but a standard that can also inspire ongoing reform of that tradition.[8]

Christian thinkers have adopted various themes for understanding the revelation of God. These have included a number of good insights such as a proper emphasis on creation, fall, and redemption. The Protestant Reformers stressed a proper understanding of the relationship between justification and sanctification. Other traditions have centered their theology on the role of the church and the sacraments in giving us grace. Orthodox theology has focused on deification, or "participation in the divine nature" (see 2 Peter 1:4). For me, the theme that captured my mind was the role of divine sovereignty in providence and salvation. This theme became the organizing principle of all my theology. But as important as all of these central themes are, none of them does full justice to the storyline of the Bible: Christ is at the center of all life and theology, and his story is rooted in divine love!

Adopting this love-centered perspective will feed missional-ecumenism. (For that matter, it will feed every aspect of your life in Christ.) Love alone will give me the grace to follow Jesus into deeper unity. *This love-centered perspective is deeply relational.* It engages with real persons, not just ideas. "A love-centered perspective will foster our spiritual development on all of these fronts."[9] When we rightly center our mind and heart on loving God, we love others (Matthew 22:37–38). This God-Love, and only this love, will cause us to seek unity. A theology of ecumenism is helpful, but love alone is indispensable.

Keep It Simple

When I was a young man, I was told the best way to move forward in the Christian life was to keep things simple. I enjoyed complexity because my mind sought to engage complex ideas. Calls for simplicity often struck me as weak. As I grew older, I realized I had made far too much about the Christian faith overly complex.

It was actually President Jimmy Carter who helped me see this in a unique way. Carter read deeply, including a number of twentieth-century theologians he treasured, yet he always found ways to express his faith in simple ways. His teaching and writing demonstrates this profoundly. He has also demonstrated how unity can be translated into Christian mission

---

8. Chartier, *Analogy of Love*, 11. This is the finest overview I've read of a theology of love.

9. Chartier, *Analogy of Love*, 12.

and public service. Regardless of their political party, most everyone I know realizes that Jimmy Carter is a faithful, compassionate Christian. His story is that of a man seeking first the kingdom of God, a man committed to unity in the mission of Jesus. His views about some things have clearly changed over the years because he keeps reading, thinking, and growing. But fundamentally President Carter has grasped the mystery of God and his love and thus remains a humble servant of the kingdom.

The former president has frequently told a story about a time in his life when he lost the hope and joy of his Christian faith. After Carter lost his first run for governor in Georgia, having been personally attacked by a leading racist, he was profoundly despondent. His sister Ruth, a Christian evangelist, urged him to get involved in service to others in order to regain his true joy. Carter realized his sister was right and undertook a short-term missionary project. He made several summer trips to the Northeast to work with the Baptist Brotherhood. One summer he went to Springfield, Massachusetts, to do evangelism among Spanish-speaking residents. His companion was Eloy Cruz, a Cuban pastor from a small Baptist church in Brooklyn. Carter observed that Cruz was deferential toward him, but he freely did the work they were assigned by witnessing with tremendous effect. Carter was so moved by what he experienced that he asked Cruz to tell him his secret. Cruz answered, "I just try to have two loves in my heart: for God and for the person who happens to be in front of me at any time."[10]

All real effort for unity in mission must begin and end here, with these two loves. *First, we must love God. Then we must love the person in front of us.* It could not be more clear if you read the whole New Testament a thousand times. When I am now asked what stirred up God's gift in me over the years, I answer in the same way Pastor Cruz answered Jimmy Carter: The more I love God and the person in front of me, the more my vision grows into a powerful experience that seeks unity.

Consider Your Vocation

In Ephesians 4:1–4, Paul describes God's call on the lives of his readers. In classical Greek the word translated *calling* was understood as a summons to court or an invitation to a feast. This background prompts biblical scholar Lynn Cohick to write that we can "rephrase Paul here to say that God summons with a summons, or God invites with a particular message of invitation, namely the gospel message of Jesus Christ."[11] Thus the unity Paul

10. Carter, *Full Life*, 96.
11. Cohick, *Ephesians*, 183.

encourages among the Ephesians is rooted in their shared vocation to live out their inherent oneness.

Over the centuries the church has evolved in her understanding of the word *vocation*. The Protestant Reformers rightly insisted on the biblical idea that vocation was not limited to certain persons, such as priests. Rather, it included the *totality* of our life, an expression of the priesthood of all believers. Vocation was understood as *a call from God and a response to God*. God created me to know him, to love him, and to serve him. Together we are called to the same vocation: to live our lives for God and others. And this vocation is to be lived in and through Christ's mission. We serve Christ's mission when we serve one another and our neighbors. We serve Christ's mission when we use our gifts and relationships to advance the love of God. We embrace our vocation when we live missional-ecumenism as the body of Christ.

My dream of unity is rooted in an unexplainable movement of God that will ultimately impact the entire church. I believe this movement will unite us to go into the whole world. But all dreams must be turned into action through living faith if they are God's dreams. The task before all of us who love Jesus, and long for his kingdom to be made visible, is to search and pray for the unity that will remove walls. *For this to happen we must feel the scandal of our painful divisions.* My mentor and friend Fr. Tom Ryan says this well: "Being ecumenical means feeling a holy unrest at our failure to live consistent with our message, more interested in proving our 'rightness' and the other's 'wrongness' than in seeking together to know what the Spirit is asking of us and to do it."[12]

My deepest desire in writing is this—that whatever your persuasion or background, you will come to see this quest for unity is not an expediency but the call of God. It is a calling for a lifetime. It is a holy quest that springs from the very nature of Christian community. And it is a quest that must be centered in Christ and his kingdom.

A few years ago I discovered a relatively simple concept that showed me how to follow Jesus into deeper unity. Most of you will not, nor should you, make this vision of unity your *highest* priority in mission. But this work and prayer is your *duty* because you share divine life with your brothers and sisters. So how should you understand this duty and carry it out? The best metaphor I have found is called the "ecumenical tithe." Let me explain. Most Christians know what a tithe is. Strictly speaking, it means ten percent, but the term is more broadly used to describe any private commitment of a portion of my time and treasure to fulfill a duty I see as God-given. If the prayer and pursuit of unity is the will of Jesus, then I believe we all have a duty. You can *do something*. You can love God and the person in front of you. You can commit yourself to

12. Ryan, "What Does It Mean?"

give and share your time and talent for the mission of Jesus in relational unity. We can be one in love and live as Christ's humble servants.

Never Settle for Cheap Unity

Dietrich Bonhoeffer wrote a classic book, *The Cost of Discipleship*, during a profoundly divided time in Germany. His message was a powerful call to Christians to embrace the costliness of living the gospel of Christ's kingdom. He coined a phrase we sill widely use to express this loss of real discipleship: cheap grace. My friend Scott Brill has borrowed Bonhoeffer's idea when he writes about "cheap unity." Scott and I both believe there is a serious temptation to settle for cheap unity. But true unity will never be cheap. It is costly. Why? It is rooted in discipleship, which requires radical love. Here are some of the ways Scott says we settle for cheap unity.

1. Cheap unity avoids conflict. It is uncomfortable with sharp disagreement and seeks to diminish strong emotions and firm convictions. It elevates attempts to feel better over honest expressions of problems.
2. Cheap unity finds a "lowest common denominator" and stops there. It declares reconciliation too soon.
3. Cheap unity shrinks the number of people to be reconciled. It draws the circle of community too tightly and ends up having fewer and fewer real Christians.
4. Cheap unity refuses to talk about holiness. In contrast to drawing the circle too tightly cheap unity wants to ignore decisions of conscience and exclude from the conversation those who seem to be inflexible.
5. Cheap unity diminishes power dynamics and thus minimizes the cost to some (usually the minority voices) for "staying at the table." It presumes a level playing field in the conflict and suggests both sides must make the same types of sacrifices to bring about healing.
6. Cheap unity wants to move too quickly, and ignore the painful history of the past.[13]

Conclusion

In my mind I can still see those amazing pictures of people tearing down the Berlin Wall. Brick by brick they removed the wall as they sang, rejoiced,

---

13. Brill, "Cheap Unity."

and celebrated. You and I can climb specific walls we encounter, whether large or small. We can begin to take down a few bricks. You can contribute your "ecumenical tithe." You can join with those who are building bridges to establish a fellowship of burning hearts that desire the love that builds up our God-given unity.

For this dream of unity, rooted in the prayer of Jesus in John 17, I offer my fervent prayer. Over the course of my life I have realized again and again what President Carter says about faith: "Throughout [the] years, my faith as a Christian has provided the necessary stability in my life. Come to think of it, 'stability' is not exactly the right word, because faith in something is an inducement not to dormancy but to action."[14] Faith is not simply a noun. It is a powerful verb. Those who hear the Master's prayer for unity must act. But how? Great Christians like St. Thérèse of Lisieux, through her "Little Way," show us how very practical the way of holiness is. She was determined to not merely *think* about love but to *be* love. She, like Brother Lawrence centuries before, practiced God's presence by performing all her daily actions in the love of God. We can do the same.

Many Christians through the ages have dreamed and prayed for what they could not yet understand. Their faith allowed them to "do something" that made a difference. St. Bernard of Clairvaux (1090–1153) expressed what I've learned in my work for unity in an age that keeps raising new walls that separate us. "I believe though I do not comprehend, and I lay hold by faith what I cannot grasp with the mind."[15]

I give my final word to Abbé Paul Couturier (1881–1953), the French priest we saw earlier. His words have become a well-known prayer for Christian unity. This prayer is especially used in places where the Week of Prayer for Christian Unity is celebrated around the world. It is a fitting conclusion to my heartfelt appeal.

> Lord Jesus,
> who prayed that we might all be one,
> we pray to You for the unity of Christians,
> according to Your will, according to Your means.
> May Your Spirit enable us
> to experience the suffering caused by division,
> to see our sin,
> and to hope beyond all hope. Amen.[16]

---

14. Carter, *Faith*, 84.

15. Cited at the Catholic Storeroom.

16. Adapted from a prayer by Abbé Paul Couturier, who was called "the apostle of Christian unity." See abbepaulcouturier.

Glossary

Apostolic. That which possesses the sanction and authority of the apostles because of its relationship to their teaching.

Catholic/Catholicity. A transliteration of the Greek *katholikos*, which means "throughout the whole" or "general." In early church literature, *catholic* referred to the universal church—the whole church diffused throughout the world. *Catholicity* refers to the quality or state of universality, thus bringing to mind the comprehensive nature of the undivided church of Jesus Christ that gathers all of God's people into one church from many different races, languages, and cultures.

Classical Christianity. A way to describe the ancient practices and confessions of the catholic church, both East and West. The term is increasingly used as a way of referring to the importance of tradition in the history of Christianity.

Creed. A brief authoritative formula of belief, generally understood as a guiding principle for confessing the mystery of the faith.

Critical Realism. In philosophy, the theory that some of our sense-data accurately represents external objects, properties, or events, and some does not. Critical realism maintains that there is an objectively knowable reality, but it must be approached by critical perception. More and more theologians are using the term (e.g., T. F. Torrance, John Polkinghorne, Alister McGrath, N. T. Wright). Wright describes critical realism as "a way of describing the process of 'knowing' that acknowledges the *reality of the thing known, as something other than the knower* (hence 'realism'), while fully acknowledging that the only access we have to this reality lies along the spiraling path of *appropriate dialogue or conversation between the knower and the thing known* (hence 'critical')." We discover Christian truth in a context of dialogue with the truth because we (the knowers) must personally relate to the thing known (God's truth) in a relational way.

Deification. A way of understanding that God's work in our salvation involves continual transformation, both now and in the age to come. *Theosis* is the commonly used Greek word for transformation. This thinking is rarely heard in Catholic and Protestant teaching and liturgy. The idea is seen in 2 Peter 1:3–11, especially verse 4, which speaks of our becoming "participants of the divine nature." Through deification we do not become God but are "made divine." Athanasius utilized *theosis* for a range of biblical ideas like "adoption, renewal, salvation, sanctification, grace, transcendence, illumination, and vivification." *Christification* expresses this truth by centering the transformation process in Christ's renewing our human nature.

Didache. An early (second-century) anonymous manual of Christian instruction about how to live the life of faith and how to govern the church. It is one of the most important non-canonical sources we have from early Christianity.

Ecumenical/Ecumenism. From the Greek *oikoumenem*, which means "the whole inhabited world." Initially used to refer to the early general councils of the church, *ecumenical* has come to refer to Christians and churches scattered geographically and denominationally around the world.

Evangelical. "Pertaining to the evangel"—to the good news (gospel). In the Protestant Reformation, it became virtually synonymous with Protestant faith. Following various worldwide renewals and awakenings, the word came to designate Christians who believed that faith, grace, and conversion were essential to the Christian life. It is now often associated with "conservative Protestantism" and has recently been used to describe a very conservative political persuasion held by some Christians.

Filioque. A Latin term that means "and from the Son." This phrase was added by the Western church to the original Nicene-Constantinopolitan Creed, commonly known as the Nicene Creed. The addition of this word has been a source of great conflict between the Western and the Eastern churches. The original creed said simply that the Spirit proceeds from the Father but not from the Son. At the heart of the debate was a continued argument about the Catholic teaching of papal primacy. Conflicts over authority, ethnic misunderstanding and hostility, personal rivalry, forced conversions, large-scale wars, and secular motives all helped divide the church East and West.

Gnosticism. A movement in the ancient world that challenged early Christianity by emphasizing a special higher truth that only the enlightened receive from God. It taught that all matter was evil. As a result of these two emphases, it denied the humanity of Jesus.

Great Tradition. The core, elemental truths that are essential to historical and confessional Christianity (for example, the Trinity, the divinity and humanity of Christ, the authority of Scripture). C. S. Lewis spoke of "mere Christianity"—his way of saying much the same thing. Christians come from different traditions, but they hold in common the "Great Tradition."

Kerygma. The Greek word meaning "the act of proclaiming" or "the message proclaimed." The *kerygma* is the core message that announces God's decisive act and offer of salvation in the death and resurrection of Jesus Christ (see Romans 16:25; 1 Corinthians 1:21; 15:3–5). *Kerygma* precedes detailed teaching, or *didache*.

Lectio divina. A Latin term meaning "divine reading," *lectio* is a way of reading, meditation, and prayer that is intended to promote communion with God and to increase the knowledge of Scripture as God's Word. It treats Scripture not as texts to be studied but as the "living" Word of God. Traditionally there are four separate steps in this practice: read; meditate; pray; contemplate.

Logos. A Greek term meaning "word" or "message," *logos* is used in the prologue of John's Gospel to refer to the preexistent divine Word (Jesus Christ), who "became flesh and made his dwelling among us." The Old Testament spoke of *logos* as the creative power and personified self-revelation of God (Psalms 33:6, 9; 107:20; Isaiah 55:10–11). In later theology the term came to refer to reason, thus prompting some to equate reason with Christ. At the Council of Nicaea, *logos* was used interchangeably with "Son of God" as the second person of the divine Trinity.

Magisterium. A Latin term meaning "the office of the teacher." In Roman Catholic theology, it refers to the authoritative teaching office of the gospel in the name of Christ, yet as serving and not as superior to the Word of God. In this view all believers are anointed by God and should read and interpret Scripture, but only the magisterium, the whole college of bishops (as successors to the college of apostolic witnesses), united with the bishop of Rome (pope), have final authority.

Missio Dei. This Latin term meaning "the mission of God" came into prominence in the twentieth century as a way to ground missionary theory and practice in the activity of the triune God. The three persons are involved in "the sending" of the Son into the world, and thus the church is "sent" because the sending God reaches out to the world.

Missional. A relatively recent theological term that reconceptualizes the idea inherent in the *missio Dei* (mission of God). It underscores the idea that in sending us into the world as his "sent ones," God has designed that we will carry out his mission in community and action. The key text is John 20:21: "As the Father has sent me, I am sending you." Christopher Wright rightly states, "Mission is and always has been God's before it becomes ours. The whole Bible presents a God of missional activity, from his purposeful, goal-oriented act of creation to the completion of his cosmic mission in the redemption of the whole of creation—a new heaven and a new earth."

Missional-ecumenism. In formulating this term, I have taken two words and combined them into one hyphenated word. I wish to stress these two truths: (1) God is both a unity in himself and a sending God, which means eternal love passes between the three divine persons, thus the love we are called to live is found in our being in union with the three persons of the divine self-giving Trinity, and (2) God's revealed desire is that we would be (relationally) one with him in this sending and sent (mission) process—thus the term *missional-ecumenism*.

Mystery. Any truth made known to us by divine revelation and believed through faith. Some mysteries in Scripture have been revealed in a way that makes them now more clearly understood than before. Generally the term has been used to describe a truth not fully comprehended until the age to come (e.g., most Christians believe the sacraments are mysteries).

Mystical. A spiritual truth that is best related to intuitive knowledge and meditation. A mystical experience is one that is related to contemplative union or a state of overwhelming feeling.

Ontological. From the Greek *ontos* ("of being") and *logia* ("subject under discussion," "study"), *ontology* means "the study of being." The ontology of God is, therefore, his *essential being*.

Orthodox. From the Greek *orthos* ("correct," "true") and *doxa* ("opinion," "belief," "notion"). The term came into the church at the Council of Chalcedon to express the correct way of understanding divine revelation in Jesus Christ. I am using the term in this way. I also use it to refer to the churches of the Christian East that evolved into local communities after the death of Theodosius in 395, when the Roman Empire was divided into East and West. The (Eastern) Orthodox churches, which experienced division with the bishop of Rome in 1054, are in communion with each other and recognize the patriarch of Constantinople as honored among equals.

Orthodoxy. The body of doctrines taught by Scripture, such as the deity and humanity of Christ, the Trinity, and the authority of Holy Scripture.

Theologian Thomas C. Oden defines orthodoxy as the "integrated biblical teaching as interpreted in its most consensual classic period."

Papacy. The office of the bishop of Rome, the supreme pontiff of the Roman Catholic Church—the pope.

Patristic(s). The Latin word means "the Fathers" or "the study of the Fathers." Patristics refers to the theology of the early church theologians (the early Church Fathers).

Roman Catholic. A person who is a communicant in the Roman Catholic Church; or pertaining (adjectivally) to the teaching and practice of Roman Catholicism. The term *Roman Catholicism* came into general use in the Protestant Reformation to identify the beliefs and practices of Christians who accepted the pope as the head of the church, as its supreme earthly authority.

Sacrament/Sacramentalism. A Christian rite (such as baptism or the Eucharist) that is believed to have been ordained by Christ and that is held to be a means of divine grace or to be a sign or symbols of a spiritual reality. Different churches recognize a different number of sacraments.

Sect. From the Latin *secta* (from *sequi*, "to follow"), *sect* is commonly used to refer to a group that has broken away from a larger religious group and thus holds distinctive views. In this sense, the earliest Christians were a sect of the Jews. The term often refers to a group that breaks away from an older, established church or to those who follow the unique teachings of a leader who has formed a new group.

Sectarianism. Generally refers to a doctrinaire commitment to one's own views or those of a particular group and often resulting in a narrow-minded devotion. Those who disagree are condemned by sectarians, sometimes harshly. Some sectarians disavow all relationship to an established Christian church. A correspondingly negative connotation is found in the synonym *tribalism*.

Spiritual Formation. The ancient Christian concept of shaping the attitudes, beliefs, and practices that form the lives of faithful Christians. The various disciplines of the Christian life (prayer, meditation, Bible reading, fasting, etc) are used to alter the way we think and live.

Theosis/deification. A transformative process whose aim is our likeness to, and union with, *God*. This has been taught by Eastern churches as the process of complete salvific transformation. *Theosis* is brought about by the purification of our mind and body through the "illumination" of our being with the "vision" of God. The Orthodox Church sees *theosis* as the very purpose of human life: to be transformed into God-likeness.

Tradition. An ongoing coherent process in which certain core values of a community are advanced through debates with critics from the outside and interpretive refinements from the inside. Tradition is the means by which the church understands its history and collective memory of Jesus Christ.

Appendix

During my last four years as president of ACT3 Network, the board created a new movement–*The Initiative*–that continues to serve the purpose of relational and ecclesial ecumenism in a wide variety of ways. The board of ACT3 wrote a Covenant that expresses the vocation of members and friends.

The Initiative

Our Covenant

To Walk in Unity With Jesus and His Followers

We covenant together to live in an *intentional initiative*, practicing deep and growing friendship with God and others, *that the love of Jesus might exceed all divisions.*

Our Way

"I give you a new commandment, that you love one another. Just as I have loved you, you also should love one another. By this everyone will know that you are my disciples, if you have love for one another" (John 13:34–35, NRSV).

Walking together in the Way of Jesus (Acts 9:2) draws us into unity (John 17:21). We call this *missional-ecumenism.*[*]

---

[*] *Missional-ecumenism* expresses the core vision of *The Initiative*. By *missional* we understand God as a unity of persons in eternal relationship. This relationship means that God is a sending God, who loves the world. He sends his Son into the world to liberate and redeem the entire cosmos. God's revealed desire is that we be in relationship with him and one another, thus becoming the sent ones who take the good news of the kingdom to all by living in divine unity.

Led by the Holy Spirit, we will each take the initiative to:

- *work* proactively for missional-ecumenism.
- *pray* daily for a radical increase of love for the whole Body of Christ.
- *share* our lives with followers of Jesus from traditions other than our own.

We will do this by:

- Organizing or promoting at least one monthly engagement with others to *demonstrate the love of Jesus and to pursue deeper unity.* This commitment includes gatherings in many different contexts, one-on-one and in groups.
- Attending an annual gathering of *The Initiative* unless hindered by health, family commitments, or other important reasons.
- Financially supporting *The Initiative* and the wider work of missional-ecumenism.
- Inviting others to work in *The Initiative* as members or friends.

Recommended Resources

I refer to a number of useful books and resources in the text; besides the bibliography in this book, I have also compiled an ongoing list of good resources on the subject of missional-ecumenism which is available at my website www.johnharmstrong.com. Here you can also discover videos and articles about missional-ecumenism. I also recommend www.theinitiative.org where you can connect with a diverse movement of sharing in a community built on unity in mission.

Bibliography

Abraham, William. "Church and Churches: Ecumenism." In *The Oxford Handbook of Evangelical Theology*, edited by Gerald R. McDermott, 269–309. New York: Oxford University Press, 2010.

Aitken, Jonathan. *Charles W. Colson: A Life Redeemed*. New York: Doubleday, 2005.

Angel, Warren. *Yes, We Can Love One Another! Catholics and Protestants Can Share a Common Faith*. Carlsbad, CA: Magnus, 1997.

Armstrong, John H. *Costly Love: The Way to True Unity for All the Followers of Jesus*. Hyde Park, NY: New City, 2017.

———. *Your Church Is Too Small: Why Unity in Christ's Mission Is Vital to the Future of the Church*. Grand Rapids: Zondervan, 2010.

Armstrong, John H., ed. *Understanding Four Views on Baptism*. Grand Rapids: Zondervan, 2007.

———. *Understanding Four Views on the Lord's Supper*. Grand Rapids: Zondervan, 2007.

Barclay, William. *Ethics in a Permissive Society*. New York: Harper & Row, 1971.

Barth, Karl. *Church Dogmatics 1/2*. Edinburgh: T & T Clark, 1956.

Bercot, David W., ed. *A Dictionary of Early Christian Beliefs*. Peabody, MA: Hendrickson, 1998.

Birlemé, André. *Local Ecumenism: How Church Unity Is Seen and Practiced by Congregations*. Geneva: World Council of Churches, 1984.

Bolen, Donald, et. al., eds. *Towards Unity: Ecumenical Dialogue 500 Years After the Reformation*. New York: Paulist, 2017.

Bonhoeffer, Dietrich. *Christ the Center*. New York: HarperCollins, 1960.

———. *The Cost of Discipleship*. New York: Macmillan, 1963.

———. *Life Together*. New York: HarperOne, 2009.

Bosch, David J. *Transforming Mission: Paradigm Shifts in Theology of Mission*. Maryknoll, NY.: Orbis, 1991.

Braaten, Carl E. and Robert W. Jenson, eds. *The Ecumenical Future*. Grand Rapids: Eerdmans, 2004.

———. *In One Body through the Cross: The Princeton Proposal for Christian Unity*. Grand Rapids: Eerdmans, 2003.

Bray, Gerald, ed. *Ancient Christian Commentary: New Testament XI*. Downers Grove, IL.: InterVarsity, 2000.

Brill, Scott. "Cheap Unity v. Costly Unity." December 12, 2016. https://recapitulareblog.wordpress.com/2016/12/12/cheap-unity-v-costly-unity.

Bromiley, G. W. *The Unity and Disunity of the Church*. Grand Rapids: Eerdmans, 1958.
Brown, Raymond E. *The Gospel and the Epistles of John: A Concise Commentary*. Collegeville, MN: Liturgical, 1988.
Brown, Robert McAfee. *The Spirit of Protestantism*. New York: Oxford University Press, 1961.
Brunner, Emil. *The Word and the World*. London: SCM, 1931.
Buber, Martin. *I and Thou*. Translated by Walter Kaufmann. New York: Charles Scribners, 1984.
Buechner, Frederick. Quote of the Day. http://frederickbuechner.com/quote-of-the-day/2017/11/10-for-christ-and-his-kingdom.
Calvin, John. *Institutes of the Christian Religion*. 2 vols. Edited by John T. McNeill. Philadelphia: Westminster, 1960.
The Cape Town Commitment. Peabody, MA: Hendrickson, 2011.
Carey, William. *An Enquiry into the Obligations of Christians to Use Means for the Conversion of the Heathens*. Leicester, 1792.
Carretto, Carlos. *Letter from the Desert*. Anniversary ed. Maryknoll, NY: Orbis, 2002.
Carter, Jimmy. *Faith: A Journey for All*. New York: Simon & Schuster, 2018.
———. *A Full Life: Reflections at Ninety*. New York: Simon & Schuster, 2015.
———. *Our Endangered Values: America's Moral Crisis*. New York: Simon & Schuster, 2005.
The Catholic Storeroom. http://www.catholicstoreroom.com/?s=I+believe+though+I+do+not+comprehend.
Chambers, Oswald. *My Utmost for His Highest*. Grand Rapids: Discovery House, 2017.
Chartier, Gary. *The Analogy of Love: Divine and Human Love as the Center of Christian Theology*. 2d ed. Ann Arbor, MI: Griffin & Lash, 2017.
Church of Scotland. *The Confession of Faith*. London: T. Nelson and Sons, 1860.
Cleveland, Christena. *Disunity in Christ: Uncovering Hidden Forces That Keep Us Apart*. Downers Grove, IL: InterVarsity, 2013.
Clifford, Catherine, ed. *A Century of Prayer for Christian Unity*. Grand Rapids: Eerdmans, 2009.
Cohick, Lynn H. *Ephesians: New Covenant Commentary Series*. Eugene, OR: Cascade, 2010.
Cole, David L. "Future Ecumenical Challenges." In *Spirit-Empowered Christianity in the 21st Century*, edited by Vinson Synan, 237–59. Lake Mary, FL: Charisma House, 2011.
Couturier, Paul. Abbepaulcouturier.blogspot.com/p/a-daily-prayer-for-christian-unity-lord.html.
———. The Week of Prayer for Christian Unity. https://en.wikipedia-org/wiki/Week_of_Prayer_for_Christian_Unity.
Cullmann, Oscar. *Christ and Time: The Primitive Christian Conception of Time and History*. Philadelphia: Westminster, 1964.
———. *The Earliest Christian Confessions*. London: Lutterworth, 1949.
Culpepper, Polk. *Decline and Dysfunction in the American Church*. Greensboro, NC: Sable, 2015.
Dias, Elizabeth, ed. *What Did Jesus Ask? Christian Leaders Reflect on His Questions of Faith*. New York: Times, 2015.
Dulles, Avery. *Models of the Church*. New York: Image, 1974.
Ellsberg, Robert. *Blessed Among Us*. Collegeville, MN: Liturgical, 2016.

BIBLIOGRAPHY

"Evangelicals and Catholics Together: The Christian Mission in the Third Millennium." *First Things,* May 1994. https://www.firstthings.com/article/1994/05/evangelicals-catholics-together-the-christian-mission-in-the-third-millennium.

Fairbairn, Donald. *Eastern Orthodoxy Through Western Eyes.* Louisville: Westminster, 2002.

Forsyth, P. T. *The Church and the Sacraments.* 2d ed. London: Independent, 1917.

Francis, Pope. *The Joy of the Gospel.* New York: Random House, 2013.

Frédéric Ozanam. Wikipedia. https://en.wikipedia.org/wiki/Frederic_Ozanam.

Garvey, John. *Orthodoxy for the Non-Orthodox: A Brief Introduction to Orthodox Christianity.* Springfield, IL: Templegate, 2002.

Global Christian Forum. "Ministry During COVID-19—Rev. Dr. Richard Howell in India." July 14, 2020. https://globalchristianforum.org/ministry-during-covid-19-rev-dr-richard-howell-in-india.

Goheen, Michael W. *The Church and Its Vocation: Lesslie Newbigin's Missionary Ecclesiology.* Grand Rapids: Baker, 2018.

Gordon-Conwell Theological Seminary's Center for the Study of Global Christianity. "Status of Global Mission, 2014, in the Context of AD 1800–2025." https://web.archive.org/web/20141014004048/http://www.gordonconwell.edu/resources/documents/StatusOfGlobalMission.pdf.

Gros, Jeffrey, Eamon McManus, and Ann Riggs. *Introduction to Ecumenism.* New York: Paulist, 1998.

Guardini, Romano. Quote Fancy. https://quotefancy.com/roman-guardini-quotes.

Guder, Darrell L. "The Church as Missional Community." In *The Community of the Word,* edited by Mark Husbands and Daniel Trier, 114–30. Downers Grove, IL: InterVarsity, 2005.

———. *The Continuing Conversion of the Church.* Grand Rapids: Eerdmans, 2000.

Guder, Darrell L. ed. *Missional Church: A Theological Vision for the Sending of the Church in North America.* Grand Rapids: Eerdmans, 1998.

Halfacre, Philip D. *Genuine Friendship.* Woodridge, IL: Midwest Theological Forum, 2008.

Harmon, Steven R. *Ecumenism Means You, Too: Ordinary Christians and the Quest for Christian Unity.* Eugene, OR: Cascade, 2010.

Henry, Matthew. *Matthew Henry's Commentary on the Whole Bible: Complete and Unabridged.* Nashville: Thomas Nelson, 2008.

Hill, Wesley. *The Lord's Prayer: A Guide to Praying to Our Father.* Bellingham, WA: Lexham, 2019.

Hunsberger, George R., and Craig Van Gelder. *The Church Between Gospel and Culture: The Emerging Mission in North America.* Grand Rapids: Eerdmans, 1996.

Imtiaz, Saba. "A New Generation Redefines What It Means to Be a Missionary." *The Atlantic,* March 8, 2018. https://www.theatlantic.com/international/archive/2018/03/young-missionaries/551585.

Jenkins, Philip. *The Next Christendom: The Coming of Global Christianity.* New York: Oxford University Press, 2011.

John Paul II, Pope. *Ut Unum Sint* (That They May Be One). Pope John Paul II's encyclical on ecumenism, May 25, 1995. www.vatican.va/holy_father/john_paul_ii/encyclicals/documents/hf_jp-ii_enc_25051995_ut-unum-sint_en.html.

John Paul II, et. al. *Searching for Christian Unity.* Hyde Park, NY: New City, 2007.

Johnson, Luke Timothy. *The Creed: What Christians Believe and Why It Matters.* New York: Doubleday, 2003.
Jones, E. Stanley. *The Christ of the American Road.* Nashville: Abingdon, 1944.
Kasper, Cardinal Walter. *A Handbook of Spiritual Ecumenism.* Hyde Park, NY: New City, 2017.
Kasper, Walter J. *That They May All Be One: The Call to Unity Today.* New York: Burns & Oates, 2004.
Keefe, Patrick Radden. *Say Nothing: A True Story of Murder and Memory in Northern Ireland.* New York: Random House, 2019.
Keleher, Serge. "Ecumenism." In *The Blackwell Dictionary of Eastern Orthodoxy*, edited by Ken Parry, et al., 172–75. Malden, MA: Blackwell, 1999.
Kinnaman, David, and Gabe Lyons. *unChristian: What a New Generation Really Thinks About Christianity . . . and Why It Matters.* Grand Rapids: Baker, 2007.
Kinnamon, Michael. *Can a Renewal Movement Be Renewed?* Grand Rapids: Eerdmans, 2014.
Kirk, A. Andrew, and Kevin J. Vanhoozer, eds. *To Stake a Claim: Mission and the Western Crisis of Knowledge.* Maryknoll, NY: Orbis, 1999.
Koch, George Byron. *What We Believe and Why.* Northwoods, IL: Byron Arts, 2012.
Koivisto, Rex A. *One Lord, One Faith: A Theology for Cross Denominational Renewal.* Eugene, OR: Wipf and Stock, 1993.
Küng, Hans. *The Church.* New York: Image, 1976.
Kuyper, Abraham. "Sphere Sovereignty." In *Abraham Kuyper: A Centennial Reader*, edited by James D. Bratt, 461–90. Grand Rapids: Eerdmans, 1998.
Ladd, George E. "Kingdom of Christ, God, Heaven." In *Evangelical Dictionary of Theology*, edited by Walter A. Elwell, 657–61. Grand Rapids: Baker, 2001.
Leith, John. *The Church: A Believing Fellowship.* Atlanta: John Knox, 1981.
Leiva-Merikakis, Erasmo. *Fire of Mercy, Heart of the God: Meditations on the Gospel According to St. Matthew.* San Francisco: Ignatius, 1996.
Lewis, C. S. *The Collected Letters of C. S. Lewis.* Vol. 2. New York: HarperOne, 2009.
Lossky, Nicholas, et al., eds. *Dictionary of the Ecumenical Movement.* Grand Rapids: Eerdmans, 1991.
Mandryk, Jason. *Operation World.* Colorado Springs, CO: Biblica, 2010.
Manschreck, Clyde. *A History of Christianity in the World.* Englewood Cliffs, NJ: Prentice Hall, 1974.
Mead, Loren. *Transforming Congregations for the Future.* Washington, DC: The Alban Institute, 1994.
Mehta, Hemant. *I Sold My Soul on eBay.* Colorado Springs, CO: WaterBrook, 2007.
Migliore, Daniel L. "The Missionary God and the Missionary Church." *Princeton Seminary Bulletin* 19.1 (Spring 1998) 14–25.
Minear, Paul S., ed. *The Nature of the Unity We Seek: Official Report on the North American Conference on Faith and Order.* St. Louis: Bethany, 1958.
Moltmann, Jürgen. *The Church in the Power of the Spirit.* Minneapolis: Fortress, 1993.
———. "Unfinished Worlds: Jürgen Moltmann @ 90 Conference." Emory University, October 19–20, 2016.
Morris, Jeremy, and Nicholas Sagovsky. *The Unity We Have and the Unity We Seek: Ecumenical Prospects for the Third Millennium.* New York: T & T Clark, 2003.
Muto, Susan. *One in the Lord: Living Our Call to Christian Community.* Hyde Park, NY: New City, 2013.

Neill, Stephen. *A History of Christian Missions*. New York: Penguin, 1964.
Nelson, R. David, and Charles Raith II. *Ecumenism: A Guide for the Perplexed*. New York: Bloomsbury/T. & T. Clark, 2017.
Newbigin, Lesslie. "Crosscurrents in Ecumenical and Evangelical Understanding of Missio." *International Bulletin of Missionary Research* 6.4 (1982) 146–51.
———. *The Gospel in a Pluralist Society*. Grand Rapids: Eerdmans, 1989.
———. *Honest Religion for Secular Man*. Philadelphia: Westminster, 1966.
———. *The Household of God: Lectures on the Nature of the Church*. London: SCM Press, 1953.
———. *Is Christ Divided: A Plea for Christian Unity in a Revolutionary Age*. Grand Rapids: Eerdmans, 1961.
———. *The Light Has Come: An Exposition of the Fourth Gospel*. Grand Rapids: Eerdmans, 1982.
———. *The Mission and the Unity of the Church (Peter Ainslie Memorial Lecture)*. Grahamstown, South Africa: Rhodes University Press, 1960.
———. *One Body, One Gospel, One World*. London: International Missionary Council, 1958.
———. *The Open Secret: Sketches for a Missionary Theology*. Grand Rapids; Eerdmans, 1978.
———. *Proper Confidence: Faith, Doubt, and Certainty in Christian Discipleship*. Grand Rapid: Eerdmans, 1995.
———. *The Reunion of the Church*. London: SCM, 1948.
Nietzsche, Frederick. *Human, All Too Human: A Book for Free Spirits*. New York: Cambridge University Press, 1986.
O'Kane, Lydia. "Pope: Cardinal Bea a model and inspiration for dialogue." *Vatican News*, February 28, 2019. https://www.vaticannews.va/en/pope/news/2019-02/pope-cardinal-bea-a-model-and-inspiration-for-dialogue.html.
Packer, James I. *Taking Christian Unity Seriously*. Milton, ON: Anglican Essentials, 2007.
Pascal, Blaise. Blaise Pascal Quotes. BrainyQuote.com. http://www.brainyquote.com/quotes/blaise_pascal_118337.
Patterson, Stephen J. *The Forgotten Creed: Christianity's Original Struggle Against Bigotry, Slavery and Sexism*. New York: Oxford University Press, 2018
Peterson, Eugene H. *Tell It Slant: A Conversation on the Language of Jesus in His Stories and Prayers*. Grand Rapids: Eerdmans, 2008.
———. *A Long Obedience in the Same Direction*. Downers Grove, IL: InterVarsity, 1980.
Phillips, Emo. "Die Heretic." http://www.emophillips.com.
Rahner, Karl. *Theological Investigations VII*. Translated by David Bourke. New York: Herder & Herder, 1991.
Robert, Dana L. *Faithful Friendships: Embracing Diversity in Christian Community*. Grand Rapids: Eerdmans, 2019.
Rouse, Ruth, and Stephen Neill, eds. *A History of the Ecumenical Movement, 1517–1948*. Philadelphia: Westminster, 1967.
Rustin, Bayard. *Quotes and Sayings*. https://www.inspiringquotes.us.author/7283-bayard-rustin.
Ryan, Thomas. *Christian Unity: How You Can Make a Difference*. New York: Paulist Press, 2015.

———. *A Survival Guide for Ecumenically Minded Christians*. Collegeville, Minnesota: The Liturgical Press, 1989.

———. "What Does It Mean to Be Ecumenical?" May 9, 2018. http://tomryancsp.org/WhatDoesItMeanTodayToBeEcumenical.html.

Ryn, Claes G. "How Conservatives Failed the Culture." *The Imaginative Conservative*, October 10, 2011. https://theimaginativeconservative.or/2011/10/how-conservatives-failed-culture.html.

Sacks, Jonathan. *The Great Partnership: Science, Religion and the Search for Meaning*. New York: Random House, 2011.

Sanneh, Lamin. *Translating the Message: The Missionary Impact on Culture*. Maryknoll, NY: Orbis, 1993.

Santos, Jason Brian. *A Community Called Taizé: A Story of Prayer, Worship and Reconciliation*. Downers Grove, IL: InterVarsity, 2008.

Schaff, Philip. *The Creeds of Christendom*. Vol. 1. Grand Rapids: Baker, 1983.

———. *History of the Christian Church*. Vol. 7. Peabody, MA: Hendrickson, 2006

———. "The Reunion of Christendom." In *The Dawn of Religious Pluralism*, edited by Richard Hughes Seager, 93–128. LaSalle, IL: Open Court, 1993.

Schaeffer, Francis A. *The Mark of the Christian*. Downers Grove, IL: InterVarsity, 1970.

Second Vatican Council. "Decree on the Mission Activity of the Church (*Ad Gentes*)." December 7, 1965. http://www.vatican.va/archive/hist_councils/ii_vatican_council/documents/vat-ii_decree_19651207_ad-gentes_en.html.

Shenk, David W. *God's Call to Mission*. Scottsdale, PA: Herald, 1994.

Slipper, Callan. *Enriched by the Other: A Spiritual Guide to Receptive Ecumenism*. Cambridge: Grove, 2016.

Slipper, Callan. *Five Steps to Living Christian Unity*. Hyde Park, NY: New City, 2013.

Staten, Stephen Francis. "Was There Unity in the Sub-Apostolic Church? An Investigation of the Tunnel Period." MA thesis, Wheaton College, 1996.

Suenens, Cardinal Leo Joseph. *Ways of the Spirit: The Spirituality of Cardinal Suenens*. New York: Seabury, 1976.

Taizé. "A Pilgrimage of Trust on Earth." January 31, 2012. https://www.taize.fr/en_article58.html.

Tickle, Phyllis. *The Great Emergence*. Grand Rapids: Baker, 2012.

Tomkins, Oliver. "John R. Mott." In *Dictionary of the Ecumenical Movement*, edited by Nicholas Lossky, et al., 703–5. Grand Rapids: Eerdmans, 1991.

Ugolnik, Anthony. *The Illuminating Icon*. Grand Rapids: Eerdmans, 1989.

United States Conference of Catholic Bishops. "Welcoming the Stranger Among Us: Unity in Diversity." https://www.usccb.org/committees/pastoral-care-migrants-refugees-travelers/welcoming-stranger-among-us-unity-diversity..

Van Engen, Charles. *God's Missionary People*. Grand Rapids: Baker, 1991.

Van Gelder, Craig. *The Essence of the Church: A Community Created by the Spirit*. Grand Rapids: Baker, 2000.

Wainwright, Geoffrey. *Lesslie Newbigin: A Theological Life*. New York: Oxford University Press, 2000.

Walsh, Albert J. D. *United and Uniting: An Ecumenical Ecclesiology for a Church in Crisis*. Eugene, OR: Wipf and Stock, 2011.

Ware, Kallistos. *How Are We Saved? The Understanding of Salvation in the Orthodox Tradition*. Minneapolis: Light & Life, 1996.

———. *The Orthodox Way*. Crestwood, NY: St. Vladimir's Seminary Press, 1995.

Watson, David. *I Believe in the Church*. Grand Rapids: Eerdmans, 1978.
Webber, Robert E. *Ancient-Future Faith*. Grand Rapids: Baker, 1995.
Weston, Paul, ed., *Lesslie Newbigin: Missionary Theologian—A Reader*. Grand Rapids: Eerdmans, 2006.
Whitehead, Kenneth D. *The New Ecumenism: How the Catholic Church after Vatican II Took Over the Leadership of the World Ecumenical Movement*. Staten Island, NY: Alba House, 2009.
Wilken, Robert L. *The Myth of Christian Beginnings*. New York: Doubleday, 1971.
Wilkinson, Kate. "May the Mind of Christ, My Savior." Hymnary.org. https://hymnary.org/text/may_the_mind_of_christ_my_savior.
Williams, Layton E. *Holy Disunity: How What Separate Us Can Save Us*. Louisville, Westminster John Knox, 2019.
Williams, Rowan. *Christ the Heart of Creation*. New York: Bloomsbury Continuum, 2018.
Witherington, Ben, III. *John's Wisdom: A Commentary on the Fourth Gospel*. Louisville: Westminster, 1995.
Witherspoon, H. J., and J. M. Kirkpatrick. *A Manual of Church Doctrine according to the Church of Scotland*. London: Oxford University Press, 1960.
Wood, Susan K., and Timothy J. Wengert. *A Shared Spiritual Journey: Lutherans and Catholics Traveling Toward Unity*. New York: Paulist, 2016.
Wright, N.T. *Collected Essays of N. T. Wright*. 3 vols. Grand Rapids: Zondervan, 2020.
———. *God and the Pandemic: A Christian Reflection on the Coronavirus and Its Aftermath*. Grand Rapids: Zondervan, 2020.
———. *Interpreting Paul: Essays on the Apostle and His Letters*. Grand Rapids: Zondervan, 2020.
Young, Frances. *The Making of the Creeds*. Philadelphia: Trinity Press International, 1991.
Yun, Brother. *Living Water*. Grand Rapids: Zondervan, 2008.